Marking Milestones

21-Keynote Speeches
about Successful Institutions and
Outstanding Leaders

Errol Miller

minna
PRESS

ISBN 978-976-95693-9-3

A catalogue record of this book is available from the National Library of Jamaica.

Ordering Information
Quantity (Bulk) Sales: Special discounts are available on quantity purchases by corporations, associations, and others. For details, contact the publisher: sales@minnapress.com

Executive Editor: Lena J. Rose

Editor: Winston G. Wright

Book and cover design: Mark Steven Weinberger

Published in Kingston Jamaica
by Minna Press
204 Mountain View Avenue, Kingston 6, Jamaica

To my grandmother: Louise Dahl, née Aldred

To my mother: Joyce Miller, née Dahl

To my wife: Sharon Miller, née Rowe

Contents

Foreword 7

Preface 9

Introduction 13

Chapter 1 17
Calvary Baptists Have Gone And Done It Again
Opening of the Calvary Baptist Education Centre

Chapter 2 29
The Triumph of Conscience and Cause
Wolmer's Trust 275th Anniversary

Chapter 3 47
*Persistent, Pioneering, Prayerful, Participatory, Presence
in the Periphery*
The Moravian Church in Jamaica 250th Anniversary

Chapter 4 63
If These Walls Could Talk
Ocho Rios Methodist Church 175th Anniversary

Chapter 5 79
Steady, Stable and Steadfast
Savanna-La-Mar Baptist Church at 175 Years

Chapter 6 93
*Purpose and Progression in Mutual Savings from
Basic Need to Permanent Domicile*
Victoria Mutual Building Society 125th Anniversary

Chapter 7 113
Christian Laywomen: Faith, Focus, Founders and Framework
The 116th Anniversary of Alpha Academy

Contents

Chapter 8   125
Educating Boys into Men of Brave Endeavours
Calabar High School Centenary Anniversary

Chapter 9   141
Anglican Deaconesses Advancing Girls Education:
St. Hugh's, a Success Story of the Twentieth Century
St Hugh's High School at 100

Chapter 10   157
Honouring the Past: Building for the Future
Shortwood Old Students Association 85th Anniversary

Chapter 11   167
The Rescue Mission in Kingston
First Missionary Church 80th Anniversary

Chapter 12   181
God's Shepherds at Bethel
Bethel Baptist Church, Half Way Tree, 60th Anniversary

Chapter 13   189
Finding It Within Ourselves
Jamaica Teachers' Association 50th Anniversary Lecture

Chapter 14   223
Enterprise in the Seminary: Profits Serving Prophets
The Launch of the UTCWI Foundation

Chapter 15   245
An Introduction to Kingston
Presentation of the Keys of the City of Kingston
to President Thabo Mbeki

Contents

Chapter 16   249
*The Role of Higher Education in Nation Building: The Case
of the Dame of COB and Queen's College*
The Inaugural Dr. Keva Bethel Memorial Lecture

Chapter 17   271
Male Marginalisation: Retrospect and Prospect
William of Grants Town 10th Anniversary Memorial Lecture

Chapter 18   295
Sixty Years of Teacher Education: Lessons for the 21st Century
The Inaugural Conference of Teachers Colleges of Jamaica

Chapter 19   315
*The English-Speaking Caribbean in its Journey of Discovery
of our Common Humanity*
**A Reply to The Education International Albert Shanker
Education Award 2004**

Chapter 20   321
*The Spirit of the Mico is the Source of its Longevity:
The First Chancellor's Address*
The Mico University College Graduation 2008

Chapter 21   329
A Vision of UWI and Living in Life's Intersections
University of the West Indies, Mona 2012 Graduation Address

Acknowledgements   337

About the Author   338

Professor Errol Miller, transformational leader, distinguished scholar, inspiring teacher, insightful preacher, charismatic speaker, has once again provided us with an intellectual masterpiece.

The composition of such a fine selection from the myriad of speeches and presentations for which Professor Miller is renowned, could only have been guided by an inner recognition of his responsibility to persistently and consistently raise the sight of his audience whenever the opportunity was presented. The intellectual techniques he uses to connect with his audience are designed to stimulate a hunger within them to delve deeper in their quest to better understand the history of their circumstances, humanity and the particular events being celebrated.

Readers will be impressed by the clarity with which Professor Miller deals with complex concepts such as context and conscience, equality and excellence, individuality and community, reason, revelation and relevance. They will marvel at the ease with which he clarifies life's seeming contradictions that are part and parcel of our daily existence. Of particular significance, is his concept of "living at the intersections of irreconcilable but fundamental human constructs that are neither abstract nor academic."

One of the considerations which seem to undergird this collection is a call by Professor Miller to engage in deep reflections of our own areas of weaknesses that so often, we unconsciously attribute to others.

Professor Miller effortlessly ignites a fierce yearning to acquire the skills of a charismatic, intellectually stimulating and caring speaker. His advice is priceless:

> Speeches are subject to moment and mood. It is unwise to proceed regardless of the moment at which you are to speak and the mood of the audience at that time. It is a tragedy to leave an audience unsatisfied…. A speaker has to engage with the audience in a sensitive manner which includes inputs, verbal and non-verbal from the audience.

The 21 speeches selected for this book, focus on key national institutions, monuments and outstanding leaders. They engender a deep understanding of the circumstances and persons who impacted the birth, growth and continued relevance of these institutions on our daily lives. This is convincingly illustrated in the titles of the chapters and equally significant, the explanation of their enduring relevance and place in our history. The central themes of the book can be gleaned from the author's definition of the "spirit of the Mico" to which he attributes the transformation of the institution from a normal school to that of a University College. I can do no better than to quote Professor Miller. The spirit of the Mico is:

- The courage and the confidence to look beyond human frailty, flaws and faults and see the potentials and possibilities that reside in human personality and society.

- The commitment to build capacity among the vulnerable in society, especially the children of the disadvantaged and marginalised.

- The conviction that when individual enterprise, energy, enthusiasm and entrepreneurship are directed to serve the common good, not only the community benefits, but individuals find meaning and fulfilment in their endeavours.

- The spirit of the Mico is a pioneering spirit, a trailblazing spirit. It is the capability to perceive what is needed, to provide what is necessary and to risk failure in order to achieve the success that is demanded by the circumstances.

The book is a tribute to the ideas and leaders who have faithfully, creatively and collectively contributed to the building of the institutions that inform, influence and essentially determine the directions of our lives.

I highly recommend this publication to the people of Jamaica.

—Professor Sir Kenneth Hall, ON, GCMG, OJ, PhD

Outside and inside of Jamaica—on streets, in airports, in malls, at functions and elsewhere—people have come up to me and said that they still remembered elements from various speeches that I have made. Several remembered a joke that I gave and the implied exhortation. Others remembered the passion of the delivery. This has happened so regularly over the years that I committed myself to putting some of these speeches together, in a single volume, and the idea for writing this book was born.

My usual style is to speak extemporaneously because I found this to be more effective in communicating with audiences. This style required going over the speech in my mind dozens of times before the event. However, some events required written preparation even if I did not follow the text word for word in delivery. During the task of compiling my speeches, the written ones, or ones with copious notes, proved to be more easily assembled. These speeches were presented at various iconic events. I have selected 21 of these speeches for this volume.

My speaking career evolved at an early age. When I was about eleven years old, I learned from my class teacher at Half Way Tree Elementary School, the late Mrs. Lilly Brown, that I had a good speaking voice. She said that was the reason why she had selected me and would coach me to be one of the school's entries in the All Island Elocution Contest. She taught me to recite a poem titled: *Godfrey Gordon Gustavus Gore*—about a boy who never would shut the door. The only detail that I remember is that the finals were at the Ward Theatre, with its huge stage and high balcony. I won first place in my age group. In those days they did not give gold medals, only certificates. However, that experience taught me that although I was very nervous before going on stage, once I started to speak, nervousness went away.

I have since learned that reciting poetry versus making presentations from your own material are totally different. My experiences have many embarrassing moments that some of my close, lifelong friends will not allow me to forget. Many of these experiences were at Bethel Baptist Church, in Half Way Tree. The Church had a programme called 'Training Union' which required that each member of an age group make a presentation to the group once per month on a set topic. Next, were the exigencies of a young church that had to invite preachers who sometimes did not show up. One of us young men had to fill in at the last moment. However, the church became more stabilized with the appointment of a pastor, The Reverend William Edwards. He included me on the preaching roster. Soon after, invitations to speak came from other churches. Several people said, and I came to accept, that I had a gift, for speaking persuasively.

After graduating from the University of the West Indies, and getting married, my first job as a teacher was at Excelsior High School. The Principal, Mr. A. Wesley Powell, was a master fundraiser. One project was monthly paid concerts in the newly constructed school auditorium. I cannot remember how I became the stand up comic for these concerts. I do remember, however, that Mr. Bradley, an Englishman who was very involved in dramatic productions, telling me that I had a great "line of pattern", which he explained as good timing in delivery. I gave up the stand up comic routine when both teachers and students began to laugh when I said anything, even when it was not really funny. I wished to be taken seriously, at least some times. However, I have been unable to stop seeing the funny side of things, even serious things, and making jokes of them. This has often gotten me into trouble.

As a young married teacher, it was difficult to make two ends meet, especially when babies began to arrive. I saw an advertisement in the Gleaner from a well-known company for part-time salesmen. I saw this as a way to earn extra income. My application was accepted. I underwent the training. The starting arrangement was that the company would provide contact information of prospective clients and I would follow-up with a sales presentation. From these initial contacts, each salesman was expected to develop his own contact list. Commission was paid on monthly sales. At the end of the first month, several of my contacts bought appliances. However, I could not bring myself to go and collect the commission. I had severe misgivings:

Would these appliances stand up to long-term use by the clients?

Could they really afford them?

What had I used this gift of persuasion to do?

Was the money worth it?

I resigned because I could not answer these questions to myself in ways that brought peace to my soul. I made a commitment that I would only use this gift to speak about matters that I truly believed in and felt it necessary to persuade others to share those beliefs. Based on this epiphany, I have never charged a fee for speaking at any function. I have accepted gifts after speaking, a minority of which have been cash, but I have never accepted any speaking invitation, or spoken at an event, with prior agreement of material reward.

Accepting the invitation by Mrs. Fay Saunders to speak at the St. Andrew's High School Prize Giving was a milestone in my career in public speaking. It was the first time I spoke to such a large audience outside of a church setting. I was 28 years old at the time and absolutely petrified before speaking. I cannot remember what I said but it must have been well received because other invitations to speak at school events, and other functions, started to come with regularity.

The invitation most centrally related to this volume, *Marking Milestones*, came twelve years later in 1979, from The Reverend Sam Reid and the leadership of the Calvary Baptist Church to speak at the opening of the new building for their Christian Education Centre. It was the first time that I gave an address which went back into the history of the group that invited me.

The response of the audience to this address, and the resulting interactivity that was generated, is still unique in my experience. Upon conclusion of the address, conversations broke out between members of the audience. These lasted for between ten to twelve minutes before the Master of Ceremonies was able to restore order and proceed with the completion of the Programme. I later learned that parts of my presentation related to core issues that were being vigorously debated among members and well-wishers of the Church.

The impact on me was profound. I realised that addressing fundamental issues that are germane to the audience, reminding them of who they are and the road they have travelled was an approach that had real meaning for people. I adopted and adapted this approach for several subsequent special occasions.

"Speeches are subject to moment and mood...it is a tragedy to leave an audience unsatisfied."

—Professor Emeritus
the Honourable Errol Miller
OJ, CD, LLD, Ph.D

T he book, *Marking Milestones,* is a collection of 21 speeches that I gave at special events celebrating great milestones in the history of the organisations that invited me; including three of such events that are personal milestones.

In order of longevity of the organisations these are:

- The 275th Anniversary of the Wolmer's Trust
- The 250th Anniversary of the Moravian Church in Jamaica
- The 175th Anniversary of the Ocho Rios Methodist Church
- The 175th Anniversary of the Savanna-la-mar Baptist Church
- The 125th Anniversary of Victoria Mutual Building Society
- The 116th Anniversary of Alpha Academy
- The 100th Anniversary of Calabar High School
- The 100th Anniversary of St. Hugh's High School
- The 85th Anniversary of the Shortwood Old Students' Association
- The 80th Anniversary of the First Missionary Church of the Missionary Alliance
- The 50th Anniversary of the Bethel Baptist Church
- The 50th Anniversary of the Jamaica Teachers' Association
- The Kingston and St. Andrew Corporation Event presenting the Keys to the City of Kingston to President Thabu Mbeki of South Africa
- The Launch of the United Theological College of the West Indies' Foundation
- The Inaugural Keva Bethel Memorial Lecture of the College of the Bahamas

- The Inaugural Conference of the Jamaica Teachers' Colleges
- My reply at the Albert Shanker Education Prize Award Ceremony for 2004 by Education International at its World Congress held in Port Alegre, Brazil
- My address as the First Chancellor of Mico University College at its graduation ceremony in 2008; and
- The graduation address given at the University of the West Indies, Mona in 2012 when I was awarded the Honorary Degree of Doctor of Laws.

A few of the speeches were delivered almost as written. Among these are the Calabar 100th Anniversary Education Lecture, the oration when President Thabu Mbeki received the Keys of the City of Kingston, the Reply to the Albert Shanker Award; the first address as Chancellor of Mico University College and the UWI, Mona Graduation Address 2012.

The speech at the Wolmer's Trust 275th Anniversary is very close to the speech as written but not as delivered. It was about 11:45 pm when I got to speak. I promised to finish before midnight and did, inclusive of the planned joke. The standing ovation I received may well have been related to having kept that promise, than to the content delivered. In the case of the 250th Anniversary of the Moravian Church, I prepared a Lecture but the event was a banquet. I had misread the situation. Like the Wolmer's presentation, the speech delivered was excerpts of what had been prepared.

A few students at the UWI once asked me to give them a lecture on public speaking. I had to explain to them that I had not received any formal training but had learned the craft by numerous trials and many errors. What I learned is that public speaking shared similarities with love making. Speeches are subject to moment and mood. It is unwise to proceed regardless of the moment at which you are to speak and the mood of the audience at that time. Further, it is a tragedy to leave an audience unsatisfied. Speeches have to come to a conclusion that leave audiences satisfied.

In a nutshell, the speaker has to engage with the audience in a sensitive manner which includes inputs, verbal and non-verbal, from the audience. If public speaking is a performance, it is more a dance with a partner than a soliloquy. This means that at sometimes, audiences take speakers down paths that were unplanned but which enhances the speech. In the interactions, insights are gained and spoken but were neither written nor planned. Planned thoughts were forgotten and not spoken but should have been spoken. In hindsight, after the speech, some insights become abundantly clear that should have been part of foresight and preparation. Also, people contribute feedback and information that are enriching.

In addition, in the preparation for this publication I included information that was not available at the time but which now enriches the essence and the substance of the speech. For example, the Anglican beginnings of the Victoria Mutual Building Society and the fact that The Reverend William Gardner of North Street Congregational Church was the founder of the First Building Society in Jamaica. I have had a copy of the second edition of Gardner's, *A History of Jamaica,* for several decades, but never read the foreword by his brother until I came across it online, after the speech.

The essence and substance of what was spoken at the event and the final product as written in this book are basically the same. However, in some cases, what is recorded in this volume is more complete and is richer in details because the written speeches are not constrained by time and circumstance of the actual event. The speeches also include feedback following the live speech and, in a few cases, contain details that were not available at the time. Nowhere was this more evident to me than with the speech given at the launch of the United Theological College of the West Indies' Foundation. In writing the speech, I worked from a transcript of the spoken speech. I realised that in the delivery of the speech, as a result of interaction with the audience, I kept leap frogging at several points, as spelling out the details was deemed unnecessary. The audience knew the subject, got the point and responded, many times with laughter, even before I completed the thought. However, it could not be assumed that the audience reading the speech would be the same audience who heard it. Hence, the speech as written here is far more formal and complete than the speech as spoken.

In the process of preparing and delivering these speeches, and in benefiting from feedback afterwards, I have come to a more holistic understanding of our people, a greater appreciation of our history, a better understanding of education, and deeper respect for sacrifices made by individuals that seemed foolish to onlookers at the time. I have been forced to have greater deference for those whom we succeed, including their perspectives and starting points. This has made me less judgmental, yet firmer in conviction, about the values and the virtues that really count. It has also altered my understanding of time and change. Real change takes time. Transformation requires patience and persistence. Further, life is not linear nor are accomplishments of one generation guaranteed permanence. There are always persons who come along later who 'knew not Joseph'.

This volume is presented to honour the organisations and the occasions. The intention is to inform and inspire a wider audience than those who heard these speeches. I have tried, by the Grace of God, to comply with the injunction of St. Paul to the Philippians in Chapter 4 of his Epistle and Verse 8:

> Finally, brethren, whatsoever things are true, whatsoever things are honest, whatsoever things are just, whatsoever things are pure, whatsoever things are lovely, whatsoever things are of good report; if there be any virtue, and if there be any praise, think on these things.

To God be the glory.

Chapter 1

Calvary Baptists
Have Gone And Done It Again

THE OPENING OF
THE CALVARY BAPTIST CHURCH
EDUCATION CENTRE
September, 1979

Mr. Master of Ceremonies, Reverend Sam Reid, pastor, deacons and members of Calvary Baptist Church, specially invited guests, brothers and sisters in Christ you have done me the great honour of being the guest speaker at this opening of Calvary Baptist Education Centre. This we are told is to be Phase One of the move of the Church from its original and present home on Market Street to these new premises. The building of the Chapel will come later.

As a fifth generation Kingstonian, it is a particular privilege to be invited to speak in Montego Bay, the City of the West, often referred to as the Republic of Montego Bay. Having been allowed to enter without a visa, I hope that there will be no problems in leaving.

Reverend Sam and myself go back a long way. I first met him when he was a student at the Calabar Theological College and I, a student at the Calabar High School. The College had a table tennis board. At times a few of us from the High School tried to get a game at the College. Reverend Sam was a champion table tennis player. He used to beat me religiously. By that I mean that he would beat me almost all the times and the few games that I won was as a result of Christian charity on his part to prevent me from being totally discouraged.

Calvary Baptist Church. Montego Bay, Jamaica.

Founded in 1846, had amongst its membership, the daughter and granddaughter of National Hero, Sam Sharpe.

While Reverend Sam was always Baptist, I come from an Anglican family. I subsequently became Baptist through the Bethel Baptist Church. So today, as a Deacon of Bethel Baptist, I bring you greetings and congratulations from the Bethel Baptist Church at Half Way Tree; your younger sister church by far.

Although I am an educator and may have been invited because this is an Education Centre, my preparation for today has led me away from a focus on education to a focus on the Calvary Baptist Church, it's past and present. While my background is in the natural sciences I have always loved history. In Fifth Form at Calabar, the choice was between Additional Mathematics and History. I did both for the Cambridge Exams. I went to the classes in Add Math and studied the history syllabus on my own. This affection for history spurred the curiosity for looking into the history of Calvary Baptist Church, being generally aware that your church has such high prestige and long pedigree within the Jamaica Baptist Union. Then there was an incident that happened in my family that simply clinched the message for this evening.

My father is a strict disciplinarian. He is a great father but practices tough love. When I was growing up, my mother simply had to say 'I am going to tell your father when he gets home'. She would receive instant compliance, accompanied by pleas not to tell him followed by promises of never again to do whatever was the transgression. It would be accurate to say that we feared our father. What has been truly amazing is to witness his transformation from father to grandfather. Currently, one of his young grandsons is living with his grandparents. Every evening when my father comes home, JJ runs out to greet granddad. They then carry on conversations that we, the children, would never dream of having with our father.

Recently my father has had a few fender benders that have left dents on his car. The other day he had another of these. As usual, JJ went out to greet him. He saw the new dent on the car.

He rebuked my father saying: "Grand Dad, you have gone and done it again!"

I am told by those who heard the emphatic nature of this strong rebuke expected JJ to be crushed by my father. Instead, my father proceeded to give JJ a full explanation of what happened and promised not to let it happen again. The consensus among us children is that our father has gone soft. Grandparenthood has transformed him.

This evening at the launch of the Calvary Baptist Education Centre, my theme is: "Calvary Baptists have gone and done it again"!

This is not a rebuke. Rather, it is a recitation of your history within the context of your actions in Jamaica today. To make the connection, allow me to go back 133 years to the founding of the Calvary Baptist Church in 1846.

Pioneers of Revolutionary Change

The year 1846 was a momentous year in the history of Jamaican Baptists. Reverend Thomas Burchell had died, he was the pastor of the Baptist Church in Montego Bay now named after him. His death followed that of Reverend William Knibb in 1845. Knibb was the pastor of the Falmouth Baptist Church. These two English Baptist missionaries, stationed in the West, along with The Reverend James Phillippo of Spanish Town, were great leaders of the denomination as well as the most respected and revered leaders of the recently freed slaves.

Knibb was the charismatic public spokesman. Burchell was the reserved thinker and strategist. Knibb and Burchell were great friends. They shared the same radical ideas about the future of the colony and the denomination. For example, they agreed that Jamaican Baptists should move to greater autonomy from the Baptist Missionary Society and that the newly freed slaves should organise politically and be represented in the House of Assembly.

Phillippo was the prime mover in the pioneering of the free village movement and agreed with the political goals of having black representatives in the House of Assembly but was far more cautious in seeking autonomy from the Baptist Missionary Society in England. Phillippo got sick, took a leave of absence and went to England. He left another missionary in charge of the church in Spanish Town. When he returned, his brother missionary claimed the pastorate.

A court battle ensued and Phillippo lost.

Knibb sided with the missionary who ousted Phillippo in 1845. Ironically, the church in Spanish Town, that Phillippo built and was ousted from, now bears his name: the Phillippo Baptist Church. The point is, that between 1845 and 1846, death and division had robbed the denomination of its three most respected and outstanding leaders.

Calvary Baptist was born out of a division in the Montego Bay Baptist Church, now the Burchell Baptist Church, following the death of Burchell. To use contemporary terminology, Montego Bay had a First and a Second Baptist Church. Reverend Sam Reid is the real church historian, not me. Hence, he may be able to tell us what the disagreement was about. As a dabbler in history I can only say, that after emancipation, the Baptist denomination boomed in membership, finances and in influence.

Baptist churches were the largest.

Baptist missionaries were the best paid.

Large manses were built for many of their pastors.

By 1846, divisions took place as missionaries competed for pastorates. All I can say is that Calvary Baptist Church on Market Street was founded as a result of division in the Burchell Church at a momentous time in the history of the Baptist denomination.

Protection or Destruction

If 1846 was a momentous year for the Baptists; it was a disastrous year for the Jamaican economy. It was in July of that year that the British Parliament passed the *Sugar Duties Equalisation Act.*

The Act stipulated that preferential duties for sugar from the West Indies would be phased out over a six year period. After 1852, all sugar entering Britain would be charged the same duty. In other words, the protection for sugar produced in British colonies with free labour would be phased out over this period. Sugar produced in Cuba and Brazil, which still had slavery, would enter the British market on the same terms as sugar produced by paid labour in British colonies.

When news reached Jamaica that the British Parliament had passed this Act, the first reaction of planters and the sugar interest was outrage. As far as they were concerned this was nothing short of betrayal. Their strong argument against the abolition of slavery was that the cost of labour would increase the cost of sugar production and the result would be ruin of the sugar industry; the mainstay of the economy and of their livelihood. The planters' understanding was that the abolition of slavery and preferential duties for West Indian sugar were intrinsically linked.

Abolition of slavery in British colonies was the *quid* and preferential duty for sugar from these colonies entering the British market was the *pro quo.*

Sugar from places that slavery continued would not be allowed to be sold in Britain on the same terms as sugar from the West Indies. This must have been an English gentleman's understanding because this was not written anywhere. In other words, it was something like the British Constitution unwritten but common knowledge.

Planters held meetings across the island protesting the passage of the Act. Their slogan was 'Protection or Destruction'. The consensus of these meetings, and of the Assembly, was to seek to have the powerful West Indian Sugar Lobby in England work for the repeal of the Act. It is important to understand that in 1846, many owners of Jamaican sugar plantations lived in England, and an even greater number depended on income from the proceeds of the sale of Jamaican sugar.

Panic Ensues

The second reaction of the ruling planter class was panic. This was because very shortly after the passage of the *Sugar Duties Equalisation Act* the price of sugar in Britain fell quite dramatically. This meant that the earnings from sugar were also greatly reduced. To understand that this should cause panic among the planters it is important to understand how the sugar industry worked then, which is not very different from how it works now.

Before the planting season each year, Jamaican planters borrowed money from London merchants to purchase supplies that were shipped to Jamaica. The London merchants were repaid from the proceeds of sale of sugar exported to Britain from Jamaica. A sudden drop in the price of sugar in Britain meant that many planters would be unable to repay the debt owed to suppliers.

The repercussion of this would be that London merchants would not extend credit for goods to be purchased for the next planting season.

But worse happened.

Britain was in a deep economic and financial recession. Many merchant houses went into bankruptcy. The decrease in the price of sugar simply added to the problem. Several merchant houses that financed Jamaican and West Indian sugar collapsed. Credit to West Indian planters virtually dried up.

The panic in Jamaica took several forms. Remember, at that time, Jamaica was largely a sugar colony. There was no banana industry, no bauxite and no tourism. A major downturn in sugar had widespread effect in the entire colony:

1. The first expression of panic was in predictions of doom and gloom, especially from the planters and those involved in sugar production. Some planters went as far as suggesting that Jamaica should consider seceding from Britain and join the United States. This resulted in backlash from the black population.

    Joining the United States could result in a re-introduction of slavery— as it continued in the Southern states.

2. The second expression went beyond talk. This included opting out of immigration schemes to import indentured workers from India and China. If you want an explanation of why Jamaica has a much smaller population of Indians than Trinidad and Guyana, 1846 is a starting point.

    Jamaica stopped participating in the immigration scheme while Trinidad and Guyana continued. It is true that in later years Jamaica again imported indentured workers from India but the numbers involved were less. Probably of greater importance, is the fact that planters cancelled most of the plans and projects they had on stream to mechanize and modernize the sugar industry. This included plans for railways and tramways, building and modernizing sugar factories.

3. The third expression of panic may surprise you. The planter representatives in the House of Assembly, through what was then referred to as the Country Party, passed a bill to reduce the salaries of the Governor, other colonial officials and the Anglican clergy. The Anglican Church was the state church and the salaries of the Bishop, rectors and priests were paid from taxes. The argument was that with sugar in depression the government of the colony would collect fewer taxes and therefore had to reduce expenditure by cutting these salaries. However, this was really taking the fight to the Imperial Government, since most of those whose salaries would be affected had been sent to Jamaica from Britain to posts in Jamaica.

The Imperial Government had betrayed the planters, hence they were going to punish British representatives in Jamaica. The Legislative Council vetoed the *Retrenchment Bill*. Remember the Legislative Council was comprised of persons appointed by the Governor; several of them were colonial officials whose salaries would be cut. The Assembly responded by threatening not to approve any revenue needed by the Governor to run the administration of the colony until the Council passed the *Retrenchment Bill*. This led to a stalemate which lasted until February 1847, when the Assembly passed the Revenue Bill on the casting vote of the Speaker of the House.

Summary of Circumstances in which Calvary Baptist was Founded in 1846

- The death of the two most respected leaders in the Denomination and in the colony, Knibb and Burchell, both of whom were from the West.

- The embarrassing public spectacle of a court case involving two Baptist missionaries contesting who was the pastor of the Baptist Church in Spanish Town.

- Divisions among the members of the Spanish Town Baptist and the Montego Bay Baptist churches.

- Economic crisis brought on by the sudden decline of the price of sugar in Britain and the drying up of credit to the planters.

- Predictions of doom and gloom based on the passage of the *Sugar Duties Equalisation Act* and the planters view that the sugar industry, the pillar of the economy, could not survive without protection against sugar produced in Cuba and Brazil which still had slavery.

- Rumblings in the country as a result of talk by planters of seceding from Britain and joining the United States and backlash from the black population that this was a rouse to return to slavery.

- A crisis and stalemate in the government as the House of Assembly and the Legislative Council fought over the *Retrenchment Bill* and revenue to run the colony.

In the midst of these negative circumstances, some members of the Baptist Church in Montego Bay decided that the best solution to the internal divisions among the members was to found another church in the Town.

It was a positive move in negative circumstances.

It was a decisive move in confusing times.

It was a bold move considering the predictions of coming economic doom.

It was a move of faith in defiance of the facts.

It was venturing into the unknown and trusting God when many were losing heart and being paralysed by fear. The testimony that faith prevailed is here today as 133 years later we are launching the Education Centre of the Calvary Baptist Church on the site planned for the relocation of the church from its original site since 1846.

When I say, **"Calvary Baptists you have gone and done it again"**, you should begin to see that today you are repeating your past. To make the point abundantly clear let us look at Jamaica in 1979. It should not take as long to survey the present as it took to recall the past circumstances of the founding of the church. For the sake of brevity, let me sketch the broad contours of our times by just listing the main lines of the terrain:

- Crime, particularly gun crimes, continues to escalate; despite the Gun Court. Murders continue to mount. People are afraid even in their homes.

- Partisan political violence is on a scale never seen before. Each political party is claiming innocence and blaming the other for the atrocities that are becoming common place. But clearly each party is not speaking the truth. Both are involved. We are seeing whole communities under siege from rival political gangs. It is ridiculous to believe that these communities are besieging themselves. Yet every day leaders are blaming the other side about what is taking place.

- The Cold War is being played out on our shores. Some have pledged to go to the mountain top with Fidel and others have vowed to save us from that fate. Let me state my position here. Capitalism and communism are two denominations of a religion called materialism.

There is salvation in neither. Salvation is only to be found in our Lord Jesus Christ. As long as the fight is over things, we are missing the fact that we are spiritual beings living in a material world.

The spirit comes first. "But seek ye first the kingdom of God, and his righteousness; and all these things shall be added unto you". (The Bible, KJV). Righteousness must come before riches, if wealth is to be used for the purpose for which they are granted by the goodness of God.

- The war between the oil producing countries which have formed the cartel called OPEC and the oil consuming countries is also at our door step. The escalation in oil prices over the last five to six years has had a very negative effect on our economic growth and development. Jamaica has tried to counter by forming a bauxite cartel and have imposed a levy on the export of bauxite but these have had very negative consequences for us as a country as the powerful bauxite lobby in the United States has struck back.

- There has been the Crawling Peg devaluation of the Jamaican dollar where each month it declines against the US dollar. Draconian restrictions have been placed on taking US$ out of the country. The justification is to prevent what is called capital flight but it is almost making criminals out of ordinary people who are just doing very ordinary things.

- The Government has had to go to the International Monetary Fund for relief and it has imposed some tough conditions for assistance from the Fund. One of the most difficult and frustrating things about being the principal of a college at this time is the directive to cut back on expenditure and on developments in order to ensure that the economy recovers. One of the things that economists are missing, is that for countries like ours, it is education that will result in economic development. It is wrong-headed to cut back on education as a means of securing economic recovery. I tell you this frustration is shared by all of us in the teaching profession.

- Almost every week we hear of people, including friends and family, who have decided to leave the country and to migrate to greener pastures and safer surroundings. I do not know if you have heard it but a joke going around is that the last person to leave the country should remember to turn off the lights. Many people have lost their nerves and have left the country. Some have even sold their homes at bargain prices

- Predictions of doom and gloom seem to be everywhere.

I hope that this list of problems/challenges is sufficient to sketch the circumstances of our times. When I compare these times with those of 1846, while the specific elements are different, the general atmosphere and circumstances seem remarkably similar. The building and launch of this Education Centre is in defiance of the material facts. This is not just a statement in words but an emphatic statement in concrete and steel. This concrete statement declares hope despite the bleak times. It sees beyond the adversities of the present and lays the foundation to further and future witness to the Grace and Goodness of God. This is a spiritual act manifesting trust in God. It says Jamaica will be here with the lights on. It is setting the stage by establishing the means by which we will continue to serve God, no matter what.

"Calvary Baptists, you have gone and done it again". Whether you realise it or not, your actions in building and launching this Education Centre, as Phase One in the relocation of the church, is exactly consistent with the circumstance in which the church was founded 133 years ago. There is a theory in biology which states that ontogeny recapitulates phylogeny. Simply put it is that the stages that the fetus in the womb goes through between embryo and baby, mirror the stages of evolution of mammals. This theory has been discredited in biology and therefore would not remotely apply to a community of individuals. Even then, I was greatly relieved when in examining the Programme, and in listening to the welcome and greetings there was no reference made to the founding of the church in 1846. I take this as evidence that there has been no conscious effort on the part of the present leadership and membership of the Calvary Baptist Church to imitate your past. Rather, you are exercising fresh faith in the present without any memory of the past.

In Freudian psychology, there is the notion of the unconscious which is used to explain some behaviour. At first, I had difficulty understanding this notion of the unconscious until I first visited England and Europe ten years ago. Their understanding of the past is very different from ours in this part of the world. In England and Europe, modern buildings are those constructed within the last 200 years. Recent buildings are those built since the end of World Wars I and II. People do so many things routinely and habitually that when asked why, they explain their actions by saying that this is the way things have been done. We in the Western Hemisphere are very conscious peoples. We do most things deliberately and consciously. For many Jamaicans, the past is last month. We are about to tear down buildings constructed in the 1940s. The unconscious cannot explain the actions of the Calvary Baptist Church in 1979.

What then explains why "Calvary Baptists have gone and done it again"? The best explanation that I can offer is that the Holy Spirit has led Reverend Sam Reid, the deacons and the members of the church to take this course. This local church has accepted the leading of the Spirit and acted accordingly. Jesus is the same yesterday, today and for evermore. God is the 'I AM THAT I AM'. He lives in eternity. He is outside of time. When His children, in succeeding generations, seek God's leading, guidance and direction; the Father, the Son and the Holy Spirit will direct them to act in ways that are remarkably similar and consistent, even if the specifics are different.

Calvary Baptist Church, in these testing times, your actions inspire us all. It reminds us that without faith it is impossible to please God. We are assured that God is faithful. His response to faith is to make things happen. Go forth therefore with this assurance, just as your forebears did.

To God be the glory.

Chapter 2

The Triumph of Conscience and Cause

~

WOLMER'S TRUST 275th ANNIVERSARY

May, 2004

~

Mr. Master of Ceremonies, Professor the Honourable Hugh Wynter and Mrs Wynter; Deputy Governor General Reverend Weevil Gordon and Mrs. Gordon; Honourable Burchell Whiteman, Minister of Education and Mrs Whiteman; Honourable Dean Peart, Minister of Local Government, the Most Honourable Edward Seaga, Leader of the Opposition and Mrs. Seaga; Lord Bishop of Jamaica Reverend Reid, former principals of Wolmer's Schools for Girls and Boys, Miss Audrey Pinto, Coleridge Barnett and Hyacinth Bennett; Chairman of the Wolmer's Trust and members of the Trust, present principals of the Wolmer's schools; Mrs. June Spence, Mrs. Montague and Mr. Myrie, distinguished Wolmerians and guests like myself, I deem it a great honour and a humongous privilege, as a Calabar Old Boy, to be invited to be the Guest Speaker on this great Wolmer's occasion. There are not many schools in the Caribbean, the Western world or the world at large that can claim continuous existence for 275 years. I can only take it that consideration was given to the fact that my two sons, one of whom serenaded us during dinner, and most of my nephews and one niece, went to Wolmer's Schools.

Distinguished Ladies and Gentlemen all, I have to acknowledge again that I am deeply and genuinely touched by the honour that has been given to me to address you tonight. I am absolutely sure that there are many who would have wanted this opportunity. My humble prayer has been that the

Wolmer's Trust was established in 1829.

Good Lord would help me to find the thoughts and the words that would add real value to these celebrations by both inspiring and challenging you on this great occasion.

I am also acutely aware of the hour of the night. You have been dined and wined; in addition to being serenaded during dinner; you have been taken down a memory lane of music with Wolmerian connections. You have heard reports from the 250th and the 275th Committees, presentations have been made to outstanding contributors to the Trust and you have been entertained by the unique wit and humour of the Master of Ceremonies. I now stand as the greatest obstacle to your departure. I am therefore at the mercy of your generosity and promise not to trespass for a minute longer than is necessary to fulfil the obligation demanded by your invitation.

However, allow me one small digression into humour. Two small boys were very concerned that they were not very popular in their neighbourhood and had no friends outside of themselves. Following some considerable discussion they came to the conclusion that the only solution was baptism. So they immediately set off on this Wednesday morning to receive the same at the nearest church. They knocked at the door of the church and the only one present was the caretaker. They requested baptism. Acting outside of ecclesiastic authority and with deplorable malice, the caretaker proceeded to take them to the bathroom, duck their heads in the toilet bowl and declared them baptized. Delighted that they had been baptized, the boys left the church but were now somewhat confused as to which denomination they belonged. One youngster opined that they could not be Baptist because they would have been totally immersed. The other ruled out being Catholic because they would have been sprinkled.

One asked the other, "Did you smell the water down there?"

The other said, "yes," and they both were convinced that they were now *Piscopalians*.

Bishop Reid, I am taking no liberties with the Anglican Church. For any clarification, you will need to check with my friend Rupert Gallimore who told me this story.

Ladies and gentlemen, you have commissioned a history of the Wolmer's School, which my esteemed colleague Professor Patrick Byran, has so very ably written. I am in no position to speak to you as a historian or with any detailed knowledge about the inner workings of the schools or as a Wolmerian from personal experience. My formation is that of a Social Psychologist of Education seeking to understand how institutions and events shape mentalities and mindsets. What I will attempt to do, as an outsider, is to present, from information available to me, my interpretation of the essence of what Wolmer's represent. This is expressed in the title: "The Triumph of Conscience and Cause".

The Context

John Wolmer was a successful goldsmith who died in Kingston in 1729, but probably started his career in Port Royal. Up to 1692 Port Royal was one of the riches cities of the New World. It was the bullion capital of the Americas. The plunder of Spanish possessions by English privateers, and pirates, brought gold and silver from the mines of Mexico and Peru into Port Royal. The consistently good quality of the gold and silver facilitated exchange and a money economy in coins. As a goldsmith, John Wolmer was most likely involved with the use of gold for ornamental purposes as well as for exchange in the money economy that set Port Royal and Jamaica apart from all other English colonies.

Kingston was born out of the disaster that follow in the earthquake and tsunami which struck Port Royal in 1692 as refugees found respite across the harbour. Kingston was carved out of the Parish of Liguanea. Kingston was made a Parish in 1693. However, it was the devastating fire of 1703, which started in warehouses, some of which stored gunpowder; which forced many merchants and artisans to relocate to Kingston. I am only speculating, but it is more than likely that John Wolmer was among these who relocated from Port Royal to Kingston, in the decade between 1693 and 1703. In so doing, he contributed to the building of Kingston which succeeded Port Royal.

The records show that John Wolmer was married in 1705 in the Anglican Church of Half Way Tree in the new Parish of St. Andrew. The fact that the Memorial Tablet "John Wolmer" is in the Kingston Parish Church, where he was buried in 1729, is probably testimony not only to the bequest of the Wolmer's school, but also to his contribution to the parish church and its construction.

At the time in which John Wolmer lived and worked in Jamaica, and particularly in Port Royal and Kingston, men came to make it rich and return to whence they came with their fortune or to endow their offspring in England. Historians have given these exploiters of Jamaican opportunities a very generous name. They have called them absentees. John Wolmer was not an absentee. He made his fortune in Jamaica, chose to live in Jamaica, kept his fortune here and bequeathed his estate to Jamaican posterity.

There have always been these two types of successful wealthy people in Jamaica:

1. Those who made their wealth in Jamaica and then export it, and

2. Those who made their wealth in Jamaica and then re-invested it here.

Every Wolmerian should know and be aware of the fact that you are a beneficiary of that category of Jamaicans that made and kept their wealth invested in Jamaica. John Wolmer is a prototype and pioneer of this category of Jamaicans.

The Conscience

John Wolmer's conscience urged him to recognise the obligation he had to the community and colony in which he had carved out his success. His conscience urged him to ignore the misguided egotistical notion that success is solely due to the superiority of the individuals so favoured. He understood that the success of any individual is in part due to the circumstances and the happenstances of the community in which that success was achieved. The obligation arising from that understanding is to give back to that community in substance or in service. The circumstances of the goldsmith's life led him to give back in substance, the legacy that formed the Wolmer's Trust.

To better appreciate John Wolmer's exercise of conscience, it is necessary to juxtapose this against those who acted with no conscience. Increasingly historians have confirmed the conclusion of Eric Williams that it is the wealth generated in the Caribbean colonies, particularly Jamaica, that was the critical source in financing Britain's rise as an industrial power.

Economist's like Lloyd Best of Trinidad has long pointed out that Jamaica was a colony of exploitation as against the North American colonies that were principally colonies of settlement. Wealth generated out of the brutal exploitation of enslaved people on plantations in Jamaica provided annuities for many who lived the life of luxury in England. Had most of the wealth generated in Jamaica, when sugar was king in the eighteenth century, been invested in Jamaica, this country today would clearly be ranked among the most wealthy in the world. It is the lack of conscience on the part of many peers of John Wolmer that facilitated the massive exportation of the wealth created in Jamaica.

Many of John Wolmer's peers, or their children, exported their wealth without any regard for the long-term viability of this society. Their focus was personal and patriarchal, that is, on themselves and those who were members of their lineage. Acting outside the mores of his times, Wolmer's conscience dictated that his obligation was to the long term good of the colony and specifically to the community in which he lived and worked.

Today we celebrate John Wolmer's exercise of conscience 275 years after his death.

The Specification of the Cause

Lurking somewhere in the background of almost all of life's great stories is some paradox and contradiction. John Wolmer's story is no exception. While the exercise of his conscience stemmed from his sense of the obligation of success, his specification of the cause rested partly in the great disappointment of his life.

John Wolmer was married but had no children.

However, bearing in mind that at that time the 'in-thing', in the process of becoming rich, was to be a 'Grandee': that is, 'to ride hard, to drink hard, to gamble hard and have a lot of brown-skinned progeny'. In a nutshell the lifestyle of Port Royal and of Kingston was marked by licentious living. The point of significance about John Wolmer is that he had no children. I am not about to cast any aspersion on John Wolmer's character, but merely wish to note that at that time, and even today in Jamaica, not having children in the marriage does not by itself preclude a man from fathering children. Put another way, the fact that he had no children was not due to the fact that his wife, at fifty years old when they married, was beyond child bearing age. John Wolmer apparently could not have children.

The remarkable thing about this successful goldsmith, who had no children, is that he seems to have been able to empathize with men who had children but could not take care of them. Here is a successful man disappointed that he did not have a child but who could move out of the castle of his own skin and envisage the frustration of unsuccessful men who had children. Disappointed that he did not have a child to share what he could so abundantly provide, John Wolmer chose not to castigate and condemn men who had children that they could not provide for but rather to show compassion for such men and their children.

John Wolmer's disappointment in not having children, and his empathy with children who had fathers who could not take care of them, specified the cause. Succinctly put, children born into families that had fallen on hard times deserve a chance to rise above those circumstances. The assertion in John Wolmer's will is that education is the best legacy to leave children, especially those who have fathers that cannot provide for them.

In John Wolmer's times, men with means sent their children to England and Scotland for schooling. There were no schools in Jamaica for the children of men without means. The practical specification of the cause therefore was to provide a school for children of men whose hopes and strivings for wealth had been dashed—thus virtually consigning their children to ignorance.

Probably John Wolmer had an even broader understanding of the cause of education and schooling than reclamation of the children of men who had fallen on hard times. Unlike the North American colonies, Jamaica was not established by investments of Joint Stock Companies. The Puritans of New England had bought and owned the Stock Company by which they came to settle. The Southern colonies were financed by Stock Companies in England. Jamaica was established from the profits of the plunder of Spanish possession and of trade because of its strategic location. Privateers, merchants and residents of Port Royal, and later Kingston, invested much of their profits in the establishment of sugar and coffee plantations. Local enterprise, some of it illegal or even immoral, generated the investments made in the nascent Jamaican economy.

Henry Morgan, the iconic privateer, became a gentleman planter in Port Maria no doubt because of his understanding that the short-term profits of plunder had to be invested in long-term economic enterprises. Consistent with the times, Morgan was even made Lieutenant Governor of Jamaica.

John Wolmer's action seem to suggest that he had some understanding that long-term economic development could not be sustained without educational provision which fostered and developed the talents of children of men who could afford to educate their children. In other words, Jamaica's economic development could not be sustained by children who were educated abroad, some of whom never returned. While others were leaving a legacy through investments in plantations, John Wolmer decided to leave a legacy in local education and schooling.

In proposing the establishment of a charity school, John Wolmer was not acting within the mainstream of those times. The Grandee lifestyle was related to the fact that British men on leave from the restraining influence of women in general, and wives in particular, and who had almost unrestrained access to the sexuality of African women slaves on the plantation, and in town to Brown women who were largely dependent on their patronage, had little regard for schooling. Family, church and school were the institutions of community. This is what they had left behind in Britain and to which they planned to return in due time. Family, church and school did not fit easily into the get rich quick orientation of the economic exploitation or the debauchery. The calypso mentality, of which the Caribbean is often accused, was developed by European men and not Africans. Africans only gave it rhythm.

Interestingly, John Wolmer's exercise of conscience and specification of cause was given expression posthumously. Given the fact that he was acting in a manner that was so contrary to the mores of the social strata to which he belonged, John Wolmer opted for the safety of death, and the barriers this poses to dialogue with his peers, to impose the dictates of his conscience and boldly state his cause. His will stated that 2,360 pounds be set aside from his estate to be used to establish a charity school for children in the parish in which he died and that fifty pounds be used for the poor of Kingston.

In other words, John Wolmer, by his will, implied that hand-outs to the poor is for immediate relief. Investment in the economy without provision for education is myopic. Neglect of schooling for the children of the poor is shortsighted. However, investment in education, especially for children of the poor, is for the long-term good and success of all.

Two hundred and seventy-five years after his death, we celebrate the foresight and perspicacity of John Wolmer's conscience and his cause. His conscience and his cause have remained alive. They have survived instances of corruption, incompetence and mismanagement in the deployment of the assets. This is because succeeding generations of Jamaicans have connected with the conscience of John Wolmer and have kept his cause alive.

There is every indication that the posthumous declaration in John Wolmer's will captured the attention of his peers and the support of some. The Wolmer's Trust was enacted into law by the Assembly in the relatively short period of seven years. Even a casual reading of Jamaica's history reveals that there were several others who displayed a similar conscience to John Wolmer and specified an identical cause. This is evidenced by several charity schools established in Barbados and Jamaica during the seventeenth and eighteenth centuries. Many did not survive. Among those surviving are Combermere in Barbados, the oldest being over 300 years old and Mannings here in Jamaica which is somewhat younger than Wolmer's but not by many years. The question to be answered is why did Wolmer's survive?

In my view, the answer is with respect to two principal factors. First is the composition of the Trust and second is the capacity to change.

Composition of the Trust

The Trust established in 1736 was composed as follows:

- The President of the Legislative Council plus four senior members of the Council

- The Speaker of the House of Assembly plus the three members of the Assembly elected from Kingston

- The Chief Justice plus four Senior Magistrates of Kingston

- The Custos of the Parish of Kingston plus the twelve members of the Vestry of Kingston

- The Rector of Kingston and three Church Wardens of Kingston

- Six freemen of Kingston, appointed annually.

The Wolmer's Trust was composed of the senior leaders of Central and Local Government; the Judiciary; the State Church and civil society of Kingston. In other words, appointees of the Governor, politicians elected by the people, judges, clergymen and members of the public were harnessed and charged with implementing the visionary legacy of John Wolmer.

Historians point out that the 36 members of the Trust had to be contrasted with the 10 students with which the school opened. However, it is not the size of the Trust that is important but the formula of its composition. There was administrative genius in the composition of the Trust. As the Chairman of the Electoral Advisory Committee, and former Chairman of the Board of the Jamaica Broadcasting Corporation, I cannot but see the significance and success of the formula for the composition of Wolmer's Trust in considering the survival of the school founded from John Wolmer's estate. The Wolmer's Trust had different groups of stakeholders and actors watching and balancing each other in the administration and oversight of the Trust.

The Capacity to Change

I wish to put forward also that Wolmer's has survived for these 275 years because of its capacity to change while being constantly connected to the conscience and committed to the cause. Wolmer's has constantly and continuously provided education to children whose parents have fallen into hard times. Through education offered those children, the children had the opportunity to rise above the circumstances of their parents. The necessity for change has arisen from contemporary societal dispositions with respect to whose children should be the beneficiaries of the legacy of John Wolmer. To better illustrate the interplay between constancy and change in the Wolmerian saga, allow me to briefly identify and comment on the main issues and challenges that the school has had to address over these 275 years.

The Issue of Race and Colour

John Wolmer did not specify any race or colour with respect to the children that should benefit from his will. His will stated children, without any caveat. However, the school established was for poor white boys. The social context of the times asserted that white boys whose parents had fallen on hard times were the only ones to be rescued through charity. The first manifestation of the conscience and the cause was therefore limited to the segment of the Jamaican society about which the oligarchy regarded as deserving of charity.

The inclusiveness of John Wolmer's will was counter-posed by the exclusiveness of its enactment in 1729. Then the question arose, what about Jews? There was nothing in the will of John Wolmer that excluded Jews, only the interpretation of the first executors of the conscience and the cause. Conscience prevailed and the cause was extended to include Jews. At the beginning of the nineteenth century as people of colour advocated for their civil rights, the same question was raised about Browns, mulattoes, Red Eboes, in other words people who look like me. In the first decades of the nineteenth century, conscience again prevailed and the cause was extended to include Brown boys to be admitted to Wolmer's. With emancipation, the question of including Blacks was posed. Again conscience prevailed and race was no longer a barrier to admission. Indeed, by the 1860s, Wolmer's had its first Black headmaster, Reverend Robert Gordon. He did not last long, but the issue of race had not only been addressed with respect to students but also with respect to teachers.

Issue of Gender

John Wolmer's will had said 'children'; his executors first implemented it for boys. Again this interpretation was constrained by the ethos of the times which largely excluded girls from education. In those times, white girls were expected to be wives and mothers and therefore not needful of an education that would allow them to rise above the fallen circumstances of their parents. Finding men of means and marriage was the route out of their social predicament. In this context, physical assets and feminine charm were more important than education. But in time, as social attitudes changed towards the education of girls, the question arose, why not girls?

There is historical evidence that seems to suggest this the gender question was addressed and solved in the eighteenth century; then unsolved and resolved again in the nineteenth century. I am not about to enter into this argument, except to say that solving problems, dissolving solutions which again creates the problem and then solving the original problem again is a common feature of Jamaican history. Indeed, it is a paradigmic Jamaican practice. My point is that Wolmer's faced up to the exclusion of girls which marked its founding and changed so that by the time of its entry into the twentieth century there were Wolmer's Girls and Wolmer's Boys Schools.

The gender inclusiveness of John Wolmer's will had been realised despite the gender exclusiveness of the establishment of the school in 1736.

The Issue of Kingston

John Wolmer died in Kingston. His will did not stipulate any particular parish in which the school should be established, except that it should be the parish in which he died. Legend has it that it was his friends that ensured that he died in Kingston. It would appear that John Wolmer was part of a circle of people who were of the view that the fast growing town of Kingston, which had replaced Port Royal as the centre of commerce of the island and the bastion of defence of the colony needed a school.

When Wolmer's was established in 1729, Spanish Town was the capital and Port Royal was the famous place. John Wolmer and his friends had lived the transformation of Kingston from being a refuge centre located in cattle and pig pens into a modern town set out on grid with East, West, North and Harbour Streets defining its borders. The school was first established on Harbour Street. Later, the school was relocated up town to Parade, across the lane from Kingston Parish Church. As a boy growing up in Kingston, and attending Central Branch Elementary School on Church Street, I remember people referring to that location as" Old Wolmer's Yard".

The factual point to note about Kingston and Wolmers is that the official boundaries of Kingston were legally changed to accommodate the location of the school at its current location. Where the Wolmers Schools are now located was originally in St. Andrew. As the city of Kingston grew and Wolmer's with it, the school was moved further up town to the present location. The parish boundary of Kingston was changed to ensure that this location fell within Kingston, because Wolmer's had to be in Kingston.

Not only has Wolmer's changed for Kingston but Kingston has been changed for Wolmer's.

From a place of cattle and pig pens, Allman Pen, Slipe Pen, Campbell Pen, all now called towns, Kingston has become a great city. It has swallowed up most of St. Andrew albeit under the subterfuge called the Corporate Area. So most of St. Andrew has become Kingston 5, Kingston 6 up to now Kingston 20. Wolmer's over these past 275 years has been an inseparable part of Kingston, inclusive of its magnificence and misery, it triumphs and its tragedies. There is no extrication of Wolmer's from Kingston. The only option is constructive and creative engagement with challenges and crises of Kingston.

The Issue of Level of Education

Wolmer's was established as a charity school offering elementary education. In the year of its 150th anniversary, the Jamaica School Commission was established with a mandate that included the transformation of Trust schools, like Wolmer's, into high schools. Those charged with directing the affairs of the Wolmer's Trust at that time stoutly resisted this change. Younger Trusts like the Munro Dickenson Trust readily responded so that Munro and Hampton were transformed into high schools. Wolmer's, the oldest, was the last to make the change in the 1890s resulting in the present structure of Prep. School, Boys' School and Girls' school. To get a full understanding of the issues involved in making this it will be necessary to read Professor Patrick Bryan's book, *Jamaica People: 1880-1902*, or *Jamaican Society and High Schooling*, written by myself. The point is that John Wolmer never specified a level of schooling, hence this openness allowed Wolmer's in the end to extend the conscience and the cause to both elementary and secondary education, that is, whatever level of schooling that would advance the upward social mobility of its students.

To return to the question: "Why did the conscience and the cause survive and prevail at Wolmer's?" First was the inclusive formulation of John Wolmer's expression of his conscience and his cause. The legacy bequeathed was simply for schooling children of parents who had fallen upon hard times. It seems to have come from John Wolmer's heart and therefore was uncluttered with limitations and caveats associated with the head. Second was the genius of the Assembly in composing the Trust with stakeholders and actors who would watch each other in order to ensure integrity in the execution of the bequest.

Third was the capacity of succeeding generations of executors of his legacy to remain faithful to the conscience and the cause while at the same time making changes in response to challenges emerging in the society as it was being transformed.

It is my belief that many of the charity schools that did not survive the embezzlement, mismanagement or exhaustion of the cash that founded them, were too prescriptive in the expression of conscience or narrow in the specification of the cause, were too vulnerable to capricious executors and did not develop and foster the capacity to change in responding to the transformations taking place in Jamaican society.

As we celebrate the 275th Anniversary of the founding of the Wolmer's Trust, let us recognise that we are basking in the glory of constancy in the expression of conscience and commitment to cause matched with the overall and long-term integrity of the Trust and the capacity to change constructively in responding to societal transformation. All who have served the Wolmer's Trust deserve commendation for this monumental achievement across generations. All who would now, and in the future, join in this enterprise, dare not depart from the tradition that has been so painstakingly and successfully crafted and shaped in guiding this institution to this point in time.

The Call to Conscience and Cause

In this banquet hall tonight are some of the living legends who have benefitted from the legacy of John Wolmer's practical expression of his conscience and his specification of cause. I run no risk of contradiction by saying that you are all successful people and that some of your success can be attributed to the education you received at one of the Wolmer's schools. If this night is to be more than a sentimental moment when you reunite with fellow students of your time and with nostalgia recall events, teachers, students and happening at Wolmer's in your time, if this week of celebration is to conclude with self-reflection and commitment then every one of us, Wolmerians or not, must recognise like John Wolmer did, that conscience dictates that those who are successful recognise that their success does not only reside in their own brilliance or superiority but in the support and sacrifice of the community that nurtured them. Conscience dictates that the successful of any community give back in service and substance or both to that community.

Every community, society and country must nurture and develop elites in order to survive and to prosper. Those elites must run the full spectrum of human experience and endeavour including academia, sports, entertainment, morality, business, the performing arts and the creative arts, among others. The problem in human society is not in having elites, this is a necessity. The problem is for any elite to attempt to reproduce itself from only among its own children and clients. Every generation needs to produce its elites from among all of its members, irrespective of the social circumstances of birth. The moral responsibility of all elites is to identify, foster and support the emergence of talent, aptitudes and natural endowments in succeeding generations irrespective of where those children may come from socially. John Wolmer recognised this and in his time answered the call to conscience and cause.

Allow me to add another controversial element which is not rooted in morality but in demography. The affluent, in countries like Jamaica and affluent countries around the world, are not procreating in numbers to replace themselves. Consistent with the refinement of this evening, the rate of production of wealth by the affluent is inversely related to the rate of their reproduction of offspring. The converse is also true with respect to the poor and marginalised. Because children are the future, continued prosperity demands high quality and appropriate education for the children of the poor and marginalised.

Wolmer's was not set up as a school for the social elite. However, it must be immediately conceded that from its inception Wolmer's has catered to children of the social elite. It is a common occurrence that the social elites have often been among the first beneficiaries of provisions made for the marginalised. Moreover, catering to children of the social elites have had it benefits in both financial and social terms. But let there be no mistake Wolmer's was set up to open up opportunities for children of poor parents to rise to elite status on the basis of aptitude, talent, merit and character. The education of children of the elite and affluent in the same schools as those of the poor and marginalised is to the great advantage and benefit of all.

You see, schools must always be avenues of hope and liberation. Schools must be blind to the social and economic backgrounds of students but must be visionary in terms of what students can achieve and be as a result of the education received within their walls. By education I am not speaking narrowly of knowledge and facts, examinations passed or failed, but also of the identity conferred, the self-confidence through diverse interactions and experiences, the friendships and bonds that are formed, the insights and inspiration that are gained and the outlooks and beliefs developed to guide life's choices.

If time would allow I am sure that each of you could give personal testimony of the ways in which Wolmer's contributed to your own success in life. The fact that so many of you are here and so many of you have travelled, not only from across Jamaica but across the world, give ample evidence of what I speak. In coming up on the plane on Thursday I met James Campbell who works and lives in Guyana. He informed me that he was coming home for these 275th Anniversary celebrations. He had missed the 250th and he was not going to miss these 275th celebrations. I did not tell him that I too was coming to this banquet because I was still in fearful preparation of this speech. My point is that Wolmer's has meant a great deal to you and thousands of other Wolmerians, precisely because it has done what John Wolmer and succeeding executors of his legacy intended.

Ladies and Gentlemen, Wolmerians all, it is with trepidation but with deep conviction that I say to all of us we too must answer the call to conscience and cause. The least that you can do, as beneficiaries of the John Wolmer's will, is to join substantially in ensuring that the conscience and the cause continues to survive and prosper.

I was relieved to hear Douglas Orane outline the plans of the 275th Committee to re-capitalise the Trust by creating an Endowment Fund, to establish a Building Fund and gather funds to offset the projected deficit in operational expenditure over a number of years. At a minimum, Wolmerians should work to meet the targets set. I am sure that there are Wolmerians who would be able to determine whether $280,000,000 JMD, $4,800,000 USD, target set for this fund raising drive is any greater than the over 2,900 pounds bequeath by John Wolmer in 1729 if that amount was invested at compound interest from that time until now and adjusted for inflation.

Surely 20,000 living Wolmerians can match their founder.

Not to achieve this goal, as a minimum, would be to betray being a beneficiary of the Wolmerian legacy.

But ladies and gentlemen there is a more general challenge to successful

Wolmerians, to all successful Jamaicans, indeed all successful people of the Caribbean with respect to the call of conscience and cause. All of us who have achieved any measure of success in whatever field of endeavour in these small countries, marginal to world economic and military power but central to the history of human civilisation, owe part of our success to the support and sacrifice of our communities and countries. We stand in no different position from John Wolmer nor are the circumstances of his times so dramatically different from ours.

The small White segment lived in constant fear of violence directed against them through rebellion. To many, the answer was in joining the militia, and having a strong garrison of British soldiers and warships in port ready at call. Many strived to make it rich and then depart, even if what they left behind was ruined plantations. The Assembly was fractious and virulent disagreements among members were not uncommon. In many ways, current circumstances are not very different as people of some substance barricade ourselves behind burglar bars, install security systems with connections to rapid response units in Security companies and demand strong policing to deal with criminal elements. Neither, is the 'what is in it for me' mentality very different from the get rich quick orientation of John Wolmer's time. Further, the priority given to the economy over education still prevails.

In our time, the divide in society is not so much about race, colour and gender but with respect to class, specifically between uptown and downtown, between so-called ghetto and middle class housing areas, between inner-city and the suburbs. In this regard, the location of the Wolmer's schools in Kingston is not only a fact of history but a contemporary challenge to the conscience and the cause. I am sure that you have heard the lament that with the expansion of educational opportunities that has taken place over the last four decades and the application of merit, and not the ability to pay, as the basis of admission to high schools, traditional high schools like Wolmer's have had to cater to broader social categories than before. Even that the effect of the location of the Wolmer's schools in Kingston has caused the schools to cater to more than their fair share of students from down-town and inner-city communities.

I hope no one feels that I am striking a discordant note in these circumstances of nostalgic celebrations, but if Wolmer's is to be faithful to its legacy it cannot but confront the realities of these times within the context of the conscience and the cause. Wolmer's must continue to be schools at the social crossroads of society and in the vanguard of giving hope and opportunity to the marginalised.

John Wolmer's response to the circumstances of his times was not with respect to a military solution, or in government policy or in running away to good 'ole' Britain. His answer to the call of conscience was personal action that provided substantial resources to embrace the cause of giving hope and opportunity to young people whose social and economic circumstances gave little reason to hope and almost no opportunity.

If we are to be guided by our history, then we must realise that it is John Wolmer's type of altruistic response to the call to conscience and cause that has built Jamaica in positive ways. On the contrary, it is also necessary to recognise that it has been the tendency to depend on the security forces to solve societal problems; to ignore manifestations of hopefulness among youths; to continue with selfishness and greed which only seeks to satisfy the wishes of one's own; and the machinations of fractious partisan politics that seeks the acquisition of power as an end it itself that has brought the greatest pain and dire circumstances to our country.

I am not one of those who believe in the glorious past and the terrible present. In my view succeeding generations are faced with more or less the same moral choices. The ebb and flow, ups and downs, progress and reversal in human societies and civilisations, are determined by the balance of the choices made by succeeding generations. Therefore I see politicians who have gone into politics for the cause of advancing country and have made great personal sacrifices and I see those who are only after the fishhead for their own benefit.

I see persons and companies that are only in business to make money no matter what and I see others who are committed to the delivery of service or to the production of goods of quality.

I see people only living for pleasure and personal enjoyment and I see others who recognise that there are only stewards of their talents, time and resources and must one day answer to the One who is their Maker.

The issue for us tonight, as these celebrations of the Wolmer's 275th anniversary are brought to a close with this impressive event, is that we can be informed and inspired in our own responses to the call to conscience and cause that we face in our time, by the example of John Wolmer and all of those who through the years have kept this legacy alive in bringing hope and opportunity to those who otherwise would have had little reason to hope.

God grant us the wisdom that as we examine and reflect upon the successes and disappointments of our own lives, we can constructively respond to that inner voice of conscience with respect to our own personal obligations. Give us the courage to embrace and give practical expression to some cause that will bring hope and provide opportunity to the poor, the marginalised, the disadvantaged and the voiceless in our society especially from among the young.

For in the final analysis, in human society and experience, it is conscience and cause that triumph.

~

Chapter 3

Persistent, Pioneering, Prayerful, Participatory, Presence in the Periphery

~

THE MORAVIAN CHURCH IN JAMAICA
250th ANNIVERSARY
December, 2004

~

Master of Ceremonies, Bishop Robert Foster, Dr. Livingstone Thompson, Chairman of the Executive Board of Unitas Jamaica, members of the Moravian and other clergy, distinguished ladies and gentlemen all, tonight I have been accorded a high honour, and great privilege that can only be explained in terms of grace and unmerited favour. This Banquet is part of the celebration of 250 years of exemplary Christian service of the Moravian Church in Jamaica.

What else but grace can explain my honour and privilege to be the Guest Speaker on such an occasion? I am Baptist. I am a layman not a member of the clergy. Yet, the Moravian Church has always been ecumenical in outlook and has always included laymen in your liturgies. Understand, therefore that I am humbled by this high honour and great privilege. However, here my troubles begin.

Being an outsider I cannot honestly claim to enter fully into the joy and ecstasy of your celebrations. Such joy and ecstasy requires lived experience. You know Moravian history. You have lived parts of it. I have merely read some of this history, fellowshipped in some of your churches and laboured together with some of the Brethren. With this partial knowledge and

Moravian churches in Jamaica that are over 100 years old.

(TOP DOWN, LEFT-RIGHT)
Carmel Church, Westmoreland
Nazareth Church, Maidstone, Manchester
Fairfield Church, Spur Tree, Manchester
Small Church, Moravia, Clarendon
Lititz Church, St. Elizabeth
Mizpath Church, Walderston, Manchester
Church of the Redeemer, Kingston

photos ©J. Young, from the book, AMEN

tangential engagement, how can I meaningfully return the honour bestowed and enhance these celebrations?

This is the challenge that has exercised by mind and tormented my soul in preparation for this occasion. The best that I can offer is the articulation of my limited understanding of the essence of Moravian Christian witness and ways, generally, and specifically in Jamaica. Probably, the best that I can offer to these celebrations is what I have come to understand as the essence of being Moravian. It is expressed in the caption: *Persistent, Pioneering, Prayerful, Participatory, Presence in the Periphery.*

Moravian Origins

Forgive me if I recite what you know so well of your history but is critical to any outsider's understanding of your denomination and its work. The antecedents of the Moravian Church can be traced by to the missionary efforts of Cyril and Methodius, missionaries of the Eastern Orthodox Church, who established churches in ancient Moravia and neighbouring Bohemia, now the Czech Republic, in 850 AD. In a pioneering move, they translated the Bible from Latin into the Czech language and established a local liturgy. In the ensuing centuries, the area came under the rule of the Roman Catholic Church. Conflicts arose which took a decisive turn for the worse when Jan Hus challenged, as unscriptural, the office of Pope, the sale of indulgences and the removal of the chalice from communicants.

Jan Hus was born in Bohemia in 1369 to a poor family. After much study, Hus became Professor of Philosophy and Rector of the University of Prague in 1400. He was greatly influenced by the writings of John Wycliffe and his sermons which he preached at the Bethlehem Chapel in Prague reflected this influence. He not only came to reject many of the practices of the Roman Church but became convinced that salvation came only by the Grace of God and faith in Christ. His refusal to recant these views resulted in him being declared a heretic at Council of Constance in Switzerland and being burnt at the stakes on July 6, 1415.

The convictions of Jan Hus persisted after his death. In 1457 a group of his followers, Hussites, formed the Unity of Brethren (Unitas Fratrum) in the village of Kunvald, 100 miles outside of Prague. Unitas Fratrum, the Moravian Church, became the first Protestant Denomination, predating the formation of the Lutheran Church by 60 years. Within ten years, Moravians had established three orders of Ministry: deacon, presbyter and bishop. The church spread from Bohemia, to Moravia and to Poland. Making use of the new printing technology, developed by Johannes Gutenberg of Mainz Germany, Moravians established two printing shops that produced thousands of copies of the Bible and other religious books in the Czech language. They established schools, including schools for girls, and a grammar school teaching Latin, Greek and Hebrew.

As can be expected with any movement that dissent with and diverge from the status quo, there was push-back from the dominant hegemony. This came from the Catholic Habsburg rulers who forcibly closed Moravians schools and burnt as many copies of the Kralitz Bibles that they confiscated. Fearing further loss of religious freedom, Protestant Bohemian and Moravian noblemen started the Bohemian Revolt in 1618. The revolt was put down in 1620 at the Battle of White Mountain, following which, not only was there further closure of Protestant schools but prolonged religious persecution during which Moravians were forced to flee or practice their faith secretly. During the 30-year war, 1618 to 1648, the Moravian Church was decimated by the conflict and persecution which continued even after the war ended.

It was during this period that Jon Amos Comenius became the Moravian Bishop. He too had to flee from Bohemia. He spent most of his time outside of Czechoslovakia especially in Sweden, England and Holland. In England he sought assistance from the Archbishop of Canterbury. For those who might not be aware, Bishop Comenius is widely regarded as the first great modern educator. He first advocated universal education including education for women. He produced the first textbook with pictures and illustrations. Indeed, in his lifetime he published 154 books. He conceived of education as holistic: learning, spiritual development and emotional growth. All were interwoven into one unified whole. Comenius was commissioned and he re-organised the school system of Sweden. He was invited to become the first President of Harvard College in the United States of America, but declined because of his responsibilities as Bishop.

Bishop Comenius's heights in education was countervailed by his depth of despair concerning the decimation of the ranks of the Moravian Church and the scattering of his members all over Europe. He prayed, hoped and worked for the 'hidden seed' that would germinate to renew and return the Church to its former status and vibrancy. Quite likely his views and work in education were inspired by his desire for the 'hidden seed' to survive. The wider applications of those views and his work in education were probably spin-offs from this inspiration. However, he did not live to see the germination of that 'hidden seed'. He died in Amsterdam in 1670.

But that 'hidden seed' did germinate. The 'hidden seed' germinated on the estate of Count Nicholas Ludwig von Zinzendorf of Saxony, Germany in 1722. Zinzendorf was a progeny of one of the oldest, noble families of Lower Austria. At the Reformation, the family became Lutheran. Count Zinzendorf's grandfather sold his Austrian possessions and moved to Germany rather than submit to forced conversion to Catholicism. Nicholas studied law. He was pious. He felt a passion to establish a model Christian Community because he was critical of the dry Lutheran orthodoxy of his day and its tendency to be highly intellectual. He believed in the 'religion of the heart,' based on deep personal connection to the Living Lord, and which sought to recapture the spirituality and practices of the early church.

His chance to do so came when Christian David, an itinerant Moravian carpenter, requested his permission to allow a small number of Bohemian Brethren, who had lived underground in Moravia for nearly 100 years, to settle on his land. With Count Zindendorf's permission, the village of Herrnhut was established on his estate. It attracted more Moravian refuges from across Europe. Disagreements arose among these Brethren and by 1727 they were divided into fighting, feuding factions.

Following the founding of Herrnhut, Count Zinzendorf read the history, theology and practices of the early Unitas Fratrum and Bishop Comenius' history of the Bohemian Brethren. He found a great deal of commonality of outlook with the Brethren and his own views. Faced with the severe conflicts at Herrnhut, into which even Christian David had become embroiled, Zinzendorf took leave from his commission and returned to his estate, determined to resolve the conflicts. He did so by visiting each home and had prayers. Following those visits he called the men of the village together for a period of intense study of the Scriptures. The end product of this process of prayer and Bible study was the Brotherly Agreement signed by all men of the village on May 12, 1727. The essence of the Agreement was on Christian behaviour to be practiced in the village. This Brotherly Agreement became, following several revisions, the genesis of what is now known as the Moravian Covenant for Christian Living.

What followed the reconciliation among the feuding Brethren was a visitation from the Holy Spirit at a communion service on August 13, 1727, which the Brethren likened to Pentecost. Herrnhut was on fire for the Lord. The Brethren soon set up a watch of continuous prayer; produced daily devotions called Watchwords; and by 1732 had sent their first missionaries overseas. These were Johann Dober a potter and David Nitschmann a carpenter. They went to St. Thomas in the Danish Virgin Islands. By this act Moravians became the first Protestant Denomination to send Missionaries to the Caribbean and the New World. They were the first to send missionaries to work with slaves and the first to send laymen and not clergy as missionaries. In 1735 Herrnhut Moravians began sending missionaries to the United States, beginning in Savannah, Georgia. On May 20, 1737, Count Nicholas Ludwig von Zinzendorf was consecrated as Bishop of the Moravian Church, a position he held until his death in May 1760.

The sending of missionaries to the Caribbean and North America was highly controversial in Europe. Zinzendorf was accused of sending young men to die. In 1736 he was banished from Saxony. Preaching what he said was his last sermon, Count Zinzendorf and his wife departed for St. Thomas not expecting to return. His visit to St. Thomas was a huge success. He was able to get Moravian missionaries, who had been illegally locked up, released from jail. The treatment of the missionaries by the planters, Zinzendorf's visit and his actions gave credibility to the Moravian mission in their work among the slaves. In 1741 Zinzendorf visited Moravian missions in Pennsylvanian. By these visits he was one of only a few European nobles who had visited the Caribbean and North America.

London became one of the main port cities from which Moravians missionaries sailed to their destinations in North America, the Caribbean and other parts of the world. Sometimes missionaries remained in London for protracted periods prior to sailing. As their numbers grew, private dwellings were not able to accommodate them. A room was rented on Fetter Lane, which became the place of worship. Indeed, for a brief period John and Charles Wesley worshipped at Fetter Lane. Following a visit by the Archbishop of Canterbury in 1742, the British Parliament passed the Act of Toleration which allowed the room on Fetter Lane to be a recognised place of worship.

Count Nicholas Ludwig von Zinzendorf was not only pious, compassionate and charismatic but he was obviously very astute. His personal and family connections to the Danish Court of King Christian VI had facilitated sending missionaries to St. Thomas and Greenland. However, the emergence of Britain as a world power with colonies in New World presented great missionary opportunities. Moreover Britain was Protestant. Britain needed settlers for their expansion and would prefer Protestants. Zinzendorf cultivated a lobby in the House of Lords in England that included the Prince and Princess of Wales, some Bishops, proprietors of property in the New World, and among the mercantile interests. Further, he developed a compelling case based on Moravian evidence for the House of Commons. Hence in 1749 the British Parliament passed the Act recognising the Moravian Denomination as an Ancient Protestant and Episcopal Church descended from the Bohemia Brethren of the fifteenth century. Immediately following the passage of this Act, Count Zinzendorf leased Lindsey House in Chelsea, which became the headquarters of the Moravian Church worldwide. Also, in 1749 Saxony rescinded the ban on Bishop Zinzendorf and invited him to return and set up other settlements like Herrnhut.

It is against this background that three Moravian missionaries: Zacharias Caries, Thomas Shallcross, and Gotlieb Haberecht from Herrnhut arrived in Jamaica, via London in December 1754, to establish the Moravian witness on the plantations of the Foster brothers in St. Elizabeth. Another batch of the 'hidden seed' was germinating, spread from rural Germany to rural Jamaica: Amazing! Yet some who advocate South/South relations think that they are forward thinking.

As we celebrate 250 years since Moravians missionaries arrived in Jamaica let us recall that this came:

- 904 years after East Orthodox missionaries, Cyril and Methodius, established the church in Moravia and Bohemia
- 339 years after Jan Hus was burnt as the stakes for the convictions that inspired the denomination's core beliefs
- 297 years after his followers established Unitas Fratrum in Kunvald outside of Prague
- 32 years after the germination of the 'hidden seed' at Herrnhut and
- 27 years after the Moravian Pentecost.

The recounting of these years should remind us that God's timeframe is different from today's instant expectations. He lives in eternity, and works in mysterious ways, His wonders to perform over timeframes that boggles the finite mind.

By the time Moravian missionaries arrived in Jamaica the character of the denomination had been defined by its history. Its antecedent was in the margins of Eastern and Western Christianity and its birth and existence had been in the periphery of societal power in Europe. It was not a state church with political clout. As such, the denomination had known the vicissitudes of persecution and accordingly developed the trait of persistence despite adversity imposed from without and conflicts that arise from within. Probably, it is persistent existence in the periphery that has cultivated the pioneering spirit that created so many Moravian firsts in Christian service.

Certainly the community has had to depend upon prayer and not power, practical Christian living and not doctrinal orthodoxy to maintain the integrity of its witness as well as to ensure survival. It would seem that persistent prayerful presence in the periphery had not only nurtured a pioneering spirit but had engendered participation in decision-making, regardless of social status in the community or position in the hierarchy of the church. Accordingly, artisan and aristocrat, laymen and clergy have been party to the path taken at several crucial points in the history of the church. In a nutshell, the character of the Moravian Denomination prior to arrival in Jamaica was persistent, pioneering, prayerful, participatory presence in the periphery.

It is within this framework that tonight we celebrate the Moravian 250 year history in Jamaica. For I wish to show that in its 250 years of Christian work and witness in Jamaica, the Moravian Church experience has been consistent with its character and history prior to arriving in Jamaica.

To begin with, for the two hundred and fifty years in Jamaica, the Moravian Church has been mainly a rural denomination with the over-whelming majority of its churches located in four parishes: St. Elizabeth, Manchester, Westmoreland and St. James; and usually with chapels in close proximity. It has never been a Kingston and St. Andrew centred denomination. Churches in Kingston, St. Andrew and Portmore have been the consequence of individual Brethren migrating to these population centres and the Denomination following them. Churches in these centres have been founded as a secondary consequence and not a primary objective of the denomination. In terms of location in relation to commercial, economic, social and political power the Moravian Church has continued its history of residing principally and persistently in the periphery. The fact that this banquet is taking place here in Kendal, Manchester tonight is not accidental or incidental it is indicative of and consistent with the history of the Moravian Church in Jamaica and the character of the Moravian Denomination generally.

The first eighty years was marked by ups and downs, by adversity and several setbacks, through which the Denomination persisted. During this period, the death rate among missionaries was high. Gotlieb Haberecht, arrived in 1754 and died in 1755. Many missionaries followed him to the grave. Yellow fever, malaria and typhoid were rampant in these early years. It is estimated that about one third of missionaries who came died here. However, that did not stop them from coming. Then there were disagreements among missionaries about matters such as Baptism which did not help the cause. Further, some of the practices followed elsewhere did not sit well in Jamaica. For example, in other colonies missionaries own slaves. This did not sit well with slaves in Jamaica. This was further compounded when in order to ensure their financial independence, missionaries in 1755 accepted the offer of the Foster family, received permission from the Worldwide Unity Board, purchased 700 acres at New Carmel in St. Elizabeth and operated it with the assistance of 30 to 40 slaves. Eventually in 1823 the missionaries sold the property.

However, the greatest challenge faced by the Moravian Mission in these first 80 years was slave uprisings and rebellions. Suffice it to say that the history of slavery in Jamaica is generously punctuated by violent episodes of resistance by slaves. The difficulty presented by slave uprisings and rebellion for Moravian missionaries was that it threatened both the relationship with the proprietors of plantations and also the relationship with the slaves. While all missionaries of non-conformists denominations worked in the intersection between slave owners and slaves, the situation of Moravians was more tenuous.

The Moravian mission was constrained by several different imperatives:

- First, was the article of faith not to bear arms, not unlike the Quakers. This article was recognised by the Act of the British Parliament of 1749. In 1763, Moravian missionaries pleaded exemption from service in the militia. The estate petitioned the Legislature which did not intervene

- Second, was its relatively recent history of the consequences of rebellion, known as the 'hidden seed'
- Third, the Moravian church was foreign, depending on the goodwill of British proprietors in Jamaica and in England
- Fourth, several of its missions were located on plantations. Finally, its doctrinal position and practice were to follow the teachings of the early church to be obedient to earthly masters as well as to God. Hence, Moravian practice was to seek the general well-being of the slaves, treat them as partners within the congregation, offer sound religious instruction and avoid military service as well as involvement in slave riots and rebellions.

Notwithstanding these constraints and practices, when slaves rebelled all missionaries were suspected and were often accused by the authorities. To defend against such accusations required showing that none of their members participated in rebellions and uprisings. Preventative measures to ensure this defence were teachings and actions to dissuade members from advocating against or participating in actions to resist slavery. This sometimes put Moravian converts among the slaves at risk of violence for not participating or supporting such advocacy and action, as was the case in the Sam Sharpe rebellion of 1831/32. However, the pattern set in 1760 when no Moravians were implicated in the widespread rebellion, was more or less the case in subsequent uprisings.

However, these measures and patterns did not completely insulate Moravian missionaries from being accused of instigating or supporting violent resistance by slaves. This was the case with Reverend Pfieffer, stationed at New Eden in St. Elizabeth, who was court marshalled in Mandeville in 1832, following the Sam Sharpe Rebellion. Plantation attorneys had a score to settle with Pfieffer because he reported them to plantation proprietors for not allowing the slaves time for worship on Sundays.

Allow me to say that as I read Buchner's account of the Moravian experience, during and in the aftermath of the 1832 Sam Sharpe rebellion, and also Reverend Pfieffer's personal account, I could not miss the number of occasions on which it is stated that the only recourse was prayer. Indeed, this was belief in action in circumstances where violence was not far away; he had no arms; was locked up, denied visitors, had little knowledge of the law and his rights; had limited mastery of the English Language and was threatened with summary execution.

What else but the answer to prayer can explain his miraculous escape from harm?

In the hindsight of history, and in the context of this 250th Anniversary, it is not possible for Moravians to celebrate collective spectacular or heroic advocacy or actions taken against slavery, or by slaves, comparable to those of Baptist and Methodist persuasions or by Maroons. However, what we must all celebrate are consistent self-sacrifice and sustained pioneering actions of the Moravian Mission and Moravian Church, which have contributed to the long-term common good of Jamaican people, the country and of the Christian Gospel.

The Moravian Church in Jamaica has numerous firsts of which it can be justly proud, particularly with respect to education. These are known to you but for the benefit of outsiders allow me to numerate the pioneering efforts including those in education:

1. Moravian missionaries were the first to arrive in Jamaica, nearly thirty years before George Lisle of Baptist fame arrived in Jamaica in 1783 and 35 years before the first Methodist missionaries arrived in 1789. They were therefore the pioneers of missionary work among slaves starting with their work at Bogue in St. Elizabeth.

2. Moravians were the first to establish Sunday Schools which afforded slaves not only religious instruction but taught them to read and write. Sunday school was not a one-hour event, but a Sunday activity lasting several hours. Accordingly, Moravians are pioneers in the teaching of literacy to the mass of people in Jamaica.

3. Moravians were the first to establish day schools and evening schools that offered instruction to slaves.

4. Lititz Elementary School was the first such school established for the children of slaves.

5. The School at Refuge, established in 1832, was the first institution to offer teacher training that was established in Jamaica and the Caribbean. It pre-dated Mico College.

6. While the existence of the School at Refuge in Trelawny was short-lived, Bethlehem Teachers College, founded in 1861, was the first teachers' college established for women in Jamaica and the Caribbean.

7. Following Emancipation, Moravians were in the forefront of establishing schools for ex-slaves.

8. Fairfield Teacher Training College, near Montego Bay in St. James, for men, founded in 1839, was among the first such colleges established in Jamaica, the others being Mico and Calabar.

9. The work of Moravian missionaries in Jamaica in the post emancipation period, in building and operating schools and colleges, and in building churches, catapulted the Jamaican Mission in the 1850s to be the largest Moravian Mission worldwide at that time. This was an achievement celebrated at the centenary anniversary in 1854.

10. The pioneering work of Moravians following Emancipation in establishing free villages, which allowed former slaves to chart a new life outside of plantations, is well documented. So too is the work in establishing public water storage and catchments in Manchester and St. Elizabeth; parishes known for drought.

11. Professor Laurie Reid, an outstanding Moravian educator, public servant and Music Director, produced the Common Entrance Examination every year after it was established in 1957 until it was replaced by GSAT in the late 1990s. Allow me to acknowledge that Professor Reid was one of two supervisors for my Ph.D. Hence, I am therefore a beneficiary of tutelage by a Moravian pioneer in higher education in Jamaica.

Hopefully these examples are sufficient to establish that in Jamaica, Moravians have been true to the character of the denomination as being bold in pioneering new paths, in devising new approaches and measures, and in taking positions and actions well in advance of the time at which they were commonly accepted. Further, that this has been particularly so in the field of education. As such, Moravians in Jamaica have been worthy of being connected to the legendary Jon Amos Comenius—the Moravian trailblazer in education.

Hopefully also, I have highlighted the fact that the Moravian Denomination, consistent with its historical character, has persisted in Jamaica as mainly a rural church without any pretentions of political and economic power derived from large urban centres.

Again, I hope that I have made the connection between bold pioneering, persistence in the periphery and prayer as being central to your *modus operandi*. To complete the theme of Persistent Pioneering Prayerful, Participatory Presence in the Periphery as the character of the Denomination to be celebrated at this 250th anniversary, I must address the issue of 'participatory'. Here I am particularly handicapped because I have no verifiable knowledge of the internal workings of the denomination and its individual churches. Hence, I must depend on its external participatory relations.

Allow me to start in the field of education. There were several denominational teacher training colleges that were established prior to 1875. Only one has survived: Bethlehem Moravian Teachers College. The only other teachers' college to have survived is the Christian but non-denominational Mico College.

One of the principal factors that contributed to Mico's survival was that in the denominational rivalry that prevailed, especially toward the end of the nineteenth century, its non-denominational character allowed the competing denominations to send their male members to be trained as teachers with assurance that 'sheep stealing', would not be a major risk.

It seems that Bethlehem survived because of a variation of this factor. Bethlehem was a denominational college with a non-denominational approach to the training of teachers. Enrolment at Bethlehem was never restricted to Moravians. Hence, the college trained teachers were members of other denominations. This was consistent with the Moravian history of promoting unity, fellowship and cooperation with other denominations.

In the field of theological education, Moravians did not have their own institution. Moravians developed working relations with both the Anglican and Presbyterian churches which allowed Moravians to be trained as Ministers at their theological colleges, St. Peter's and St. Colm's.

The Moravian church in Jamaica operated in sync with this spirit of fellowship, and. Moravians have always been prominent leaders, partners and participants in inter-denominational bodies:

- Moravians were among the founding members of the Jamaica Council of Churches in 1921. The late Bishop S. U. Hastings was twice the President of this Council

- Moravians were founding partners of the United Theological College of the West Indies, probably the greatest ecumenical accomplishment of churches in the Caribbean. The late Bishop Hastings was the first Chairman of the Board of this College

- The late Reverend Robert Cuthbert was, for several years, Executive Director of the Caribbean Conference of Churches at the time when Caribbean churches sought stronger relations.

An interesting footnote to the ecumenical and cooperative outlook of the Moravian church in Jamaica is illustrated in an event in 1911. The first Moravian church established in Kingston was in 1893 on Hanover Street. The church was destroyed in the great 1907 earthquake in Kingston. The congregation continued to operate out of two sheds until the Church of the Redeemer was opened in 1918 at Duke and North Streets.

In 1911, the church approached Archbishop Enos Nuttall of the Anglican Church and received permission to hold a service of consecration at the St. Georges Anglican Church on East Street. Archbishop Nuttall, a Methodist missionary who became Anglican, was a towering figure not only in the Anglican Church but in education. I suspect that in giving permission for this service of consecration the Archbishop, not only took account of relations in theological education, but was reciprocating past acts of ecumenical cooperation with the Moravian church.

Allow me to conclude with a confession and two opinions. Before delving into the history of the Moravian Denomination I was well aware of the great Bishop and legendary educator, Jon Amos Comenius, but knew nothing of Count Nicholas Ludwig von Zinzendorf. The more I have read about him and his work the more I have been personally inspired by the example of his life. Here was a man who came to understand that all that he was and had, was to be put to the service of our Lord and Saviour Jesus Christ. In his case, it was nobility of birth; connections with the powerful of Europe; wealth;

charismatic personality; oratorical skills; legal training and acumen; organising ability; foresight; energy; and lifelong commitment. What a life of stewardship!

Allow me therefore to adopt one of Bishop Zinzendorf's personal tenets. It is that every Christian denomination has a unique and special contribution to make within the body of Christ. This applies to the Moravian Denomination in general and to the Moravian Church in Jamaica over the last 250 years.

Let me add to this a considered personal opinion. Fundamental change begins in the margin, in the periphery. The margin, periphery, is a social fact not a pathological or terminal condition. The history of ciivilisation can be written in relation to the creativity, inventions, innovative ideas and risk taking ventures of the marginalised. It is constructive engagement when confronting the adversities of peripheral existence that generates new thinking, new ventures and pioneering efforts. When such engagements are inspired by the Grace of God and faith and dependence on Him, the results are transformative and empowering. Herein lays the explanation for our celebration of 250 years of Moravian witness in Jamaica.

But the manifestations of transformation and empowerment are not only societal it is also personal. Three examples of Jamaican Moravian believers should suffice:

1. **Noel Keith Montieth,** born in modest circumstances in the Darliston area of Westmoreland; schooled in the Moravian school there, continues his education and becomes an outstanding teacher; noted administrator as Principal of Maud McLeod High School, Cornwall College and G. C. Foster College of Physical Education and Sports; beloved President of the Jamaica Teachers' Association; Senator in the Jamaica Parliament; recognised for his integrity; Minister of State in the Ministry of Education; and upon retirement from teaching, Minister of the Moravian Church.

2. **Lawrence H. E. Reid,** born in modest circumstances in Walderson, Manchester; schooled at the Moravian school at Mizpah; continues his education and becomes an outstanding teacher and principal; obtains his Ph.D. from London University; becomes an international expert in education testing and measurement and one of the first Professors of Education of the School of Education, University of the

West Indies; serves on numerous boards including the Electoral Advisory Committee where he chaired the Technical Committee that developed the Electronic Voter Identification and Balloting Issues System, the first such system in the world for which Jamaica obtained the United States Patent; was the outstanding Director of the choir at the Church of the Redeemer; and served on the Executive Board of Unitas in Jamaica for several years.

3. **Selvin Uriah Hastings,** born in modest circumstances in the Darliston area of Westmoreland; educated in the Moravian school in the area; continues his education and is ordained a Minister of the Moravian Church; is elected to the Executive Board in 1951 and subsequently served as President; is consecrated Bishop in 1961 the first Jamaican Bishop of the Moravian Church; becomes a member of the Executive Board of the Worldwide Moravian Church and served as both its Chairman and Executive Director. Bishop Hasting was the first Jamaican to be the leader of a major Christian Denomination worldwide.

Persistent, Pioneering, Prayerful, Participatory, Presence in the Periphery is transformative and empowering at both the corporate and personal levels. The fruits of transformation and empowerment have to be celebrated with the sure knowledge that it is the Grace of God alone and faith in Jesus Christ that is their source. As we draw inspiration for the celebration of these past 250 years, let us all, Moravians and other believers be committed to be faithful and fruitful stewards of the Grace of God and of our Lord Jesus Christ.

Chapter 4

If These Walls Could Talk

~

OCHO RIOS
METHODIST CHURCH
175th ANNIVERSARY
March, 2003

~

Master of Ceremonies, Reverend Bentley Headley and other members of the clergy, brothers and sisters in Christ, it is an honour and a pleasure to be asked to be the guest speaker at this Banquet celebrating the 175th Anniversary of the Ocho Rios Methodist Church. One hundred and seventy five years of Christian witness, in one place. Indeed, this is a matter for great celebration.

Introduction

We are witnessing some very interesting developments in technology, where machines are becoming smart. You can now programme your VCR to tape one television programme while you are watching another, or to tape a favourite show while you out attending a function. Many machines, like the VCR, have memory.

I heard a very funny story lately of this gentleman who had bought the new latest model car fully loaded, as they say. His gardener had the responsibility of washing his car, new or old, every morning, because the gentleman insisted that his car had to be sparkling shine and clean. Moreover, the gardener took great pride in doing this task and looked forward to his first wash of this brand new car. Before starting to wash the car he decided to

The Ocho Rios Methodist Church, St. Ann, Jamaica. Established in 1828.

take a look at the dashboard to see all the features. So he put the key in the ignition and turned it on. However, he had left the door open and his legs outside. Whereupon a voice came on and said, "Close the door". He was frightened. Later he told someone, "Imagine Mr. Name buy a new car that can watch mi and talk to mi if mi do something wrong."

As I thought about this 175th anniversary I wondered what "if the walls of the Ocho Rios Methodist Church had memory and could talk"? If these walls could talk, what particular memories would they remind us to celebrate on this very special occasion in 2002? Some of these memories would have been what happened before the chapel was built. Others would have happened outside of the church but of which preachers, class leaders and members spoke about inside the church. That is hearsay, not accepted as evidence in court, but definitely a part of the oral history of any church. Then again, these walls could talk about happenings within them to which they could give evidence.

I am well aware that there are happenings these walls have witnessed that they would prefer not to talk about or celebrate. These happen in the best regulated families and even in very pious, zealous and loving churches. Such are more subjects of introspection and instruction than celebration. Hence, since 175 years is a very long time and so much has been heard and witnessed by these walls, and to avoid any tug on my jacket by the Master of Ceremonies or sighs of fatigue from you brothers and sisters, let me reduce what these walls could say to a short-list.

The Coming of Methodism to St. Ann and Ocho Rios

I received your invitation to the banquet through my esteemed colleague at the University of the West Indies and your ardent member, Miss Meta Bogle. I hope there that she will forgive me for trespassing on her area of expertise, Reading. As you probably know, I have done a bit of research on the poor performance of boys in school. On one occasion while examining how some boys had answered multiple choice questions on an often used Standardized Reading Test, I came across a most instructive matter.

One question was: Who is a boss?

Among the choices given were: Manager, Worker, Brute and two others that I do not recall.

Most of the boys answered 'Brute'. This was marked wrong on the Test.

The expected right answer was Manager. However, from then, every time boys at stop lights in Kingston call me 'Boss' I know exactly what they are really calling me.

The stereotype and characterisation of a 'boss' as a 'brute' goes directly to slavery and to planters and their overseers on plantations. But like all stereotypes it is not universally true. These walls would remind us that

Methodism came to St. Ann through a planter and not a missionary. The Lord uses unlikely sources in His work of redemption. Stephen Drew was a planter and lawyer/magistrate. He was the proprietor of the Belmont Estate in the hills above St. Ann's Bay. It is not clear how he came to know the Lord as his Saviour, but he did.

One story is that on a visit to England he came across the writings of John Wesley and was greatly influenced by Wesley's writing. On his return to Jamaica, he began to have daily prayers with his family and the slaves on his estate and read from the writings of Wesley. Reverend John Shipman had been the Methodist missionary at the Montego Bay and Falmouth circuit but had been moved to Spanish Town. Drew knew of Shipman. In 1817 Drew paid a Macedonian visit to Shipman at Spanish Town to learn more about the Lord and for guidance on how to start a mission at Belmont.

It was in response to this visit that Shipman visited Belmont. The Jamaica Archives show that Reverend John Shipman baptized 39 Negroes at Belmont, St. Ann, on January 1, 1818. Six children aged 3 to 8 years were among those baptized. All others were 12 years and older. Sixteen were classified as Africans, 21 as Creoles and two as 'Creole a Sambo'. As someone who has studied Caribbean pigmentocracy I find the 'Creole a Sambo' classification intriguing. At the time imported slaves were classified as Africans. Slaves born on the plantation were Creoles. 'Creole a Sambo' seems to have been a shade of colour/complexion resulting from a union between a Mulatto and an African.

Although these were not the first slaves to be baptized by Methodists in Jamaica, the records of Belmont are the oldest Methodist baptisms on the records of the Archives. Synod placed the work in St. Ann with the Falmouth Circuit. Although the distance between Spanish Town and Ocho Rios is shorter than the distance from Falmouth, Mount Rosser has always posed a challenge to transportation between the two.

By 1821, premises had been purchased and a chapel was established in St. Ann's Bay. Living quarters for a missionary was provided at Belmont. Preaching stations were established at Runnaway Bay, Dry Harbour and Ocho Rios. A seasoned missionary, William Ratcliffe, was assigned to the work in St. Ann. Give thanks for the faith and faithfulness of the planter Stephen Drew, who did not fit the mould or the stereotype of planters and overseers. Give thanks for John Shipman and the Methodist Missionary

Society for their immediate response to Drew's faith and fervent actions. Recognise that Methodist witness in Ocho Rios to the Gospel of Jesus Christ started several years before the church was built in 1827.

Before going further with the story leading to the building of the Church in 1827, these walls would insist that we recall the general story of non-conformist missionaries in Jamaica and specifically remember the early history of Methodists before this church was built. These walls would tell us that they heard that after the arrival of Dr. Thomas Coke in Port Royal, and his work to establish Methodist Missionary activities in Jamaica, Methodist Missionaries had been subjected to great opposition and resistance in Kingston, and Morant Bay. Dr. Coke and Methodist missionaries were not the first non-conformists to arrive in Jamaica. That first goes to Moravian missionaries who arrived in Jamaica in 1754. Their missions were largely confined to estates and villages in St. Elizabeth, Manchester, Westmoreland and St. James. Second were Baptists in 1783 with the arrival in Kingston of freed American slave Reverend George Lisle in Kingston.

Methodists, however, were the first to confront the slave-owning planter oligarchy of Jamaica, directly and frontally, not only with respect to their lifestyle but more critically with respect to the source of their wealth and status in Jamaica. Wesleyan Methodists were opposed to slavery doctrinally. Methodist missionaries were officially debarred from owning slaves. They were also forbidden to marry any lady who owned slaves. They were obligated to preach against slavery.

Methodist missions began in Kingston in the face of opposition. But it was in Morant Bay in 1803 that it faced its wealthiest, most powerful and most formidable foe: Simon Taylor. He was then the supreme oligarch of Jamaica. Simon Taylor owned plantations but more significantly he was the most successful plantation attorney, managing plantations for plantation owners living in England. He was the wealthiest man in Jamaica and in the British Empire. Taylor was Custos of St. Thomas in the East and therefore Chairman of the Vestry and Chief Magistrate of the Parish; member of the Assembly, Chief Justice of the Court of Azzizes and Lieutenant General of the Horses Militia. Wealth, political power, judicial authority, constabulary responsibility and military might were concentrated in Taylor's hand.

In 1802, Methodists decided to venture out of Kingston into Morant Bay. They had ventured into Taylor's domain. Preaching began in April. By July they formed a society of 30 members which grew to 90 by November. In December 1802, the Hon. Simon Taylor originated and instigated the passage of "An Act in the Assembly to prevent preaching by persons not duly qualified". The Act was signed into law by Governor Nugent on the very day it was passed by the Council. In essence, the Act debarred non-conformist missionaries from preaching to coloured and black, freemen or slaves, without a license.

On January 4, 1803, John Williams a free man of colour, and owner of property in Morant Bay, applied to the Magistrate of the Court of Quarter Sessions for a license to preach, but was denied. On the next day he met with a few friends in his house, sang a few hymns and engaged in prayer. He was arrested and summarily tried by five Magistrates who concluded that singing hymns and praying amounted to preaching. Williams was promptly sentenced to one month in jail. When news of Williams' imprisonment reached Reverend Campbell, the ordained Methodist missionary who had been granted a license to preach in England, he thought that Williams was denied the application to preach because he was a layman. He rushed to Morant Bay and applied for a license to preach, presenting his credentials from England. He was informed that the license granted in England did not apply in Jamaica. He was denied and similarly imprisoned. On release from jail after one month, Williams was then charged and convicted, this time for having preached in his house without a license

The matter was appealed to the Supreme Court. Stephen Drew lawyer/ magistrate of St. Ann represented Reverend Campbell. He presented cogent legal arguments to the effect that the *English Toleration Act of 1689*, and its subsequent amendments, recognised non-conformists denominations, including Methodists, and this applied in Jamaica. The Chief Justice found merit in Drew's argument. However, the matter was determined by majority vote and the Assistant Judges ignored the Chief Justice and ruled against Stephen Drew and his client Reverend Campbell. The Assistant Judges had no legal training. They were planters or merchants, some engaged in business with Taylor. The Court also determined that license to preach granted in England did not apply in Jamaica. Further, separate licenses were needed to preach in each parish, places of preaching had to be licensed and the hours in which preaching was allowed were specified.

In 1804 the King-in-Council disallowed *The Jamaican Act of 1802*.

However, in 1807 the Kingston Common Council passed an Ordinance, with the same objectives of the Act of 1802, but took account of the grounds on which the Crown had disallowed the Act of 1802. The effect was that preaching by non-conformist missionaries was banned in Kingston, and Morant Bay and elsewhere. Further, in the Assembly in 1810, a Bill about the clothing of slaves included clauses similar to those used by the Kingston Common Council. By delaying the submission of this Legislation to England, where it would be disallowed by the Crown, the law remained in effect in Jamaica until 1815, when it was finally disallowed.

Put succinctly, Taylor was able to align the Assembly, the Legislative Council, the Governor, the Kingston Common Council, the Vestries, the Courts and constables to effectively stop preaching by non-conformist missionaries, thus severely restricting their public evangelistic efforts.

Taylor died in 1813. What Taylor and his associates did not anticipate were the unintended consequences of their actions:

- First, the complicit and corrupt manipulation of the law offended the consciences of some of their own. For example, in 1820 a young Anglican priest attempted to follow in Simon Taylor's footsteps. However, the Custos of the Parish informed the young priest that if he wanted to drive the Methodists out of St. Thomas-in-the-East he would have to preach them out, sing them out or pray them out

- Second, their consistent coercive tactics used in enforcing the unjust decisions of denying license and places to preach would enhance the legitimacy and credibility of the non-conformists missionaries among whites of modest means, free coloured and blacks, and among slaves especially in towns. Methodist missionaries made many converts and they spread across the entire island. Preaching is not the only means of Christian conversion

- Third, as humans we are not immortal.

These walls would remind us that the Rector of the St. Ann Parish Church, Reverend G. W. Bridges, did not learn any lessons from the experience of Simon Taylor so he repeated them. Methodist missionaries came to St. Ann in 1818 at the invitation of Stephen Drew, lawyer and planter, who by then had become a Methodist. Methodists were the first non-conformist missionaries to arrive in St. Ann. Their missionary efforts had proceeded without incident or opposition; that is, until Reverend Bridges arrived.

Reverend Bridges was among the strongest supporters of slavery and the most vocal and vehement opponents of the Dissenting denominations. He was appointed Rector of St. Ann in 1823. On Christmas Day 1825, he preached an incendiary and inflammatory sermon against dissenters that got immediate response from members of the St. Ann militia on duty. On Christmas night, militia men armed with muskettes shot up the house where William Ratchiffe and his family were sleeping. Miraculously, neither the missionary nor his wife and children were harmed. As would be expected, those shots were heard around the colony. Imagine shooting up a house of a minister of religion on Christmas night? This was unheard of in 1825. Reverend Ratcliffe had done a good job over the period of three years. Membership in the circuit stood at 301. However, Reverend Ratcliffe and his family left shortly thereafter.

What was not anticipated was the response received by his successor, probationary missionary, Joseph Grimsdall, during 1826. Brown and black people, free and slave, and some whites turned out in droves to hear this young preacher who knowingly braved the hostile intent manifested in the shooting.

And preach he did.

The Lord blessed his preaching. Hundreds were converted. The local oligarchy was outraged. Intimidation had not succeeded. From shooting they turned to abuse of the law. Abuses included bullying of regular chapel-goers, including slaves, by the Chief Constable who reported the slaves to their planters and overseers for spurious reasons. The Chief Constable also labeled all Methodists – white, coloured and blacks, free or slave, as law-breakers and watched their every move.

Grimsdall was warned for preaching without a license to preach in the Parish of St. Ann, although he had a license to preach in England. He therefore qualified himself, applied for and obtained a license at the next Quarter Sessions Court. He was subsequently charged for preaching at an unlicensed place in Ocho Rios and preaching to slaves during unlicensed hours in St. Ann's Bay. The first charge was dropped when Grimsdall agreed to stop preaching in Ocho Rios until the license for the preaching place, which had been applied for, was granted.

Although he had followed the letter of the license, to preach in St. Ann, he was sentenced to 10 days in jail on the second charge. He was confined in the most unsanitary conditions imaginable and without a single item of anything in the cell. Three months after his release, he was charged for marrying two negroes, without their master's consent, although several years previously the Colonial Office had explicitly declared that this was not a legal offence. While there were no legal grounds for prosecution it was sent as a test case to the Supreme Court. Before that case was heard in the Supreme Court at Spanish Town, Joseph Grimsdall died on December 15, 1827 at age 32. His death was attributed to pneumonia contracted in the unsanitary conditions of the cell in which he was confined. Joseph Grimsdall became a martyr. These are the circumstances surrounding the founding of the Ocho Rios Methodist Church in June 1827.

Reverend Isaac Whitehouse succeeded Reverend Grimsdall. He faced the same harassment, prosecution and persecution. He also was charged on spurious grounds, jailed and locked up in the same cell as Grimsdall, despite protests against such treatment. Whitehouse survived. When the illegal actions taken by the constable and magistrates of St. Ann reached the authorities they were squashed and those involved censured. The missionaries prevailed.

Allow me to mix metaphors. The shots fired at Reverend Ratcliffe and his family back-fired. The martyrdom of Reverend Grimsdall and the continued illegal prosecution and persecution of Reverend Whitehouse established the authenticity and sincerity of the missionaries. People became more receptive to the Gospel that they preached. Souls were saved. The church membership grew. By 1831 the membership of the circuit was 1,030, surpassed only by the Kingston and Morant Bay circuits.

The Ocho Rios Methodist Church was founded 175 years ago in turbulent times marked on the one hand by violence, intimidation, harassment and abuse of power by the local vestry authorities in St. Ann. On the other hand, by courage, defiant faith, self-sacrifice and bold persistent proclamation of the Gospel by Methodist missionaries.

Jesus said, 'I will establish my church and the gates of hell will not prevail against it.' The Ocho Rios Methodist Church triumphed over the trials, tribulations and tragedies of its founding.

These walls could testify that the 1830s was a tumultuous decade. The years immediately following 1828 were relatively uneventful. However, all that changed after the Sam Sharp Rebellion, December 1831 to January 1832. It was bad enough for the dissenting missionaries to challenge and confront the licentious lifestyle common among the ruling elite. It was worse that they opposed slavery and supported the anti-slavery movement in England. The planters believed that replacing free with paid labor, would lead to their economic ruin. However, the greatest objection was to the preaching of the Gospel to slaves. They feared that the teaching of the Gospel could promote revolt similar to that of Haiti in 1797, which followed on the precedents of the French Revolution in 1789 and the American War of Independence in 1776.

The Sam Sharpe Rebellion, then called the 'Baptist War', turned that fear into panic and panic into state terror. Reverend Bridges and his cohort formed the Colonial Church Union in January 1832. Its written objectives were to use constitutional means to expose the falsehoods of the anti-slavery movement and defend the established church and the Church of Scotland. However, the actions that followed the end of martial law on February 5, 1832 were anything but constitutional.

Although it was called the 'Baptist War, that did not stop Methodists and Moravians from being persecuted. Some stood and were counted despite the risks involved. It was Reverend. Henry Bleby, Methodist Minister of Montego Bay, who ministered to Sam Sharpe after he was sentenced to be hanged. It was to Reverend Bleby that Sam Sharpe made his final and famous declaration: 'Minister I would rather die on yonder gallows than live in slavery. For his service to Sharpe Bleby home was destroy and he was tarred. It was the courageous action of his wife that saved his life when she tackled the man who was trying to light tar which covered her husband.

Four Methodist missionaries were imprisoned: Bar, Greenwood, Wood and Murray. Dozens of the chapels were burnt. Most of the thatch houses that slaves built on estates for class meetings were either torn down or burnt.

Fear was everywhere.

The only response of the faithful to these atrocities was prayer. And pray they did. To stop the continued atrocities of the Colonial Church Union in St. Ann, the Governor, the Earl of Musgrave, Governor at the time, relieved Colonels Hilton and Brown of their command of the militia, suspended several magistrates and stationed troops in the parish.

These walls would tell us that the answer to prayer was almost beyond belief. Not only was the Colonial Church Union declared illegal and its organisation disbanded but in 1834 there was the declaration that slavery would be abolished following a period of Apprenticeship.

Fear was transformed into hope that the freedom, prayed for over many years, was finally in sight. Church attendance was uninhibited. Schools started to be built. Hope became unadulterated joy and rejoicing when 'full free' came on August morning 1838.

The differences between 1832 and 1838 were mind-boggling.

Allow me this aside. Life has several twists that prompt us to wonder. In 1837 the Reverend Bridges was watching from the beach when the boat in which four of his daughters and some friends were sailing suddenly capsized. All were drowned and their bodies never recovered. He was inconsolable. He locked himself in a room with toys and memorabilia of his daughters. It was a Methodist missionary and John Sturge, a Quaker, who offered comfort and counsel that restored him to life as normal as could be following such a tragedy. In a tract titled "A Call to My Parishioners" Reverend Bridges confessed that in his love for the creature he had forgotten the Creator, the overruling hand of God in human affairs and recommitted himself to faith in and service of the crucified Saviour. It was care and kindness shown by non-conformists after great personal tragedy that helped to restore Reverend Bridges' commitment to the Gospel and to God.

For Methodists, the benediction of the decade was the Jubilee Year of 1839. The first 50 years of Methodist missionary work in Jamaica were heroic, inspiring and triumphant. What a time of rejoicing that was. From the eight members of the first class established by Dr. Thomas Coke in Kingston in 1789; Methodists numbered over 20,000 members served by 31 missionaries. Mr. William Harris, a free black man born in America, was in that class. He had become a renowned class leader and circuit steward. He was the only one still alive from that founding Class. He was on the platform at the Coke Chapel in the Jubilee service there. There was thanksgiving for the abolition of slavery, for all the missionaries who had served, many of whom had died in service of the Lord in Jamaica and for the many who had come to adhere to the teachings of the Lord.

The Next Hundred Years of Methodism in Jamaica

The next hundred years of Methodism in Jamaica was mixed. The years immediately following emancipation were exciting and challenging times. The village of Ocho Rios soon had three schools: Anglican, Baptist and Methodist. Children started to go to day schools while several adults started to attend evening school and almost all went to Sunday School, which did not only teach the Bible but also taught children and adults to read.

Education brought hope.

What was challenging was planters' attempt to try to continue slavery in a new form. They were required to pay wages for work. However, they paid low wages. They charged people high rent for living in the very houses they had built during slavery and also for plots of land that they had cleared and cultivated over many years. However, many ex-slaves had saved their limited earnings to purchase land. So they left the plantations, built houses and planted cash crops to make a living.

The hopes and aspirations of what freedom would bring started to be dashed in 1846 with the *Sugar Duties Equalisation Act* in England. Subsequently, many plantations failed and were abandoned. At the same time, this provided the opportunity for ex-slaves to buy and set up free villages. The economy got so bad that the Assembly said it had no money. Prisoners were let out of jail as a cost-saving measure. However, the biggest blow came in the form of the cholera outbreaks in 1852 and 1854. People died like flies. These walls could tell of funerals almost every day although St. Ann was not as hard hit as Kingston, St. Andrew, St. Catherine, St. James and St. Mary.

Looking back, aside from providing for the personal liberty of the enslaved, probably the greatest change that the abolition of slavery brought about was the change in lifestyle, in all sectors of the society. People started to live in settled communities based on church, school and in many instances, small holdings. They established families through marriage. Those who did not marry immediately formed stable concubinages, which became the norm in contrast to the licentious lifestyle of slavery. These entities brought children with wholesome habits even if the household means were modest. The churches promoted marriage and were successful to an extent but economic consideration hindered marriage in the minds of many.

If these walls could talk, it would remind us that the Morant Bay Rebellion in St. Thomas-in-the-East had island-wide and West Indies-wide repercussions. The Native Baptists who led this rebellion could read and write; judging from the number of petitions they wrote. But what it showed more than anything else was that the Assembly was so intent on preserving the status and interests that they could not govern the colony. When Crown Colony Government took over, many changes that ordinary people hoped for were made. The militia was disbanded; the Constabulary Police Force was established. The school system was expanded so that many more children could go to school and more teachers were employed. The Anglican Church was dis-established so that the state-church system was no more. Public health inspectors were employed. Hope was renewed. The Methodists got into the act and created the Barbican High School for Girls in St. Andrew and the York Castle High School for Boys in Brown's Town. Indeed, a few families from Ocho Rios set their eyes on sending their sons to York Castle.

But division, dissent and differences were gathering among Methodists:

- The first sign was small breakaway factions which formed different brands of Methodists and other traditions of the Wesleyan movement that made their way into Jamaica. Names that come to mind are United Free Methodists, Wesleyan Holiness, African Methodist Espicopal Church, with which the great son of the Parish and National Hero, Marcus Mosiah Garvey was associated. However, there are enough such groups among Baptists for me to try to understand than to add to similar divisions among Methodists. You know these much better than I. The point to note is that by the closing decades of the nineteenth century and early decades of the twentieth century, Methodism brought to Jamaica by Dr. Thomas Coke, was no longer the exclusive representation of Methodist Christianity in the country.

- The second sign was dissent among Methodist missionaries. This is exemplified by the case of Enos Nuttall. He had come to Jamaica as a probationary Methodist missionary, aged 22, who left the Methodist Church after being put down for some of his ideas. He was ordained as an Anglican priest. He became the most beloved, respected and effective church leader in Jamaica for nearly 30 years as a result of being able to implement those ideas in the Anglican Church.

- The third sign was that by the centenary in 1889 the Missionary Society that had been the main sponsor of the work in Jamaica began to look to mission fields in other areas of the world, mainly Asia and Africa. The Missionary Society which had been the main funders of the work in Jamaica, and the West Indies, believed that the church in the West Indies, including Jamaica, should become more self-sustaining. The work in the region had benefitted for more than a century of support. It was time to be weaned of external support from the Missionary Society.

In the transition, as the Missionary Society reduced its funding, the West Indies Conference was created to chart its course. Methodist efforts waned for at least the first four decades. Barbican High School for Girls was closed in the 1880s and York Castle High School for Boys was closed in 1899. At that time York Castle was the best high school in Jamaica. Lack of finances was given as the justification for its closure.

Probably, one of the events that these walls would remember occurred, at the turn of the twentieth century with the death of the great Queen Victoria, Missus Queen, in 1901. It was Missus Queen who had signed and sent the 'free paper' in 1838. She had reigned for 63 years. Her death shook the colony and the Empire. People in St. Ann had written Queen Victoria in 1864 asking for Crown Lands to cultivate and although their request was not granted, she had replied to their letter. Many events were held to mark the mourning.

There was fear of the future.

Another event would be the great earthquake in Kingston in 1907 followed by a great fire. This also generated great fear across the colony. Despite the doubts and difficulties, life continued.

Ocho Rios and Methodism: Changes Since the 1940s

By the 1940s, the Methodist Church was firmly in local hands. It had been weaned of missionary support and was self-supporting. Further, some outstanding Methodists, ministers and laymen, took leading roles in the life of the country. Chief among these were the Sherlock brothers, Phillip and Hugh. Phillip was a first a member of the Irvine Committee tasked with drawing up the framework for the University College of the West Indies, then appointed to establish a major department of the University College and finally elevated to run the University as Vice Chancellor. Hugh established Boys Town to provide opportunity for some of the disadvantaged boys of Kingston.

In 1946, the Methodist, Synod resolved that the Church had an obligation to re-establish York Castle as either a boys or co-educational high school. This was accomplished with the opening of the New York Castle as a co-educational high school in 1952. The Church also provided the premises at Atrim in Kingston and became the owner of Excelsior High School founded by A Wesley Powell and located on North Street. In 1962 the Church opened Morant Bay High School in Morant Bay.

The church was on the move again, only now locally led and financed.

One of the first things that these walls would say to us is that at the same time the Methodist Church was manifesting new vigor, new voice and new vision within the Jamaican society, Ocho Rios was also changing. Ocho Rios was a fishing village long before 1818. It remained a fishing village up until the 1940s. St. Ann's Bay was the capital of parish administration and had a port, with wharfs. But Ocho Rios always had more natural resources. However, it was the building of the deep water pier by Reynolds Mines with the conveyor belt to Lyford in the 1940s that began to change the fishing village. The conveyor belt brought bauxite from the mines to be loaded on ships at the newly built pier. By so doing Ocho Rios in the 1940s and 1950s acquired an industrial element.

However, the major change has come with the development of tourism through which the fishing village and Bauxite port were transformed into a tourist resort town and conference centre and more recently into a port for cruise ships. It is these developments over the last 60 years that has transformed 'Ochi'. As a result, the town has become a magnet attracting persons from all over Jamaica. Ocho Rios is one of the towns that have experienced the pressures of internal migration as it has struggled to accommodate both temporary and more permanent residents, not to speak of local vacationers and tourists.

Concluding Comment

The Ocho Rios Methodist Church is 175 years away from the tumultuous circumstances surrounding its founding. Gone are the days of an established church which controls the local militia, local magistrates and local government. Slavery is no more. Jamaica is now politically independent. Methodism with its history of social inclusion, evangelical fervour, systematic approach to the development of mind and spirit, caring disposition for the marginalised and connexional practices can flourish in the context of national and personal freedom. However, freedom, ease and material well-being can dampen the soul, dull conscience and debilitate fervour. You just have to read the Old Testament books of Judges, Jeremiah and Ezekiel to come face-to-face with moral and spiritual pitfalls of life in the Promised Land.

As Ocho Rios seeks to meet the challenges of population growth, the accommodation of transient workers, the comforts and needs of tourists, local vacationers and conference participants the issues are different. However, the same faith in our Lord Jesus Christ, fervour in serving his mission in bringing the Kingdom of God to past, faithfulness in daily living and practical holiness are demanded... just as they have over these last 175 years.

May God's richest blessings be with you now and always.

~

Chapter 5

Steady, Stable and Steadfast

~

SAVANNA-LA-MAR BAPTIST CHURCH
AT 175 YEARS
October, 2010

~

Mr. Master of Ceremonies, Honourable Owen Sinclair, Custos of Westmoreland; Reverend Carlton Wilson, pastor, deacons, members of the clergy, specially invited guests, brothers and sisters in Christ, greetings and salutations. I am honoured beyond measure to be invited to be Guest Speaker on this very special occasion, celebrating the 175th Anniversary of the Savanna-la-mar Baptist Church. This invitation is surely a matter of grace, unmerited favour, as I can think of nothing on my part that would merit this invitation. I am a Kingstonian. My parents are Kingstonians. Three of my four grandparents are Kingstonians. My fourth grandparent, who migrated from Manchester, left there at an early age. I do not know if you can imagine the disadvantage of this heritage. One of them is that at summer time, and other holidays, there were no country relatives for me to visit and spend time. It also means limited personal knowledge of Jamaican life outside of the city of Kingston. Knowingly, you have invited a rank outsider to celebrate this great anniversary with you.

However, we are brothers and sisters in the risen Christ, saved by the blood of the Lamb, kept daily by the enabling of Holy Spirit and directed by the love and divine purpose of the Father. We are Baptists to boot, holding firmly to the sacraments of Communion and Baptism by full immersion, to

The Savanna-la-mar Baptist Church, Westmoreland.
Established in 1835, it was destroyed by fire on the
23rd November 1839 and rebuilt in 1840.

the autonomy of the local church, and the priesthood of all believers. Therefore, there is great joy in celebrating these 175 years of God's sustaining grace in the witness of the body of believers, located in the town of Savanna-la-Mar in the parish of Westmoreland. To God be the glory great things He has done.

As an outsider to Savanna-la-mar, but sharing the same faith in God, our Father and our Lord Jesus Christ and in the circumstances of sharing in the celebration of your 175th anniversary; I have tried to understand the historical, geographical and social context in which you have given witnessed to the Christian faith. Indeed, this invitation has given me the opportunity to continue to learn more about Western Jamaica and about 'SAV', as Savanna-la-mar is affectionately called.

I have to confess immediately that my curiosity to learn more about Westmoreland and Savanna-la-mar did not begin with your invitation. My father was a journalist. He was one of few reporters who was present to write eye-witness accounts of the riots in Frome in 1938. I grew up hearing some of these stories, including some that were not printed in the press. However, it is as Chairman of the Electoral Commission that Westmoreland and Savanna-la-mar have found focus in my thoughts, especially in the conduct of the recent exercise in the drawing of constituency boundaries. Savanna-la-mar is located in the Constituency of Central Westmoreland, which attracts attention as one of the fastest growing constituencies in Jamaica. The key to understanding politics in any area is to probe into the history of the people of that area. I am not here engaging in any partisan politics but rather admitting that the obligation of being a steward of the electoral body is to be informed and wise.

The Town of Savanna-la-mar

As you all know, Savanna-la-mar existed before the parish of Westmoreland. Emerging evidence is that Bluefields is the site of one of the earliest Spanish settlements in Jamaica starting from Columbus's second voyage. Bluefields' sheltered anchorage and constant fresh water stream made it a supply-point for ships. Savanna-la-mar, as a Spanish settlement, appears to have its origin as an offshoot of Bluefields. Shephardic Jews from that second voyage of Columbus were among its first residents, judged by records of a synagogue and remnants of a Jewish cemetery in Savanna-la-mar. In a nutshell, Savanna-la-mar, as a settlement, had its origin before the British conquest in 1655.

Westmoreland as a parish came after the British Conquest. It was declared a parish in 1703 in the second round of the declaration of parishes. Westmoreland was carved out of St. Elizabeth. Its area covered all of the Southwestern section of the island. In 1723, Hanover was carved off from Westmoreland. When Westmoreland was declared a parish in 1703, Banbury in Georges Plain was named the capital. Savanna-la-mar became the capital in 1730 and owe this position to the success of the sugar plantations in Georges Plain and by being a port town.

It must be remembered that up until the latter part of the nineteenth century, transportation around Jamaica was largely by sea. Those mountain ranges that run down the centre of Jamaica posed serious challenges to overland travel, from east to west. Savanna-la-mar as a port town featured not only in the export of sugar and rum to Britain, the import of supplies from Britain and the North American colonies on the Eastern Seaboard; but also in the network of coastal towns providing cross-island local transportation. Savanna-la-mar was the major port-of-call on the South Coast. Savanna-la-mar's rise to being the capital of Westmoreland in 1730 marked its eclipse of Bluefields as a port town and of Banbury as the administrative centre of the Parish. Savanna-la-mar came in second on both counts, but having gained these advantages has kept them.

As the parish capital, Savanna-la-mar was given a fort that was never completed. The fort was built at the end of Great George Street which is probably the most defining feature of this town of the George's Plain. From its inception, Great George Street was among the widest and straightest streets in Jamaica. Indeed, the history of Savanna-la-mar can be written around Great George Street. The street probably owes its wide and straight feature not only to the fact that there were swamps on both sides of the Town, constraining lateral extensions but also to the fact that the road system was from the Port to the plantations on the Georges Plain, with Great George Street as the main artery. Savanna-la-mar benefited, in 1738, from the bequest of Thomas Manning, a planter who left land on his Burnt Savannah plantation for the establishment of a free-school but which the Assembly, by legislation, shifted to Savanna-la-mar. By this Act of the Assembly, Savanna-la-mar boasts the second oldest school in Jamaica and one of the oldest in the Caribbean, Manning's High School. It also benefitted from the construction of the St. George Anglican Church in 1739 which became the Parish Church and the location of the Vestry, the seat of local government in the Parish.

In completing the early history of Savanna-la-mar, it is necessary to mention three additional facts:

First, Savanna-la-mar was not the healthiest place. Swamps breeding mosquitos, and the prevalence of malaria and other such vector-borne diseases ensured that those who lived and survived in this town were hardy people with strong physical constitutions.

Second, Savanna-la-mar was no stranger to disaster. This is marked by the fact that in 1780, the fiftieth year of being the capital of Westmoreland, it suffered a triple natural disaster between October 2nd and 3rd. A storm surge killed all the onlookers who had gathered at the seashore to see a very unusual configuration of sea and weather. This was followed by a great hurricane that totally destroyed the port. Then there were repeated shocks of an earthquake which spread across Westmoreland, Hanover and St. James destroying almost all buildings in Westmoreland and Hanover. The death toll of the triple disaster was over 4000. The response was resilience and recovery. The people of Savanna-la-mar rebuilt, with some assistance, St. George Church, Manning School, the port, their homes and places of commerce.

Third, towns in Jamaica before the abolition of slavery had a distinctly different economic focus and social composition from plantations. Plantations were focused on the growing of sugar cane and the manufacture of sugar. They were principally composed of white planters, overseers, bookkeepers and slaves, predominantly black, who worked between the fields and great house. Towns were focused on commercial activities, and capital towns on governance through courts, vestries and a few constables. Towns were more cosmopolitan in social composition. They included whites, free people who were Brown, Black and Jewish and slaves of both complexions engaged in jobbing. Where schools existed they were found in towns. Some towns namely Kingston, Montego Bay and Falmouth had newspapers but Savanna-la-mar does not appear to have had a newspaper in the eighteenth and early nineteenth century.

By the end of the eighteenth century, the character of Savanna-la-mar had been set. Savanna-la-mar was not the pioneer or trailblazer but it kept and maintained what it got: capital, port, school and churches. The people knew hardship and adversity but were resourceful and resilient when faced with disaster. The town was cosmopolitan, it embraced diversity. These shaped the character of Savanna-la-mar: *Steady, Stable and Steadfast.*

The Founding Baptist Church and Construction of Chapel in Savanna-la-mar

The history of Christian denominations in Jamaica has many chapters that are still to be written. What is known is that the Anglican Church was the state church and therefore had presence in several areas of Jamaica before the other denominations, this included presence in Savannna-la-mar. The Moravian missionaries were the earliest of the non-conformist denomination to begin work in Jamaica. They started work in St. Elizabeth in 1754 which later spread into Manchester, Westmoreland and St. James; but worked mainly in the hills of those parishes, establishing churches in close proximity to each other. Savanna-la-mar was not on the Moravian radar.

The Baptist missionaries came to Jamaica next in the persons of Reverend George Lisle in 1782 and Moses Baker in 1783. They came from the United States. Reverend Lisle worked in Kingston. He baptized Baker who was employed and later tasked by a Quaker in St. James to give religious instruction to his slaves. Having pioneered Baptist work, Lisle and Baker invited the Baptist Missionary Society in England to join them. Baptist missionaries from England arrived in 1814.

Methodist missionaries came next. Among them were Reverend Dr. Thomas Coke who arrived at Port Royal in 1789 and proceeded to Kingston. Reverend Coke also went to Montego Bay to preach. Baptists and Methodist missionaries were more assertive than Moravians in challenging the licentious lifestyle of the planter elite and in opposing slavery. However, all were united in the common cause of preaching the gospel to slaves.

Baptist and Methodist missionary expansion across Jamaica followed similar patterns. Starting with work in Kingston in the east and Montego Bay in the west; they advanced from those points along the coast, both having established works in Spanish Town, the capital. Methodism seem to have taken greater hold in the towns, while that of Baptists on the plantations. While both denominations attracted converts from all racial segments, their congregations mirrored the social compositions of the social spheres in which they attracted their greatest followers.

I have not been able to discover, definitively, whether Baptist or Methodist missionaries came to Savanna-la-mar first; although the odds are in favour of the Methodists. What is sure is that Reverend William Knibb arrived in this town in 1828 and lived and worked here for two years. There is also evidence that Reverend Thomas Burchell from Montego Bay joined in the Baptist effort here in 1829. What is important for us to note tonight is that the church started years before the Chapel was built. This 175th Anniversary, marks the opening of the Chapel not the commencement of the church. The body of believers existed before the building that housed their gathering together.

What I find most intriguing is that the Savanna-la-mar Baptist Church was founded by two of the greatest leaders of the Baptist church in the nineteenth century. Knibb was the most charismatic and eloquent of the Baptist missionaries who came to Jamaica. Burchell was among the most strategic thinkers. They combined under the leadership of the Spirit to found this church. Yet their impact was not as immediate as happened elsewhere. Indeed, Knibb was invited and accepted the call to be pastor of the Falmouth Baptist Church in 1830 and is forever associated with the work there. Hopefully someone will be provoked to research this matter. I only offer a hypothesis that could be tested. The hypothesis is that the hardy, steady and stable people of Savanna-la-mar are pre-disposed to contemplate, test and consider things before embarking on change. Impulsiveness does not appear to be part of the disposition of Savanna-la-mar.

It is necessary to note, that this 175th Anniversary of the building and opening of the Chapel in 1835, is one year after the announcement of the proposed abolition of slavery in 1834 and after the implementation of the Apprenticeship system. Baptists were given great credit for this monumental change that was to come. Indeed, membership in Baptist churches began to soar. In other words, the building and opening of the Chapel came at the time when the Baptist denomination began to significantly increase its membership island-wide; as restrictions of religious activities by missionaries were being removed and the denomination's authenticity as an effective advocate against slavery and the conditions of slaves was not in dispute.

For those who have forgotten Jamaican history, between 1830 when Knibb left Savanna-la-mar and 1835 when the Chapel was built, let me remind you that in late December 1831 and January 1832 there was the Sam Sharpe rebellion, then referred to as the "Baptist War". Sam Sharpe was a deacon of Reverend Thomas Burchell's church in Montego Bay. Both Burchell and Knibb were accused, arrested but later cleared, of complicity in the rebellion.

In the immediate aftermath, numerous Baptist and Methodist chapels in the West were burnt or otherwise destroyed by planters and their allies. The reason that Savanna-la-mar did not suffer this fate was that the chapel had not yet been constructed. The more far-reaching impact of the Sam Sharpe rebellion was greater pressure by the abolitionists in England resulting in the decision of the British Parliament to abolish slavery; after a period of so-called Apprenticeship.

The point here, is that the Savanna-la-mar Baptist Chapel was not built as a harbinger of change to come but rather was built consistent and congruent which the consolidation of Baptist missionary work that was surely on the way, which contours had been clearly defined. One hundred and seventy five years later we can all testify to the soundness of the decision made by the believers to build and open the Chapel in the immediate circumstances of apprenticeship as the final step to the abolition of slavery which would bring with it freedom, generally, and freedom to worship, in particular.

In keeping with the character of the town, Savanna-la-mar Baptist church has known tragedy. Four years after its opening the chapel was destroyed by fire. Equally consistent with the resilient character of the town, the chapel was rebuilt and reopened in 1840. Further, it survived the devastating hurricane of 1912 and stands today as a National Heritage site with its simple but elegant architecture.

On the Outskirts of Major Developments

In celebrating this 175th Anniversary, come with me very quickly, and look at major developments in Jamaica and their direct impact on Savanna-la-mar and by implication the witness of the church in this town. It is easier to simply list these changes:

- Immediately after the abolition of slavery there was a movement of some of the newly emancipated to leave the sugar plantations, and set up free villages mainly in the hills, and very often, on unprofitable estates that were up for sale and bought for the purpose of sub-division as free villages. This was largely led by Baptists with Knibb, Burchell and Phillippo in the forefront.

- The free village movement was about fundamental changes in lifestyle, economic activity, mentality and community infrastructure from that which was operated in slavery on the plantations. In Westmoreland, Bethel Town is one such example. Others of the emancipated did not totally separate from the plantation. They set up villages in relatively close proximity to plantations. Several of these villages, in time, became sugar towns of which Frome is a prime example. Savanna-lar-mar as a coastal town and parish capital was only marginally impacted by this major socio-economic and socio-political movement. It remained stable and steady as an administrative capital of the parish and the major coastal transportation point on the south coast.

- The Morant Bay Rebellion of 1865 was almost on the opposite side of the island and therefore merely a news item. Under Crown Colony Government which followed; the number of parishes was reduced from 22 to 14. Westmoreland was unaffected and unaltered by this reduction. However, Savanna-la-mar benefited from the fact that in the 1880s re-organisation of the school system, Mannings was upgraded from a free-school at the elementary level to being a high school, thus further elevating the importance of the town as a centre of education. At that time there were only eleven public high schools in Jamaica. Mannings was one of the eleven and one of only three co-educational high schools.

- The debate as to whether slave labour was more efficient than free labour in the production of sugar became an academic matter, when in 1846, the British Government passed the Sugar Duty Equalisation Act which allowed sugar from slave states such as Cuba and Brazil to enter the British market on the same duty regime as sugar from British West Indian colonies. The pattern then was for each plantation to have its own sugar factory. The new circumstance was to the great disadvantage of small estates operating on marginal land located far from ports. Schemes were proposed to mitigate these disadvantages from the beginning of the 1850s. These included growing cane sugar on more fertile lands, better soil conservation, railways to transport sugar to the ports and central factories that could produce sugar for plantations in their vicinity. Sugar plantations on the Georges Plain were only minimally affected by the challenges. The lands were fertile and they were close to the port in Savanna-la-mar. However, by the 1930s the eleven small factories of the sugar estates on the Georges Plain were antiquated, production costs were high and each estate having its own factory, was no longer viable. A central factory, proposed 80 years before, was among the most feasible options. The closing down of these antiquated factories, with the attendant loss of jobs and unemployment, along with lower wages and the economic depression of the 1930s ignited the social unrest and the Frome riots of 1938. These factors were the catalyst for major political and economic changes which followed in the post-war period.

As I mentioned before, my father was one of the few journalists who covered and gave eyewitness accounts of the Frome riots and I grew up hearing some of these accounts. One of these was of a man who some rioters identified as deserving a good beating who when he was grabbed to receive the beating made a joke which the rioters found to be really funny. They all laughed. They let him go with the warning that next time he may not be so lucky. My father's lesson to us was that humour was an asset, especially in difficult situations. The point not to be missed about this iconic event in Jamaica's history is that it occurred in Frome, about five miles from SAV.

Savanna-la-mar was on the periphery and not at the centre of this turning point in Jamaica's history.

The tourist industry is one of the major developments in the post-war period. However, the centre piece of that development in Westmoreland is Negril, ten miles west of SAV. Although Savanna-la-mar is affected positively and negatively by this proximity, the fact is that both effects are indirect.

Another major development is that of the bauxite and alumina industry. The bauxite and alumina industry stops in St. Elizabeth.

If we were to encapsulate major movements and developments in Jamaica's history over the last 175 years; it would be fair and factual to say that Savanna-la-mar has not been the first or the prime mover or the focal point or genesis of any of these major changes. At the same time, this town has benefitted indirectly from all of them. Further, SAV has made do with whatever it has been bequeathed. In other words, the last 175 years is not fundamentally different from when the town was established in 1730.

To illustrate the point, here's a current example which is sure to get me into trouble, but what is a little trouble anyway? The matter is so familiar to you that I am sure that you can immediately verify its accuracy. At the present time driving from Montego Bay through to Negril and then passing through Negril on the way to SAV good roads end somewhere outside of Savanna-la-mar, probably around Sheffield. Coming out of SAV and driving to Mandeville good roads begin after you cross the border from Westmoreland into St.

Elizabeth. So good roads are coming elsewhere in Jamaica but they have not yet reached and cross Savanna-la-mar. Yet the town appears to be doing the best with the roads it has. There have not been roadblocks and demonstrations in Savanna-la-mar demanding good roads as is common in other parts of the country. What exists is a bustling town getting on with business, unhindered by the challenges of the conditions and limitations of the road system. On my most recent trip in which I passed through SAV it took me close to 45 minutes to cross the town, traffic was so backed up. I was made to understand that this is not unusual, especially in the afternoons. It is only in Montego Bay or Kingston, much bigger urban centres, that you would encounter the same type of traffic challenges. In other words, Savanna-la-mar is characterized with stability and steadiness despite the circumstances.

Sugar is no longer shipped from Savanna-la-mar, however the town still remains the capital of Westmoreland, after 280 years. Currently, Savanna-la-mar is located in the constituency of Central Westmoreland. The Electoral Commission has recently concluded the periodic review of constituencies into which Jamaica is divided as required by the Constitution. Central Westmoreland is one of the five largest of the 63 constituencies. It is one of the Constituencies into which people are migrating from other parts of the country.

Savanna-lar-mar is at the heart of Central Westmoreland and therefore must be experiencing the pressures from internal migration which in turn are creating new challenges for the town and the churches. As a growing urban centre, problems characteristic of urban dwelling are surely being manifested which will test the character of Savanna-la-mar and that of the Savanna-la-mar Baptist Church.

Celebrating the Witness of the Savanna-la-mar Baptist Church over 175 years

Tonight we are celebrating the feat of the Savanna-la-mar Baptist Church, of bearing witness to our Lord Jesus Christ continuously as a body of believers in the town of Savanna-la-mar for 175 years. This is truly remarkable, given the common tendency about Protestants, including Baptists, for congregations to split with one group remaining at the original church site and the other going down the road to build another chapel. Thanks be to God, Baptist believers in Savanna-la-mar have stuck together as one body although, over these 175 years, differences must have arisen.

From my line of argument, you hopefully can accept the suggestion that Savanna-la-mar Baptists over the years have captured the essence of the character of the people of this town.

It would appear that the people of Savanna-la-mar may take note of the spectacular but are not carried away by it; that they are not unmindful of the extraordinary, the unusual and the exceptional but they do not base their lives on these; that they may show interest in the exotic but are not mesmerised by it; that they may be struck by idiosyncrasy but understand the nature of its peculiarity, and that they acknowledge the heroic but appreciate that it is not a continuous state of being. Put another way, Savanna-la-mar people see virtue in routines; wisdom in standard ways of doing things; good sense in the ordinary; daily necessity in duty and beauty in things we often regard as common. In other words, Savanna-la-mar people have a down-to-earth and grounded approach to life.

The Word of God is absolutely and universally true. The Lordship of Christ is independent of time and place. God's power to transform lives has no boundaries or limitations beyond faith in the Lamb of God. At the same time these are not abstract concepts. The Word of God has to be lived and interpreted, the Lordship of Christ has to witnessed and the saving power of the risen Lamb has to be manifested to people of different places and at different times in ways that are consistent with their understanding of life. Believers in Christ of the Savanna-la-mar seem to have come to faith through matters of practical holiness seen in the lives of believers before them, who in turn are inspired and empowered by the Holy Spirit to live such convincing lives.

Paul in his letters to the Corinthians, Ephesians and Romans, list some twenty gifts of the Spirit given to churches for the work of evangelism and the edification of the saints. The gifts given to members of a particular church appear to be those that the Spirit determines are essential to the witness of those believers at that particular place. Currently it is very popular to place great value on the spectacular gifts of prophecy, miracles, healing, word of knowledge and tongues. Overlooked are gifts of discernment, help that is practical assistance, mercy, giving, administration and teaching. Looking at the history and record of the Savanna-la-mar Baptist Church over the last 175 years it would appear that these latter gifts have been the one most manifested.

Concluding Comment

It is a matter of real speculation, what would be the situation, if the members who built the chapel in 1835, and those who rebuilt if after the fire in 1839, were to come back to Savanna-la-mar in 2010. The changes over the last 50 years are spectacular enough, much more that of 175 years. Just take one item, television. The island got television in 1962. There was only one channel, JBC. It came on air at 4.00 pm and closed off at midnight. It was in black and white. Further, the television set had to warm up for a few minutes before pictures came on. Now there is instant colour TV over 24 hours with multitudes of channels. This is not to mention radio, telephone, cell phones, traffic lights etc. etc.

I think that they would probably recognise Great George Street. However, they would be blown away by the buildings that now reside on both sides and the business they do. Once they are on Great George Street they could find the chapel. They would be most familiar and at home with the Order of Service, the preaching of the Gospel and the conduct of Communion.

It is the spiritual, and not the material, that binds us together across generations and in Christ.

God continues to grant the Savanna-la-mar Baptist Church his continued blessing in succeeding years until Jesus come again in triumph. Until then, by the enabling of the Holy Spirit, may the body of Christ, Savanna-la-mar Baptist Church, continue to be steady, stable and steadfast, looking on to Jesus the author and finisher of our faith.

To God be the glory.

Victoria Mutual Building Society,
Corporate Office, Half Way Tree, Jamaica.
Established in 1878.

Chapter 6

Purpose and Progression in Mutual Savings from Basic Need to Permanent Domicile

～

VICTORIA MUTUAL BUILDING SOCIETY 125TH ANNIVERSARY

November, 2003

～

Master of Ceremonies, Mr. Roy Hutchinson, Chairman and Members of the Board of Victoria Mutual Building Society, Mr. Karl Wright, President and Chief Executive Officer and members of the Management Team, recipients of awards, specially invited guests, ladies and gentlemen; it is a real and personal privilege to be invited as the guest speaker at this Award Banquet celebrating the 125th Anniversary of the Victoria Mutual Building Society. I have been a member of Victoria Mutual for the past 37 years. The first house I bought was through Victoria and also the home in which my family and I now live. Although we have paid off the mortgage, we still maintain savings in the Society because we believe that just as we have benefited from the savings of others, our savings should assist others to achieve the same goal of home ownership. Participating in this celebration is therefore, not merely an event but it has personal meaning in thanksgiving for an enduring concept and for a most successful exponent of that concept.

In joining the celebrations of this the 125th Anniversary of the Victoria Mutual Building Society; I feel constrained to remember its founder; to review the circumstances of its beginnings; to take account of the basis for its name; to try to glean some understanding of why VMBS has survived and prospered for a century and a quarter, and to point to lessons learned that may be instructive to its future. Follow me on this journey.

The Founding and Naming of Victoria Mutual Building Society

Victoria Mutual Building Society was founded by the Venerable Archdeacon Reverend George William Downer and a few other clergymen in 1878. He was then Rector of Kingston Parish Church. He was the founding Chairman of the Society and Reverend A. H. Neito its founding Secretary. Who the other clergymen were, most likely all Anglicans, is not yet public knowledge.

Reverend G. W. Downer was born in Jamaica on October 1, 1837 in a family that originated in Scotland but which came to Jamaica in 1760 via Long Island, New York. They first settled in Snow Hill, Portland but later moved to Kingston where William was born. By Professor Edward Brathwaite's terminology, Reverend Downer was a creole Jamaican. He was ordained a deacon of the Anglican Church in 1860 and a priest in 1861. He married Helen Jane Nelson and they had three children, two girls and a boy. He first served in Stewart Town and then at the Cathedral in Spanish Town before becoming Island Curate of St. Gabriel's Church in Four Paths, Clarendon, where he served for 10 years. In Clarendon, Reverend Downer did pioneering missionary work among Indians who had come to Jamaica as indentured workers but remained as workers on sugar estates in Clarendon. When the Morant Bay Rebellion occurred the Downer's were at St. Gabriels'. Helen Jane was among the Ladies who wrote a Memorial to Governor John Eyre thanking him for putting down the Morant Bay Rebellion in 1865. William became Rector of Kingston Parish Church in 1873 and was Rector for 35 years. He retired in 1908 and died on March 21, 1912.

During his long tenure at Kingston Parish Church, Reverend Downer engaged in many and varied activities. He was a member of the Royal Lodge 207, the Bishop's Nominee to Synod, Chairman of the Kingston Parochial Board of the Anglican Church and Patron of the Christian Union Established Church Society founded in 1844. He renovated the church, which had over 1300 members and was then the second largest congregation only surpassed by St. George's Church on East Street which had over 1500 members. He reached out to the Chinese who had remained in Jamaica and had shops in Kingston. He was a contemporary of the great Reverend Enos Nuttall. They were nominees together to the Synod. After Nuttall was consecrated as

Bishop in 1880, Downer became one of the Bishops' nominees to Synod and subsequently Archdeacon.

Downer and his family were loyalists and royalists. Queen Victoria was on the throne in England and at the pinnacle of her reign in the1870s with almost universal acceptance among her subjects. It is therefore not surprising that in founding the building society in 1878, Downer memorialised the reigning British sovereign in the name Victoria Mutual Building Society. For very different reasons, loyalty to the British Crown has been part of the glue that has held Jamaican society together. Downer of Scottish ancestry, and creole upbringing, invoked the name of the English Queen many years and long before her Jubilee Anniversary in 1897, when it was common to do so.

The Origination of Building Societies in Jamaica, their Core Values and Rapid Spread

Reverend William J. Gardner, in his book, *A History of Jamaica*, first published in 1873, stated that the first building society was founded in 1864 by a 'few friends anxious to promote the well-being of the working and middle classes.' On Page 470, Gardner gave critical details of this first building society. He stated:

> Its income at first was small but in 1871, profits were for the first time declared, and shares, upon which sixteen guineas had been paid by installments of four shillings per month for seven years, were found entitled to five per cent interest making 20 pounds, and a bonus of five pounds nine shillings and six pence in addition. The safety of the project thus proved, great numbers has since joined and its income in 1872 was about twenty thousand pounds. It is purely mutual in its character, and provided many people with excellent homes they could have obtained in no other way.

Reverend Gardner died in 1874 at the age of 49.

After Reverend Gardner's death, his brother, Aston W. Gardner continued the work. In his introductory note to the Second Edition, *A History of Jamaica*, he provided information about the ministry and the work of his late brother. He wrote that Reverend William Gardner was the founder of the first building society in Jamaica. In other words, Reverend Gardner was the leader of the group of friends who, in 1864, were anxious to promote the well-being of the working and middle classes. Neither Aston nor William Gardner gave the name of this first building society but it was most likely the Kingston Benefit Building Society.

The authenticity of Reverend William Gardner, pastor of the North Street Congregational Church, as being the founder of the first building society in Jamaica is supported on three grounds:

- First, the stated goal of all building societies established from 1872 onwards was to assist the 'working and middle classes' or 'middle and working classes' or the 'working classes' in house purchase and home improvement. In the late nineteenth century, terms of 'middle class' and 'working class' had definite social and historic meanings although both classes occupied more or less similar economic and financial space. They were the classes that earned income but not enough to purchase property without accumulating savings.

- Second, the financial formula for all building societies after 1871 was member acquisition of a twenty pound share through payment of four shillings per month for seven years. The number of shares to which members subscribed varied according to means and intentions.

- Third, the *modus operandi* for all building societies was mutual saving by members for a prescribed period before benefits were declared and paid. In today's terminology, between 1864 and 1871, Gardner and his other anxious friends, provided proof of concept of building societies as a viable, feasible and workable means of house purchase and home improvement for people who otherwise could not afford a home.

The Rapid Spread of Building Societies

After 1871, the building society concept spread rapidly. Reverend Henry Clarke was the earliest adopter in leading the effort to found the Westmoreland Building Society in 1872, followed by Reverend Cork in 1874 with the founding of the St. James Benefit and Building Society. Indeed, by 1900, almost every parish had a building society; for example, the St. Ann Benefit and Building Society; the St. Elizabeth Benefit and Building Society; the Manchester Mutual Building Society; the Trelawny Benefit and Building Society and the St. Mary Benefit and Building Society. As was the case with Victoria Mutual, not all building societies invoked the name of the Parish in

THE CORE VALUES OF THE PROTOTYPE BUILDING SOCIETY CAN BE CAPTURED AND SUMMARISED AS FOLLOWS:

1. Membership as a requirement of participation in the society

2. Consistent saving by members as the means of purchasing shares over time

3. The pooling of members' saving and the prudent investment of pooled savings

4. Accountability and transparency with respect to investments of pooled funds

5. Declaration and sharing of benefits to members as the source of at least the down payment for house purchase or home improvement

which they were established. For example, the Jamaica Permanent Building Society was also founded in 1878 as well as the Brown's Town Benefit and Building Society and Falmouth Benefit and Building Society.

It is important to note some important facts and common features of these early building societies:

- First, the idea of building societies originated in the church by a missionary of the Congregational Church, spread quickly by Anglican clergy but also included other groups. In other words, the early building societies had strong connections with the church and gave every appearance that they were firmly grounded on an ethical base.

- Second, consistent with being mutual societies, all the building societies founded in the latter three decades of the nineteenth century established common, clear and transparent processes for management and accountability. These included electing officers such as President/ Chairman, Secretary and Treasurer; appointing trustees; appointing auditors; appointing arbitrators; naming their banker and holding annual members' meetings.

- Third, Professor Patrick Bryan in his book, *The Jamaican People, 1880-1902: Race, Class, and Social Control*, noted that the largely white oligarchy of the times were largely represented in the structures of the building societies. While this was true, account must be taken of the fact that "respectability politics", so labeled by Robert Osborn and Edward Jordon in mid-nineteenth century, was still in vogue at the end of the century. Building Societies in their infancy clearly made use of the politics of respectability. Clergymen and men of known financial means and high reputation often shared the directorships; men of known financial means and high reputation were most often trustees; while clergymen were most numerous among the arbitrators. An example of this pattern is Edward Andrews, who had been Stamp Commissioner and Island Treasurer. After he retired from the public service in 1911, he was elected Chairman of Victoria Mutual and served until the time of his death in November 1915.

Victoria Mutual Building Society was not the first or even the second building society founded in Jamaica or even in Kingston. It was founded after the building society prototype and paradigm had been proven and adopted. The unique feature of Victoria Mutual Building Society that must be included in these 125th anniversary celebrations, is that among all the building societies established in the latter decades of the nineteenth century, it is the only one that has retained its original name and character continuously until today. Because this is a Victoria Mutual event, it would not be appropriate for me to trace the history of any other building society, still operating in contemporary times, and how it was formed. Suffice it to say that VMBS is unique among building societies in Jamaica in retaining its original name.

Political and Social Context of the Spread of Building Societies in the 1870s

To get a better understanding of the rapid mushrooming of building societies in the 1870s, we need to take a peek into the political and social context of that decade:

1. **Social Unrest.** The Morant Bay Rebellion was a 'small settlers' uprising. 'Small settlers' was the euphemism that was adopted by those ex-slaves who with high expectation and enthusiasm left the

plantation, bought lands, set up village communities with families, churches, schools and small farms to produce food for the domestic market. They moved to qualify themselves for participation in the political process by owning land that made them eligible to vote.

2. **The Morant Bay Rebellion.** By 1865, small settlers' hopes and aspirations were transformed into frustration and disillusionment and they were more often referred to as the 'working class'. The oligarchy had deliberately disenfranchised them with respect to eligibility to vote; discriminated against them in the courts; burdened them with a high proportion of taxation; limited their access to education; failed to implement basic public health measures even after disastrous outbreaks of cholera and yellow fever; and ignored their protests and objections to these injustices and neglect. The literate petition-writing small settlers of St. Thomas exploded in riot in Morant Bay in 1865. Governor Eyre responded with draconian measures and brutality which was far in excess of the violence of the riot. These included the execution of Paul Bogle, George William Gordon, Samuel Clarke, several elementary school teachers and many members of the Native Baptists and the burning of their houses and churches. The oligarchy panicked as they feared another Haiti was at hand. The Assembly dissolved itself and invited Crown Colony Government in 1866.

3. **Reform Begins.** Governor, John Peter Grant who succeeded Eyre as Governor; literally adopted the small settlers'/working classes grievances as his reform agenda for the colony. These included the reform of the judiciary; the abolition of the militia with its exalted ranks; the setting up of the Jamaica Constabulary Force; the establishment of a public health system; the expansion of the teachers college/elementary school system; and the disestablishment of the Anglican Church in 1870. The State would no longer pay the salaries of Anglican deacons and priests, maintain the buildings and subsidise operations of the church. The expenditure saved would be applied to State reforms. The Anglican Church from 1870 had responsibility for the remuneration and conditions of service of its priests. This was another blow for priests because they had sustained a pay cut in the austerity measures that were implemented during the economic and financial crisis of the 1850s.

4. **Inequities in the Jamaican Society.** From the inception of colonialism, Jamaican society was marked by socio-economic divisions based on some combination of citizenship, race, class and gender. Every action to address any of these bases of inequality was met by reaction to preserve the status quo. The reform agenda of early Crown Colony government was no exception. The central theme uniting the grievances of the 'small settler/working class was greater opportunities for upward social mobility, equal treatment under the law and more equitable taxation. The Crown's attention to this central grievance was met with demands by the other segments of the society that perceived that their positions were threatened.

Allow me to illustrate from the field of education. Expanding elementary education, improving its quality and upgrading the standard of elementary school teachers, raised concerns among the traditional middle classes that educational standards were being equalized since their children only received an elementary education. Accordingly, there was great advocacy for the reform of the charity school system which served this segment. As a result, by the end of the 1870s, many charity schools had been transformed into high schools and preparatory schools: for example, Munro, Hampton, Mannings, Ruseas, Titchfield, Beckford and Smith now St. Jago, and Jamaica College were built as the premier high schools of the colony. Further, the Cambridge University Examination system and the Jamaica Scholarship were introduced and made part of the infrastructure of high schooling. The apartheid that was evident between charity schools and elementary schools was deepened: elementary schools and teachers' colleges as one system and preparatory and high schools as a parallel and more privileged system.

My Hypothesis. I cannot speak with the same authority about building societies as I do about the education system. Further, not being a trained historian the best I can do is to offer a hypothesis that the disestablishment of the Anglican Church in 1870, which cut off State funding, had great medium and long term consequences for economic and socio-economic well-being for the Anglican clergy. The proof of concept of the viability of the building society idea, pioneered by Congregationalist William Gardner and friends, and confirmed in 1871, came at a very opportune time. Early adopters of the building society concept like Reverend Henry Clarke of Westmoreland, Reverend Cork of St. James and Reverend Downer of Kingston, not only saw the common good of the idea but they were also very mindful of its benefits to the clergy in the post-establishment era. Given the fact that the Anglican clergy had always been part of the ruling oligarchy, these leaders in the church were able to mobilise the support of persons of established wealth, known financial expertise, and high rank in the society to become part of the building society's infrastructure. This involvement of supporters from within the oligarchy enhanced the acceptability of the building society idea generally and contributed to its acceptance and rapid spread.

This is only a hypothesis formed from my amateur and cursory exploration of available material. Victoria Mutual at 125 should commission a study by qualified historians to explore the origin and spread of building societies in Jamaica. Understanding these roots is critical to continued evolution of this movement. However, a better understanding of the origination and rapid spread of the building society concept, in the closing decades of the nineteenth century, do not account for its continuation into the twentieth century.

It is therefore critical to also address the question: Why have building societies survived? I wish to offer a three part answer.

Shelter: A Basic Human Need

The three basic biological needs of the human species are food, shelter and a mate. Food is needed for daily bodily sustenance. Shelter is needed for protection from the elements. Mates are needed for the reproduction of future generations. What this means is that there will never be a generation of any human beings anywhere or at any time who will not need to satisfy these species requirements, even though there may be individual exceptions. Put another way, any generation of human beings of any particular time and at any specific place who collectively choose to ignore these three basic needs will not survive. Bluntly put, among humans the food business, the shelter business and the reproduction business will never be out of business. Building societies have an elemental connection to the need for shelter.

Over time, humans have satisfied this basic need for shelter by living in caverns; in   rocks; in caves; under trees; in trees; in tents; in dwellings constructed with mud, stone, ice, thatch, dung of animals, wood, bricks or some combinations of these and in more modern times of concrete and steel. Historically, the responsibility to provide shelter rested with the patriarch of the family, the lineage, the clan or the tribe who discharged that shelter responsibility on communal property. As governance evolved, cities grew and governments acquired ownership of communal lands and as land ownership was privatized, people without lands captured government and private property to provide shelter for themselves and their families. Indeed, capturing is a well-known practice in Jamaica. This is why homelessness, people without shelter, is not as common a phenomenon in Jamaica as now being highlighted in the more well-regulated cities of the US. Jamaica has far more landless people than homeless people. Indeed, some shelters constructed on captured lands are most impressive, although without funding from VMBS.

I am unable to resist the temptation of telling how my understanding of homelessness was radically changed. While on sabbatical leave from UWI in 1988, as a visiting professor at Stanford University, I ended up in hospital because I did not know I had duodenal ulcers or the signs of such ulcers. It was both a frightening and funny experience at the same time, although I laughed upon reflection of the experience. I walked into the emergency room. My blood pressure was taken sitting; then standing; nursing and doctors started running and immediately I was put on a stretcher with a tube put up my nose, an IV drip placed in one hand and a connection to an ECG machine on the other hand. That I was frightened is an understatement. I had never been in hospital and did not know that the hospital gown was to be put on back ways. I had put it on front ways. Being over six feet it became a mini-dress opened in the front. I must have looked ridiculous but I did not know that at the time. The embarrassment was retroactive. This probably accounts for the fact that I never went back to the Stanford Hospital after I was discharged.

I was admitted to the hospital. On the next bed to me was a man who told me that he was homeless. His story was eye-opening and jaw-dropping. He was retired and in receipt of a small pension and social security. However, the combined monthly income was not sufficient to cover his rent and living expenses. His income could only adequately cover food and other living expenses. To make ends meet, he had given up his apartment; put his furniture, clothing and other belongings in storage; found a few corporate buildings with shower facilities which if he entered late in the afternoons he could avoid detection at the time of closing. He took his shower in the mornings and left before the time of the earliest arrivals. He rotated between these buildings during the course of a week. His great concern was that he had left some items in the building in which he slept on the night before being hospitalized. If they were found it could lead to tightened security that would decrease his options in continuing his weekly routine. Previously, I had thought that homeless people were destitute and in most cases somewhat deranged. This man was rational, resourceful and resolute in seeking to maintain his middle class lifestyle that included a daily shower. He was providing shelter for himself in a most ingenious manner.

The provision of shelter for citizens of a country or city is not the province of building societies. This is the challenge of local or central government. The establishment of our own National Housing Trust is yet another attempt to address this challenge by adopting some of the principles of building societies. This has come after the failure of government housing schemes, many of which have fallen victim to capture and the mentality that if it is government there is no compulsion to pay. At the same time, the majority of persons who compulsorily contribute to the National Housing Trust from their earned income will not qualify for loans to acquire houses. In other words, the provision of shelter and home ownership are not one and the same thing. Hence, the satisfaction of the basic need for shelter in modern society and the obligation of the state to address this need for its citizens may be by other means than only home ownership.

Home Ownership:
The Widespread Human Aspiration

While the building society idea is connected to the basic human need for shelter, the primal impetus and driving force for home ownership comes directly from the widespread aspiration of most people to own the shelters in which they live. This aspiration and impetus has emerged as human society shifts from its historical organisation of blood-bonded kinship collectives as the unit of social organisation; shifting from the extended family, the lineage, the clan and the tribe owning communal property to private property and individual ownership independent of family or lineage, or clan or tribe.

Home ownership, owning the shelter in which one lives, has meaning to individuals in at least three interrelated ways:

1. Sovereign control over the space in which one lives and how one lives in that space, physically and socially. The common and emphatic expression, 'This is my house' demonstrates this meaning.

2. Status and stability in relating to the community in which one lives. One's home establishes the boundary and a border in relating to others in the community.

3. Reward and justification for work, especially in circumstances in which work is not personally meaningful, enjoyable or satisfying. The goal of owning a home through income from working, mitigates the daily grind in hopes of the expected achievement.

Owning a home through a lifetime of work has become a standard for assessing equity, fairness and worth in compensation earned from various occupations in society. For example, if teachers, nurses, police officers, ministers of religion and mid-level civil servants are unable to own a home after a lifetime of service then their compensation is deemed inequitable in comparison to their service to the society. The United States has wonderfully sanitized terms for emerging problems. One of this is the working poor. A definition of the working poor that strikes me personally is: someone who is living in a home that he/she could not now purchase on market. This speaks to the differential in the increase in the cost of housing compared to that in salaries and wages.

Teachers, nurses, civil servants, police officers, Ministers of Religion and middle managers of the private sector have been the traditional clientele of building societies. They are numbered among those who aspire to own their own shelter and are obliged to do so within the context of mutuality; in the pooling of their resources over time. Increasing income inequality in society could become a real challenge for building societies and place them in a situation not much different from the NHT; in which the majority of their savers may not be able to quality for mortgages.

Housing as an Expression
of Permanent Domicile

In the interest of time, the most economical way to establish the connection of building societies to expressions of permanent domicile by Jamaicans is by quoting a famous poll by the legendary, Professor Karl Stone, and extending its application. Professor Stone did an opinion poll which showed that 63 percent of Jamaicans would migrate if given the opportunity. This caused great public lament. However, that poll also showed that 34 percent would not migrate because they had gone abroad and returned. To me, the policy implication is abundantly clear: The Government should immediately embark upon a scheme to assist the 63 percent that wish to migrate to do so. The medium and long term impact of such a policy would be greater commitment to the building of country and the nation by those who return.

The sentiment and emotion of the 34 percent are penned elegantly by the English poet, Sir Walter Scott in his poem, *Breathes There the Man with Soul So Dead*:

> Breathes there the man with soul so dead,
> Who never to himself hath said,
> 'This is my own, my native land!'
> Whose heart hath ne'er within him burn'd
> As home his footsteps he hath turn'd
> From wandering on a foreign strand?
> If such there breathe, go, mark him well;
> For him no Minstrel raptures swell;
> High though his titles, proud his name,
> Boundless his wealth as wish can claim;
> Despite those titles, power, and pelf,
> The wretch, concentred all in self,
> Living, shall forfeit fair renown,
> And, doubly dying, shall go down
> To the vile dust from whence he sprung,
> Unwept, unhonour'd, and unsung

Jamaica, like the rest of the Western Hemisphere, is populated by people who came from elsewhere. There is no Homo Sapiens, Caribbeanensis or

Americanensis. Indeed, over the course of Jamaica's history this sense of native land has risen for Africa, Europe, India, China and the Middle East. The sense of Jamaica being a native land compared to Africa, Europe, India, China or the Middle East has been slow in coming, but is not recent, although not yet a sentiment of the majority who were born and live in this land.

There is general agreement on a number of features about Jamaica. The island is beautiful. The flavor of food grown here is fantastic. The water taste great. The climate is wonderful. The mountains are majestic. The beaches are alluring. The sea is warm. However, for many the aboriginal sense of belonging is reserved for elsewhere. For many of us who have journeyed elsewhere we have found that we no longer belong there. We are Africans without tribes, Indians without caste, Chinese without dynastic connections and Europeans without class. We have lost the Old World distinctions that make Africans, Africans; Indians, Indians; Chinese, Chinese; and Europeans, Europeans. Further, some of us are so mixed in Old World ancestry that it makes no sense to claim any exclusive connection with any part of that antiquity.

You can see the sentiment of 'Jamaica being homeland' writ large in houses built, and being built, across the island. You can see them especially on the hills of most parishes. They are mansions. Do not for a moment think that they only look good on the outside. Enter them and you will find first class fixtures, beautiful furniture and the latest name brand equipment. These houses are statements that Jamaica is our permanent domicile. Jamaica is where we belong. I can see the coy smiles which loudly declare that these houses are not built from income saved in building societies. I agree that some of these houses are constructed from other sources, some of which should remain nameless. But building societies are also implicated in this sentiment of 'Jamaica being homeland'.

I call to the witness stand officers of the branches of Victoria Mutual, and other building societies, in London, Toronto and New York which have garnered savings from the Jamaican Diaspora. I also call to the witness stand officers of the Society to give evidence under oath that savings from the Jamaican Diaspora have gone to construct five, six and seven bedroom houses in instances where only mother and father returns to live in these houses, but there are bedrooms rooms reserved for their children and grandchildren when they visit periodically. Some of these returning residents have laboured abroad for many years and have sold their houses in London, New York and

Toronto in order build these concrete and steel statements of Jamaica being their permanent place of belonging.

Slowly over the centuries, through such contrary influences as sex, the church, and rum inspired bacchanal, increasing numbers have formed common identity which claimed Jamaica as their homeland. After the end of the Second Maroon War in the late 1790s, many Maroons were transported to Sierra Leone. In 1841 many Maroons returned to live in Jamaica as their home. In the latter part of the nineteenth century, people born in Jamaica, started to migrate to Central America, then in the twentieth century to Cuba, the United States, England and Canada. With each migration, some remained in the countries where they went, often establishing Jamaican communities. With every wave of migration there were those who returned with a greater sense of Jamaica being their homeland. The identification of Jamaica as a permanent place of belonging has always found expression in home construction. Indeed, one of the motives for working abroad has been to earn the resources to build that dream house. This propensity accelerated after Independence in 1962, with some reversal in the late 1970s when many sold their homes and migrated especially to Florida. Retroactively, the words of Eric Donaldson could be applied to the actions of these Maroons:

> This is the Land of my birth
> This is the Land of my birth
> This is Jamaica my Jamaica
> The land of my birth.

As another aside, note that over the last twenty years, two new terms related to Jamaica being homeland have become parts of the Jamaican lexicon, with even legal meaning. First is "returning resident". Second is "deportee".

A 'returning resident' is someone who migrated at some earlier stage of life, has enjoyed financial success abroad and voluntarily comes back to live the sunset years in Jamaica, usually in a home purchased as a result of success abroad.

Deportees are mostly children of those who migrated, and are still living abroad, but are forced to return because of legal infractions with the authorities and having little means of ensuring their upkeep. Unlike deportees, returning residents usually have savings with building societies. The fact is that whether voluntarily, or by force, both returning residents and deportees live in Jamaica as permanent residents.

Victoria Mutual, and other building societies, has flourished since independence from the aspirations of Jamaicans inside Jamaica to own homes as well as from Jamaicans in the Diaspora making statements about Jamaica as the place of permanent domicile. When I became a member of Victoria Mutual in the mid-1960s there was only one office, now the headquarters at Duke Street. Today Victoria Mutual has several branches in Kingston and across Jamaica, plus overseas in London, New York and Toronto. There is indeed much to celebrate about Victoria Mutual at 125.

What of the Future?

In any celebration, it is mandatory to look backward and prudent to look forward.

Over these 125 years, Victoria Mutual has seen natural disasters such as the Great Earthquake and fires of 1907, Hurricane Charlie of 1951 and wild Gilbert of 1988. I was stranded in Curacao, on my way back from Aruba, when Gilbert struck. I was on the first flight from the Southern Caribbean when the Airport was reopened. I could hardly believe my eyes at the devastation. Most striking were the stately and elegant homes of Beverly Hills, Norbrook and Cherry Gardens whose walls were still standing but their roofs, doors and windows had taken flight. Less elegant houses on the flats were in no better condition. Giant trees were uprooted and those still standing had lost most of their foliage.

From the back porch of my home I could see parts of Kingston that I had never seen before. Three weeks later I went to London for a month and when I returned I could not believe my eyes. The foliage was back in all its green glory. My back porch view was blocked, again. The less elegant houses on the flats had zinc roofs, although not their original zinc. Gilbert had conducted an informal exchange of zinc for roofs. The elegant houses were still in distress. Their owners had to wait on insurance. Gilbert brought to the fore the resilience of Jamaica; plants and people. Also on display was that indomitable spirit, determined to continue despite the circumstances.

Close to home, Victoria Mutual has felt the effects of the financial disaster of the recent past. To those who may not remember, there was an economic recession following the Gulf War when the United States responded to Iraq's invasion of Kuwait. Somewhere in the mid-1990s on returning from an overseas trip in which economic distress was evident in several countries, I remember asking my wife, 'what do we in Jamaica know that the rest of the world does not know'?

My wife is an economist, and after a discussion, the conclusion was that money in the bank was of no value in a financial collapse. We decided that the most important asset to preserve was our home. We pull all our savings which, fortunately, was sufficient to pay off the balance on our mortgage. The records of Victoria Mutual can confirm this. The financial collapse did come. Locally-owned banks were wiped out. The insurance industry was decimated. Government, which previously was in no strong financial position, attempted to bail out certain banks and insurance companies leaving taxpayers with huge debts to pay in succeeding years. A notable causality of this financial crisis was Jamaica Mutual Life Assurance Society, Mutual Life, founded in 1844 and named no less a person among its directors than National Hero, George William Gordon. Longevity by itself is no guarantee of the future. Victoria Mutual was affected by this crisis. I am not sure if the Society had a near death experience but in 1998, Chairman Vayden McMorris announced that the worst had past.

Jamaica is vulnerable to natural disasters. It is also vulnerable to the boom and bust cycles of modern money economies. Knowing this, we are wise to engage in long-term strategies that mitigate the major risks of what may be inevitable.

Victoria Mutual was born out of the church. I must confess that as a young saver in the society, I believed that Victoria Mutual was connected to the Brethren Church. The late Karl Richards then Elder of Galilee Gospel Hall was then general manager. It is delving into history that has revealed the Society's Anglican genesis. Probably the church connection is the foundation of the reputation for integrity that Victoria Mutual has had over these many years. President and CEO Karl Wright has continued to enhance that image of trust and uphold that nobility of character that engenders public confidence in the affairs of the Society. This is a priceless legacy that must never be compromised.

As a Calabar Old Boy, I cannot but observe that Victoria Mutual has had a fair share of Wolmer's Old boys in top positions. Seeing that my two sons and almost all my nephews are past Wolmerians, I am constrained in adopting the roasting tradition of that great school, the oldest school of the country. I will only say that the Wolmer's connection does not seem to have done the Society any harm. With the objectivity that Calabar engenders, let me observe the fact that the oldest school in the country located in Kingston has, over the last 125 years, contributed leadership to the oldest building society also located in Kingston. This underscores that truth that the best talent in our schools, possessed not only the competence but also the character, and integrity to play a critical role in the survival of our institutions in the past and for the future. It behooves us all to continue to invest in education.

Listening to friends in business, I hear such ideas and phrases as 'vertical integration'; 'subsidiaries'; 'group of companies'; being 'asset rich' and 'cash poor' leading to problems with cash flow; wealth management and making money work for you. I grew up being told that you should work for your money. Now money is supposed to work for you. So as a simple teacher, I have begun to take a little closer look at the idea of money as worker.

I am not thrilled by what I am seeing.

Money seems to be a very careless employee. It keeps coming back with less than you sent it out with. Money seems to be very fickle. Depending on who is handling it, money keeps taking off with some persons whose touch it seems to like, never to be seen again. The degree of unfaithfulness of money is unbelievable. It will take off with relatives, close friends and church brothers leaving only anguish in its wake. Money is moody. It often refuses to circulate, leading to problems with something called 'liquidity'. Sometimes it goes on 'strike'. This interrupts lending and borrowing, leading to little or no returns. My point is extremely simple. Victoria Mutual is well advised to engage in the most careful interrogation of some on these high financing ideas.

Allow me to conclude with a few exhortations.

Victoria Mutual cannot rest on its laurels, it would be folly to think that its future is automatically secure because:

- It has survived as a distinct building society for 125 years, maintaining its original name
- It has flourished over the last forty years by connecting to a basic human need

- It has its impetus in the widespread human aspiration of home ownership, and is a beneficiary of the increasing tendency of Jamaicans at home and abroad to see Jamaica as their native land; constructing lavish homes to make this statement emphatic.

Moving forward into the twenty-first century, Victoria Mutual must continue to stay close to its core business:

- Members who save should be able to withdraw their funds when they want it
- Members should be able to qualify for affordable mortgages
- Be mindful of venturing into areas that could bring the Society into ruin.

A building society is not a commercial bank or an investment bank or an insurance company. It is not set up for the profits of shareholders. Building societies are, in essence, cooperatives focusing on the common goal of home owners.

My final word is to those who manage the affairs of the Society:

You are a steward not an owner. The Society is not yours. You are accountable to the owners. As a steward you are required to be faithful. Strenuously avoid the temptation to run the Society for your own benefit. The Society is for the benefit of members. As a steward you must be fruitful. The Society must show increase as a result of your stewardship.

Bless God for Victoria Mutual at age 125 and may God continue to bless Victoria Mutual for the years to come.

Sister Mary Bernadette Little, RSM, CD. 1920-2014

Since its founding in 1894, the Alpha Academy has produced many alumnae who have joined the Order of the Sisters of Mercy and have made outstanding contributions to its work. Sister Mary Bernadette served as the first Jamaican headmistress for 30 years.

Chapter 7

Christian Laywomen: Faith, Focus, Founders and Framework

~

THE 116TH ANNIVERSARY
OF ALPHA ACADEMY
May, 2010

~

Introduction

Let me begin by congratulating the Sisters of Mercy for the founding of Convent of Mercy Academy, Alpha in 1894 and for being involved in education and child development in Jamaica for 130 years. Visions that survive their founders and persist for over a century, with every prospect of continuing for as long as we can see in the future, are very special. Marking each milestone of this journey takes on important significance. I therefore deem it a considerable honour and privilege that you have invited me to share this occasion with you on this first Monday morning in May.

The event has been billed as a "celebration of nostalgia". Alumnae no longer called old girls, from here and abroad, are meeting to tour the facilities, reconnect with colleagues of past eras, reminisce on their days at Alpha and interact with current students. My gender precludes me from being an old girl. The closest that I can come in nostalgic remembrance is in what my mother tells me – that I was born on Emma Ville Crescent, off Norman Road, in the vicinity of the General Post Office just down the road and the fact that I grew up for the first ten years of my life on Laidlaw Street, off Seaforth Street which is just across the road. I remember playing at Issa Park which is the premises that now house the Jesse Ripoll Primary School. Many are the days that I walked past, or took the bus or the tramcar past Alpha Academy on the way to or from downtown Kingston. Alpha as a place is etched in my childhood memory.

There is another reason why I am so happy to share in this celebration. I sincerely hope that the Sisters of Mercy don't mind me saying this, but over the last 20 or more years I have been included among those persons to whom the Sisters send a Christmas Card. It is one of the cards that I actively looked forward to receiving. My assumption is that if I am on the list to be sent a card, I am also on the list for prayer. On receiving the card, I am comforted that I am still in their prayers. This stems from something that happened in 1986.

I was part of the leadership of the Jamaica Teachers Association and we were involved in a fierce battle with the Government over matters concerning education and teachers' pay. The outcome was not assured and even some persons who you thought were friends were keeping their distance, just in case we were on the losing side. One day I was in the office and was told that there was a Nun outside to see me. When she came in she said that she did not want to waste my time, but she had just come to tell me that she and some other Nuns were praying for me. In the brief conversation that we had it turned out that she had taken a bus from May Pen into Kingston to deliver this word of encouragement and support. I cannot tell you what this meant to me. I know that we are here today to celebrate the founding of a great school and the work of a particular Order of Religious Women. However, I hope that we include in those celebrations, and in the nostalgia, recollections of those small but indelible acts of kindness, love and encouragement that Sisters of all Orders have done, even to those of us who are not Catholic.

On anniversaries it is important that we engage in four processes:

- Reviewing the history
- Recalling the context
- Reflecting on their meaning; and
- Recognising the lessons to be learned for our time and for the future.

As briefly as I can, in a keynote address, please allow me to take you through these four processes.

Reviewing the History of Alpha

Permit me to review the history of Alpha that you all know so well. Three young women, Justina Jesse Ripoll, Josephine Ximenes and Louise Dugiol, decided to establish an orphanage in Jamaica. With what savings they had, and with Jesse Ripoll putting up most of the money, they purchased the 43-acre Alpha Property on South Camp Road. On May 1, 1880, Jesse Ripoll pushed open the wicket gate, and with an orphan girl in one hand and a statue of the Holy Mother in the other, she and her friends walked up the bushy path to the "Cottage". About three years later, the Orphanage was open to boys and out of that came the birth of the Alpha Boys School.

After 10 years of difficulties and privations of all kinds, and failing to receive any Government assistance, in December 1890 the Sisters of Bermondsey in London responded to the invitation of the three founders to join them in the work that they had started. On February 2, 1891, the three founders received the Habit of the Order of Mercy: Jesse took the Religious Name of Sister Mary Peter Claver, Louise took the name Sister Mary Joseph and Josephine took the name Sister Mary Margaret.

In 1894, the Convent of Mercy Academy at Alpha was established as a girls' high school. Sister Mary Joseph died on January 31, 1895 just after its founding. She lived to see the birth of the Academy but not to share in its development. However, Sister Mary Margaret continued to be a part of Alpha until her death on August 19, 1944 and Mother Peter Claver until her death on December 10, 1949 at age 97 years.

Reviewing the History of the Founding of the Sisters of Mercy

In September 1827, Catherine McAuley and two companions, undertook the management of an institution established at Baggot Street, Dublin, Ireland, founded to assist destitute women, orphans and poor schools. The institution was financed from a fortune that Catherine had inherited. Initially, there was no intention to establish a religious order. Further, there was resistance because these laywomen were performing tasks that were usually carried out by Nuns. Catherine and her associates were required to make a choice between being a secular institution or a religious order. They opted to be a religious order. The hierarchy of the church agreed to the establishment of a non-cloistered Order. Hence the Order of the Sisters of Mercy was founded in Dublin in 1831, with Sister Mary Catherine as its Superior. Sisters of Mercy were called the walking nuns for their practice to care for the poor in their homes, and in hospitals and for providing shelters for the homeless. They established day and night schools that catered to the poor. The nickname 'walking nuns' was not a term of endearment or one of approbation. Rather, it was a derisive description of what was considered an oddity: nuns operating outside of the cloister of the convent. Like other Orders of Religious women, Sisters of Mercy take the vow of poverty, chastity, obedience and evangelical counsel, but in addition, Sisters of Mercy take the vow of service.

In 1838, some English ladies, including Lady Barbara Eyre, went to Ireland for the purpose of establishing a congregation in England. The Convent of Mercy in Bermondsey, London was established in November 1839. Lady Eyre was the first to be received into the congregation and was one of its main benefactors. This was the first Convent of Mercy established outside of Ireland and the first established on a public highway in England. Mother Catherine McAuley herself participated in the founding of this first convent of the Sisters of Mercy in England. The need was for the education of children and the visitation of the poor and the sick.

The Convent of Mercy at Alpha is therefore a grandchild of the founding Convent in Dublin, Ireland. Since its founding in 1894, the Alpha Academy has produced many alumnae who have joined the Order of the Sisters of Mercy and have made outstanding contributions to its work. Allow me to name three: the legendary Sister Mary Ignatius Davies who worked for sixty years at the Boys School, the beloved Sister Mary Bernadette Little who served as principal of the Academy for more than three decades, and the versatile Sister Mary Paschal who transformed St. Catherine High School in Spanish Town and did sterling work at the St. Joseph's hospital.

Recalling the Context of Founding of the Order and of Alpha

Catherine McAuley was born on September 29, 1787. She grew up during the times when great social changes were occurring in Great Britain and Ireland in the wake of the Industrial Revolution. In this new social order, people were migrating from rural to urban areas, where the expanding industrial centres had not yet put in place appropriate infrastructure. There were demands for new levels of literacy and numeracy. In addition, there was exploitation of the poor.

Famine in Ireland further compounded the social problems as greater numbers deserted the land for urban and industrial centres. She also grew up in times when in Ireland and Great Britain, expressions of the Catholic faith were made in quiet terms, against the prevailing Protestant forms of religious expression.

Catherine was the eldest of three children. Mr. McAuley died in 1794, when Catherine was only seven and her mother passed on a few years later. The orphan children were passed from one relative to the next, who became their guardians and also invested the family patrimony for the benefit of the children. To cut a long story short, in 1822 when one of her guardians, Mr. Callahan, died, he bequeathed his entire estate to Catherine. When she came into full possession of this inheritance, two years later, Catherine determined that she was obliged to use this fortune for the benefit of the poor. In this regard she was following examples set by her father, whom she adored. Fortune, faith and fatherly example combined to lead Catherine to the founding of the Sisters of Mercy. Catherine had the experience of being an orphan with cash. She included in her life's mission to provide for orphans without cash.

Shifting from the founder of the Sisters of Mercy to the founders of Alpha, it must be noted that Justina Jesse Ripoll was born in 1858. She grew up in times of great economic hardship and social injustice in Jamaica. The circumstances of these times are well documented in Jamaica's history.

In 1865, National Hero, Paul Bogle, led his famous march from Stony Gut in St. Thomas to the Capital in Spanish Town to petition for greater justice in the administration of the law. Failure to respond in a constructive manner led to the Morant Bay Rebellion, that monumental event in Caribbean history. Young Jesse was seven years old at the time. Born in Jamaica of a Portuguese mother and a French father, Jesse saw human suffering and violence in her formative years. In her twenties she came into an inheritance. As was the case with Catherine McAuley, Jesse Ripoll decided to use her fortune to the benefit of the poor and dispossessed in the Jamaican society, especially orphans.

The 1880s and 1890s were other periods of challenge and change in Jamaican society. Following measures to ameliorate the concerns of the descendants of the slaves, following the Morant Bay Rebellion, including public funding for elementary education and training colleges, the Middle Classes began to advocate for better educational opportunities for their children. This led to the development of public secondary education. The first efforts focused on secondary education for boys. By the 1890s many influential persons, within the society including the Assembly, became very concerned about the level of education of women and girls. This prompted the founding of several girls' high schools including Alpha. In a nutshell, in founding Alpha, the founders of the orphanage and the Sisters of Mercy combined to respond to a felt need in the Jamaican society.

Reflecting on its Meaning

If we are to go beyond the surface of sentimentality and nostalgia, what are we celebrating on this Monday morning, May 3rd 2010? Yes, we are gathered together in McAuly Hall, here at Alpha celebrating the 116 anniversary of Alpha Academy. But what does this really mean? McAuley Hall is named after Catherine McAuley who along with two other Catholic laywomen established an institution on Baggot Street, Dublin, Ireland to serve destitute women, orphans and the poor, which led to the founding of the Sisters of Mercy in 1831. We are here at Alpha the property that three Jamaican Catholic laywomen, led by Jesse Ripoll, purchased in May 1880 to start an orphanage for poor children. Our particular focus this morning is the founding of the high school for girls by the combined efforts of Jesse Ripoll, Josephine Ximense and Louise Dugiol and the Sisters of Mercy of Bermondsey, London. These dates make events but we should be celebrating more than events and the passage of time since they occurred. The fact is that these events mark much more than dates.

When we look beyond the surface of sentimentality and nostalgia, and dates marking the founding of the Sisters of Mercy, the Orphanage at Alpha and the establishment of the Alpha Academy, there are at least four deeper factors that were at work:

1. Christian faith of laywomen exercised in difficult times. In times of economic hardship, social turmoil and political uncertainty it is not

unusual for persons to become despondent nor is it unusual for persons to look to the authorities for answers. Neither in Ireland in the 1820s, nor in Jamaica in the 1870s, could it be said that Catholic laywomen were numbered among the powerful or represented the authorities. In reality they came from sections of society that were not expected to light candles in the social darkness that prevailed.

Yet, it was these Catholic laywomen who exercised Christian faith in acts of practical holiness that created hope and opportunity for many whose future and circumstances appeared bleak. They did not set out to change the entire world, rather they reached out in the communities in which they lived and acted on behalf of the marginalised who they could reach. Their faith created visions. They then worked to bring vision and faith to reality. Those actions created hope as they brought relief to the suffering, opportunities to the young and set examples that others would emulate.

Today we are celebrating faith backed up by works that continue to create hope for so many who are not even aware of the visions of which they are the beneficiaries.

2. Focus on others rather than self. Catherine McAuley and Jesse Ripoll inherited legacies that they could have used for their own personal comfort and enjoyment. After all, they were single women without husbands to provide for them. Yet their concern and focus were not about themselves. Their concern and focus were the marginalised in society, especially orphans, destitute women and children.

    Contrast this with the so-called investment bankers of Wall Street who by their greed and amoral actions have generated so much suffering on innocent people across the world. I do not know if any of you watched executives of Goldman Sachs testifying before a Senate Committee last week. They saw nothing wrong or immoral in what they did. They justified their actions on the grounds that their customers represented institutions and their executives were well versed in what was going on. Therefore, it did not matter if Goldman created financial products that it sold to those customers without letting them know that Goldman itself was betting that those products would fail.

Clearly, these highly educated financial wizards of Wall Street had forgotten two basic things. First, investment banking should be about supporting businesses that are creating products and services with the potential of adding value and benefits to customers and investors. Second, they and their customers were not betting their own money. What these very knowledgeable and clever executives had done was to create nothing but a casino in which the game was really about who among them would become the wealthiest. The truth is that what these selfish executives have done is to generate great suffering not only in the United States, but all around the world, including here in Jamaica.

In contrast, Catherine and Jesse and their associates invested financial legacies that they inherited for the benefit of those who were financially destitute and those legacies have created spiritual, social and economic benefits that have brought returns far greater that the amounts invested.

Today we celebrate those gifts that have kept on giving because those legacies were invested for the benefit of others and not self.

3. Personal sacrificial service rendered over time. The remarkable thing about Catherine McAuley and her associates, and Jesse, Josephine and Louise is not only did they give of their substance to the institutions that they founded but they gave of themselves. A one-time financial contribution of whatever amount is worthy of commendation. But much more difficult and demanding is the giving of one's self daily, to that which we have committed. Daily personal sacrifice requires monumental discipline and determination. This is because life-long commitment to any cause has to face disappointments, difficulties, doubt, disasters, disease and the death of loved ones and faithful colleagues.

Louise saw the founding of the Orphanage, the Boys School and the Academy. But she died in January 1895. Jesse and Josephine lived into the 1940s: Josephine died in 1944 and Jesse in 1949. They had to deal with the death of Louise and all of the other components of long term self-sacrifice. However, they had the joy and satisfaction of seeing what started out as a modest effort grow into a major educational establishment with far-reaching impact on the entire

Jamaican society. Yet, they did not see the explosive growth and development that took place in the latter half of the twentieth century with the Boys School, the Infant Schools, Primary School and High School.

Today we celebrate self-sacrifice, life-long commitment to a cause, and daily giving, unstintingly to others.

4. An institutional framework that provided continuity. Almost every good in society comes through individual initiative, imagination, ingenuity, inventiveness, innovation and individual effort, enthusiasm, energy and enterprise. Yet, if these remain solely as individual pursuits, they invariably die with the particular individuals involved. Continuity of individual endeavours has an essential social component. In former times it was the family, the tribe, the clan or the caste that provided the social framework for continuity. The modern social framework for continuity is the institution: the school, the college, the university, the church, the mosque, the temple, the synagogue, the convent, the club, the political party, the union, the corporation or the company.

Essentially, institutions gather together the individual contributions of each generation, mould them to be more than the parts and pass this collective contribution on to the next generation. The institution does not guarantee continuity because there is always the risk of individuals of a particular generation, who make up the institution, departing from the core values and ethics of the institution, or not making the appropriate adjustments to the conditions of a particular time. Rather, institutions increase the probability that individual efforts in a particular era will survive into the future.

Today we celebrate the institution of Alpha Academy and the institution of the Sisters of Mercy in Jamaica and around world. For 116 years and for 179 years, the individuals who have comprised these institutions have kept them faithful to the founding principles and relevant and appropriate to changing times.

I hope that as the Alpha Alumnae, present students, principal and teachers and Sisters of Mercy reflect upon the deeper reasons for which we are gathered we take due note of the virtues of Christian faith, our obligations to the marginalised of society, the demands and rewards of personal sacrifice and the value of an institutional framework.

Recognising the Lessons for Our Lives

This event has been billed as one of nostalgia as Alumnae revisit familiar places of the campus, reminisce on past times, reconnect with old friends and remember Alpha in your times. I trust that in reviewing the history, recalling the context and reflecting upon the meaning I have taken you beyond nostalgia and brought you face-to-face with the faith, the focus, the sacrifice and the framework of which you have all been beneficiaries. But if we end here, we would not have completed the processes of celebrating anniversaries.

The other day I was watching the Catholic Channel on TV. A father and son were being interviewed. The point was made that has stuck with me: God has no grandchildren, only children. God only has children: he has a direct relationship with each one of us in our time. The faith, focus, sacrifice and framework of Sister Mary Peter Claver, Sister Mary Margaret and Sister Mary Joseph belong to them. We need to exercise our own faith in these times; focus on the needs of the marginalised in our communities at this time, make our own personal sacrifices and contribute to holding together the institutions to which we belong in our time.

There can be no question these are difficult days in Jamaica. Economic challenges are everywhere to be seen. Political problems are too numerous to mention. Social conditions, especially violence in families and communities, are more than disconcerting. The questions we need to ask of ourselves are:

What vision do we have for making some things better in the areas in which we have resources and influence?

What faith have we exercised or need to exercise to bring that vision to reality?

What acts of practical holiness are we engaged in to back up the faith that we have?

What hopes are we bringing to those who can see no future?

Are we only complaining about the dark or are we resolved to light candles to put out the darkness?

Do we see the poor and marginalised as problems or as having problems?

To those of us who are fully engaged with vision, faith, focus, and our frameworks, how are we dealing with the disappointments, doubts, disasters and disabilities that invariably afflict long-term and life-long commitment to causes?

One lesson to be drawn from the 116th anniversary of Alpha Academy, is that the life that is truly worth living is the life sincerely engaged with giving hope to the hopeless, bringing relief to those who are suffering, providing opportunities to the young especially those from disadvantaged circumstances, giving voice to the voiceless, defending the weak against the powerful who would seek to oppress them and engaging in acts of practical holiness that are not for publicity or personal gain but for the upliftment of those we seek to serve.

Another lesson is that it is faith in God and dependence on his grace and sustenance that enable us to live a life worth living. In this regard, fellowship with others who are likewise committed and dependent on God is critical support and essential communion that carries us from day-to-day over all tribulations and triumphs.

Finally, it is the life worth living that transcends the years, the decades, the centuries and possibly reaches into eternity. It is the life that makes the difference in families, communities, institutions and countries. It is the life that creates real joy and happiness because of its transformative power. Its worth is not measured in monetary terms because its value is priceless. Thank God for the lives of Catherine McAuley, Jesse Ripoll, Josephine Ximenes and Louise Dugiol and all those Sisters of Mercy and their associates whose legacies, contributions and sacrifices have created and sustained Alpha Academy.

Alpha Academy and the Sisters of Mercy will continue for decades and centuries to come, if like their founders, those who come under their influence and inspiration live lives worth living.

The Chapel; Calabar High School, Kingston, Jamaica. Established in 1912.

Chapter 8

Educating Boys into Men of Brave Endeavours

CALABAR HIGH SCHOOL
CENTENARY ANNIVERSARY
September, 2012

Introduction

Master of Ceremonies; the Right Honourable P. J. Patterson, former Prime Minister of Jamaica; Professor Franklin Knight, Chairman and members of the Board, Principal and staff of Calabar High School, specially invited guests, fellow old boys of Calabar, ladies and gentlemen; the theme "Educating Boys into Men of Brave Endeavours" seeks answers to contemporary concerns and provides guidelines for future direction. Yet, its genesis is in the School Song which is almost as old as the school. Probably, it is best to commence by attempting to tease out the main ideas informing each of the theme's three elements.

1. Educating

A mother took her four-year-old son to pre-school for the first time. She was anxious to hear how his first day went.

She asked him, "How did it go"?

"Okay" he replied very unenthusiastically.

So she followed up: "Did you learn anything today"?

"Not enough" was his answer.

"Why do you say not enough?

"Well, the teacher said that I should come back tomorrow."

The theme appears to have a somewhat longer perspective for education than the little boy's. It implies the termination of education when boys become men. However, I am not going to posit the caveat that men need life-long education if they are to engage in brave endeavours since the theme assumes high school education which is one of the markers of boys turning into men, of adolescents becoming adults.

My favourite definition of education is that "education is what you have left when you have forgotten all you ever learned in school". It is the attributes, the habits of the mind, the disposition of spirit and the outlook on life that persist after the specifics of the various subjects are no longer recalled.

2. Boys Becoming Men

Boys turning into men is a matter of biology. It is the working of genes over time, barring accidents. We need not be detained by biology given that its efficiency rate is nearly 99 percent. The theme however, is not about biological change but social and character formation, hence we will move to a more fulsome treatment when the theme is treated in totality.

3. Brave Endeavours

Some synonyms of brave are: bold, courageous, daring, dauntless, valiant, heroic, fearless, and gallant. Bravery is inner courage in relation to external deeds. It is a quality of the mind or spirit in the face of danger and peril. Being brave implies the risk of danger to self, for the good of some other, or in conformity to some ideals or consistent with some principles or transcendent experience. Bravery is doing right despite danger. Bravery and nobility are relatives.

Endeavour is defined as strenuous effort. It is exertion and striving to accomplish some goal. Brave endeavours therefore are not about specific events, but rather about long-term exertion in the face of danger, in pursuit of some noble goal.

Against this background, the central question being asked in this Symposium is: 'What ought Calabar High School to be doing to cultivate the heart, mind and spirit that would lead boys to become men who engage in strenuous exertions to achieve noble goals, in spite of and despite dangers and perils'? In essence, this question speaks to the ethos and the ethic of the lives expected of Calabar boys as they become men in society'.

Life, Society, Males and School

The theme, like the school song, is not only ambitious but lofty. Yet to dismiss its idealism is to be constrained to the misery of what is; while forfeiting an opportunity to consider the magnificence and majesty that could be. Civilisation is a product of those who embraced opportunities to contemplate what ought to be, and then constructively strive to achieve it. Yet, to proceed without a healthy dose of realism is foolhardy.

Embedded in the theme are issues related to life, society, males and schools. Each needs to be commented on briefly, separately and realistically.

Life is not linear. Its contours include twists and turns, ins and outs, ups and downs. All who travel on the way of life encounter the unplanned, the unexpected, the unimaginable; the unexplained and the unprovoked. Brave endeavours must endure the vicissitudes that come and take full advantage of the openings that come as a result. Brave endeavours are therefore not just about good intentions that are soon abandoned, but intentions that are sustained and pursued, come what may.

Society is not single-dimensional. Nothing is simply a matter of power, or wealth, or status, or culture, or belief. These dimensions intersect and interact in complexities of innumerable permutations and combinations, dependent upon period of time, people involved and the places where they are located. Further, unlike inanimate objects, human beings act with intention. They are not only acted upon but act by their own volition. This teleological element is not only the bane of social scientists in making predictions about society or offering social prescriptions but it is also the bane of politicians, preachers, pedagogues, and parents. Boys educated to be men of brave endeavours need to know from the outset that outcomes are not guaranteed. So too should all those who seek to educate and bring up boys, which, in the present context, is itself a brave endeavour. Brave endeavours ought not to be embarked upon for praise or prize, recognition or reward; but for reasons of conviction or duty or a sense of call or purpose.

Men and boys are not monolithic. They are not products of production lines. Boys and men have unique personalities. They come with multiple intelligences, combined in different sets. They come from diverse social backgrounds each with different histories and sub-cultures. Inequality is the social fact among all human beings, including men. Some are born into more centralised and privileged circumstances, others in to more marginal and underprivileged circumstances. Centrality is not a symbol of superiority nor rite of passage. Marginality is not a terminal condition nor is it an excuse for evil. Either can be a handicap or a blessing, depending upon how they are perceived. The critical issue is not the hand that is given but rather how that hand is played in the game of life.

Schools are institutions for mobilising people of different personalities, multiple intelligences, diverse social backgrounds and succeeding generations to construct a common future based on shared identity and bonds of solidarity. Schools are shaped not only by relations between students and teachers, but through relations among students, among teachers and these with their predecessors and successors. Schools, therefore, not only create identities and solidarities but are identities and have bonds which connect generations. Schools are the precursors of society of the future. Look into schools and you get a glimpse of what is to come in society as well as from whence society has come. In a nutshell, schools are microcosms of society.

Calabar High School, celebrating 100 years since its founding, is not a greenfield. If this theme is to be taken seriously, then exploration must begin within this 100-year history. What is there to be learned about educating boys into men of brave endeavours from 100 years of Calabar as a boys' high school?

Calabar at its Founding and the Tides of the Times

Much has been said about the actions taken by Reverend David Davies and Reverend Ernest Price in founding Calabar in 1912. The official story is that they did so to provide secondary education for the sons of Baptist Ministers. Both were missionaries sent out by the Baptist Missionary Society to train local clergy at the Calabar Theological College. The founding of a high school for boys was not in their job description. To better understand their action it is necessary to examine the socio-cultural context of the times.

Jamaica had undergone major social, economic and educational changes in the aftermath of the Morant Bay Rebellion. This was recognised locally and internationally. For example, In 1884 General Eaton, the United States Commissioner of Education, invited Jamaican schools to participate in the International Congress on Education and its Exhibition in New Orleans. About 30 to 40 Jamaican schools participated. The Jamaican Exhibit was awarded a Diploma of Honour. This was followed by Jamaica being among the 'civilised countries of the world', invited to the International Congress in Chicago in 1893 at which three Jamaican educators and officials were appointed as honorary Vice Presidents in the Departments of School Supervision and Elementary Education.

However, by the last decade of the nineteenth century and the first decade of the twentieth century, the tides had shifted. The status quo that prevailed prior to the Morant Bay Rebellion was being reinstated. Crown Colony Government was in the process of becoming the open ally of the planter elite. The fear of Jamaica becoming another Haiti, which had hovered for the entire nineteenth century, was then almost non-existent. Jamaica's future in the twentieth century would be its past, as a sugar colony.

The denominational elementary school system had expanded beyond the resources of churches and the ability of parents to pay. Fierce competition between the various denominations foreclosed on ecumenical action which could have mitigated the situation if denominations de-linked their proselytizing mission from the operation of schools in small districts. Four or five small schools in small villages or towns, run by different denominations, were not sustainable. Failure to concede to each other opened the door for the State to intervene in 1892.

The Denominational Elementary School System with State support was replaced by the State Elementary School System with denominational management. The inducement was free elementary education. What followed this financial boon to parents and relief to the denominations, was the closure of many small schools. This resulted in declining student enrolment, especially among boys. Further, the State withdrew financial support to denominational colleges which trained male teachers only; resulting in the closure of Fairfield Teachers' college and Calabar Teachers' College in 1899.

The context of these developments was the segregated system of education that existed at the time. Elementary schools, through pupil teachers' examinations, led to teachers' college. In effect, teachers' colleges were secondary schooling for Blacks. This segment of the system was under the jurisdiction of the Department of Education. This was the education system set up in 1834 to serve the emancipated slaves and their descendants. A few qualified teachers, after some years of service in schools, entered the theological college to be trained as ministers. These teachers and ministers were the backbone of the emerging black middle class whose ancestors were slaves.

The parallel segment of this segregated system was the preparatory school/high school system under the jurisdiction of the Jamaica Schools Commission. This segment had its roots in charity schools set up initially to serve poor white boys but evolved to be schools of the cosmopolitan middle strata composed of whites of modest means, coloureds, Jews and freed blacks. The career path for high school leavers was the civil service or business. The lines drawn between the two segments were rigid. For example, if a qualified teacher applied to enter the civil service and passed the necessary examination, he was required to immediately repay the cost of his training as a teacher. At the end of the nineteenth century it was the segment for the descendants of slaves that was re-structured by the state with the compliance of the missionaries.

Within the denominations, tension existed between the missionaries and the local clergy that missionary enterprise had sponsored and trained. The missionaries controlled the purse strings. Local clergy was demanding more say. These trophies of missionary benevolence had developed independent voice and views. They were talking back to their benefactors. Empowerment is fashionable until it is exercised. This came to a head among the Methodists missionaries who closed York Castle High School in 1899. The point that must not be missed is that from the time of its founding, in the late 1870s to 1899, students of York Castle had won the Jamaica scholarship more times than all the other high schools combined.

Surely, money could not have been the only factor accounting for the closure of this highly successfully high school, whose students were drawn from among parents of modest means of the less privileged rural strata of society. Let me put it bluntly, in the last decade of the nineteenth century and the first decade of the twentieth century the tide was turning against black men. The Crown and missionaries, for different reasons, were no longer on the page of upward socio-economic mobility for the children of small settlers, as black and brown people of modest means were called, euphemistically.

Jamaican history is replete with periods of advancements in the interest of the mass of the people followed by periods of retrenchment, retreat and return to the status quo. Calabar in 1912 was founded during one such period. Calabar was founded against the tides of the times. A boys' high school was founded by missionaries in times when schools and colleges serving blacks were closed for reasons of lack of financial support from the government and second thoughts in some missionary societies.

Calabar was founded to serve the offspring of black men, using the code words: 'Baptist ministers', 'native sons of the soil'. The founding of Calabar High School was a brave endeavour. Price and Davies clearly recognised that with the closure of the Calabar Teachers' College the matter of the long-term recruitment of qualified students for Calabar Theological College was at risk, given the segregated structure of the education system. The founding of Calabar High School pioneered a new and more direct path to sustain theological education among Baptists. It was rooted in the social capital invested in the local clergy and local teachers who had been trained by the Baptist denomination. Ministers of other non-conformist denominations almost immediately began to send their sons to Calabar High School. This brave endeavour, conceived with a seemingly narrow but long-term purpose, and against the tides of the times, has flourished beyond the conceptualisation of its founders.

Calabar, Athletics and Brave Endeavours

Arnold Bertram has written a book, *The History of Calabar High School 1912-2012*, and has documented the careers of old boys who have engaged in brave endeavours. This should provide circumstantial evidence that the indoctrination in the classroom has played some role in the education of these boys into men of brave endeavours. I will restrict myself to one process outside of the classroom that has been instrumental in shaping the lives of boys. Sports and playing fields are as important as the classroom in the education of boys. In this regard, athletics is foundational to any understanding of the shaping of the Calabar mentality.

I was part of the Team at Champs in 1955. The last event was the Class 2, 200 yards. Wolmers was leading us by half a point. They had no athlete in the event. We had Jacques, but his time was the slowest going into the final. Points were only awarded for First, Second and Third: 3, 2 and 1 respectively. Champs was at Sabina and Jacques lived in Franklin Town. The Team gathered around Jacques and one senior boy told him, "Jacques if you do not come Third, don't stop just run home". Jacques came second, and we won by one-and-a-half points. Now, fifty-five years later Wolmers repaid us. That is life.

I was also part of the Team in 1957. We were slated to win. On the Friday night, after blazing though the heats, Denis Johnson met in a car accident and broke his hand. Yet, he ran in the finals with his hand in a sling and he was placed. We did not win that year, but no one can forget what Denis did in that losing effort.

Winning or losing, the person engendering this great team spirit was Herb McKinley, legendary Olympian and Calabar Old Boy. Herb taught us that athletics was an individual sport but performing for the team, the school or the country, required the best of each and every individual. Individuality expressed in the service of community is the highest level of self-satisfaction. Success required sacrifice. Hence, to be a member of the team, you had to train hard; no matter how much ability you had. You had to warm-up and warm down properly before and after every event to prevent personal injury which would cause damage to the team.

You could dismiss this team approach to athletics by saying that it only applied to the handful of boys who made the Champs team. However, unlike the other sports at Calabar, when it came to athletics every jack-man in the school had to participate. The school was divided into four houses. Each House had a House Master and the House Captain who together enlisted every boy in the House to contribute. The overriding mantra was every individual had to contribute to the success of the House. Leading up to Sports Day, every boy had to contribute House Points by either running or throwing or jumping or all of the above; meeting set upper and lower standards. Scores were kept of each boy's contribution to his House. This was one component of determining which House won athletics. I was a good hurdler, reasonable sprinter, could hold my own throwing the shot-put and doing the triple jump. However, each year I had a near death experience in home-stretch of the 400 yards in trying to meet the upper standard. But my house, Athens, needed the points.

Athletics, as well as other sports, have contributed substantially to educating Calabar boys into men of brave endeavours. Take my classmate, Denis Johnson, a genuine human being if ever there was one. After leaving school he had a stellar career in track, equaling world record in the 100 yards four times in one month. He came back to Jamaica with the idea that many Jamaicans on athletic scholarships were not achieving their full potential because of the arduous schedule of meets and lack of concern for their well-being. The answer was to create capacity to achieve world standards here in Jamaica. Working for 25 years with Dr. Alfred Sangster at The College of Arts, Science and Technology (CAST), he pioneered a new path to the fostering of Jamaican talent, just as Reverends Davies and Price did in 1912. Jamaica is currently basking in the glory that this additional path has brought.

Mike Fennell became Head Boy shortly after I entered Calabar. However, he left school in the middle of a term because his father had died and he had to take care of family matters. That made an impression on me. Since then I have always taken an interest in his career. This includes the time when an Immigration Officer, who was giving him a hard-time at Heathrow Airport, asked Mike who he knew in England who could vouch for him. Mike's instant answer was, "the Queen". I have some vague recollection of him playing cricket but only he could tell you what success he had with either bat or ball. However, we can all agree that he has become the greatest sports administrator of independent Jamaica.

I crave your indulgence for a couple of asides. Another person to whom I was a small boy when I entered Calabar was P. J Patterson. Throughout life, no matter what I have done, I have remained a small boy to both P.J. and Mike. Some things never change. Also my belief in the transforming power of the Gospel has been considerably strengthened by the fact that Gervais Clarke, the boy at school, as a man became a priest and Canon of the Anglican Church; a miraculous transformation if ever there was one.

The Tides of the Times in the Twenty-First Century

Hopefully, I have established that brave endeavours marked the founding of Calabar as its founders acted against the tides of the times. Certainly, the book written by Bertram will give testimony of many Calabar boys who have been men of brave endeavours. I have shown that the ethos of the school in sports, particularly athletics, engender interactions between teachers, boys and past students to the end that individuality must be exercised for the benefit and upliftment of community.

Can we then be sanguine about the future?

The answer is a resounding no. This is because brave endeavours of the present and the future are dependent on the tides of the times. It is therefore critical to examine the times of the tides in the second decade of the twenty-first century and as they portend for the next few decades, with particular reference to boys and men. The world of 2012 is considerably more complex than those of 1912 and 1962. Currently, the world is in the throes of fundamental changes in several related but different ways. Allow me to sketch briefly the broad contours of these times:

From the social perspective, traditional patriarchal forms of association based on blood and gender such as dynasties, tribes, castes, clan and lineages are being superseded by nation-states, political parties, corporations, unions, schools, religious factions and clubs which disavow blood and gender and assert equality and diversity as their creed.

Government by descent is being replaced by government by consent of the governed, where sovereignty resides with the people and not the emperor, king, chief, sultan or father.

The individual has replaced the kinship collective as the unit of societal organisation resulting in greater assertion of human rights and freedoms. Individual material progress has replaced perpetuation of the lineage as one of the prime goals of life. Many men who were automatically centralised by traditional patriarchy are being consigned to more marginal positions by these social changes, which offer women more space for advancement. This is particularly the case where groups vigorously contend concerning historic injustices and where the groups holding advantage make concessions to females of the disadvantaged groups as one means of appeasement.

From the demographic perspective, the world's population is at its highest and projected to increase even higher in the next 40 years. People are living longer and remaining healthier as public health standards are raised and preventative disease measures are adopted by increasing numbers of people.

Instead of leaving legacies for the next generation, debt is left behind as older generations consume more than they earned. Poor people are reproducing at higher rates than more affluent people, and when this is combined with ethnicity the result is noticeable and significant changes in the ethnic composition of several countries of the world. Demography was a root cause of the break-up of the Soviet Union and is posing considerable challenges in the United States and Western Europe.

From the ecological perspective, the high and increasing populations are living in the same amount of space, the land to person density keeps increasing. People are living closer together, leading to more towns and cities and larger towns and cities. As the better-resourced cities attract the poor, from rural areas, the more affluent create suburbs of cities. Decaying inner-city communities are formed. Greater population density means that the option of conflicting communities to move away from each other, decreases and conflict resolution strategies are based on the assumption that conflicting communities will remain in place. The propensity to resort to violent conflict resolution measures is therefore increased.

From the technology knowledge perspective, civilisation is going through its fourth major era of transformation. Fibre optics, satellite technology, digital technology and the microchip is transforming communication, travel, work, education, banking, entertainment, medicine, trade and practically all areas of human endeavours. Ownership of land and natural resources, availability of cheap labour and capital are no longer the main arbiters of wealth. Knowledge, technological infrastructure, talent and imagination are now the drivers of wealth creation.

From the geopolitical perspective, as Fareed Zakaria has pointed out, there is the "Rise of the Rest and the Decline of the West." The hegemony of Western Europe and the United States is under challenge with the rise of Brazil, Russia, India, China, (BRIC), Korea and Malaysia.

Prior to the fifteenth century, Western European Civilisation was the least of the civilisations that had emerged from antiquity. However, in the short period of 600 years, the Renaissance, the Reformation and Industrial Revolution catapulted the West to the forefront of world domination. The United States eventually became the leader of the Western world as it emerged from colonialism; increasingly embraced democratic governance, allowed industrialization unencumbered by a landed aristocracy, attracted and accommodated migrants seeking opportunity and remained somewhat isolated from the ravages and destruction of two world wars.

As with all great civilisations, and their imperial entities, over time they become complacent, believing that they have attained the pinnacle of human progress and are the superior people contemporarily and of all times. They become comfortable because they enjoy the best lifestyle that is available and see luxury as a right. They become conservative, holding on to forms of production, ideas, methods of governing and ways of relating. Although these become obsolete or outmoded or ineffective; thus leaving limited room for invention, innovation and new ideas that change the status quo. They become corrupt as they skew access to opportunity, to favour their own. Thus, they exclude persons of merit and talent on grounds of politics or ethnicity or class or creed. In essence, they use might as right while at the same time espousing high ethical values to extract wealth from the poor by blaming the poor for their victimization.

Great civilisations are undermined from within as ruling factions fight among themselves on the false assumptions of superiority. Some become morally outraged by the corruption as inventors, innovators and creators look outside for opportunities to implement their inventions. Short term measures are employed, to retain comfort and luxury, and those who are marginalised are joined by those who are morally outraged to challenge the status quo. Great civilisations are challenged from without by peoples who have developed moral force, embraced alternative social forms, invented or utilized and applied new technological inventions and are determined to caste off the mantle of inferiority and marginality.

In 2012, all of these patterns and trends are taking place before our very eyes. These separate tendencies are intersecting, overlapping and interrelating. Some groups are embracing their implications, others are going about business as usual, and yet others want to reach back to the past. Indeed, one super-pack in the current US Presidential Elections has adopted the slogan "Restoring our Future" in other words, forward to our past. In reality, there is no option to go back to the past, no technology to unravel history. The issue is about constructing the future.

Jamaica, for the last five hundred years, has been a part of the West. In the last four hundred years, Jamaica has become a Western society of modest means. The rise of the Rest and the decline of the West present a huge conundrum. The Caribbean is an addendum in the Western Hemisphere. There is Anglophone North America, Latin America and the Caribbean. We are small, open and vulnerable economies with very limited military capability and virtually no political clout in geopolitics. The Caribbean is the only region without a representative in the G-20. At the same time, there is a Caribbean civilisation that is a work in progress and which is better identified and understood by those living outside the region than those inside. In the international forums that I have been in over the last 30 years, the twelve politically independent English-speaking countries, plus Haiti and Surinam, are the ones defined as the Caribbean. A common destiny is being imposed externally upon these fourteen countries. Yet, the mechanisms put in place internally to create CARICOM looks like a recipe for failure.

Attributes Needed by Calabar Men to Engage in Brave Endeavours

Given the tides of these times and the location of Jamaica and the Caribbean in the geopolitical ocean, the future is fraught with difficult choices and great uncertainty. Brave endeavours will be at a premium. The only opinion that I am able to offer is that our fate rests in the exercise of the power of the weak. Without military might, economic power and political clout, marginal people and societies survive and prosper by being indispensable.

What will make Jamaican and Caribbean people indispensable in the twenty-first century? My answer is attributes of the heart, habits of the mind and disposition of spirit that are needed to cope with the tides of the times. These attributes, habits and dispositions, should pervade the teaching of all subjects, inform all relationships and undergird extra-curriculum activities.

In a world where knowledge will increasingly be a main engine of wealth creation, it is absolutely critical to develop the intellect in all areas; to foster the creative imagination in expressing the entire range of human experience; and to promote inventiveness to find new ways of solving old problems as well as constructive ways of addressing new developments.

In a world in which one certainty is that information and communication technology will continue to change all facets of life, it is obligatory to master its algorithms, become highly skilled in its core competences, and become adept in innovative applications.

In a world in which exploding information, misinformation, and spin comingle, where slogans substitute for substance and wisdom is often in short supply; it is vitally essential to cultivate depth of understanding in matters. In addition, uncompromising integrity that will seek and speak truth, come to sound judgment on the available evidence and apply common sense in decision-making.

In a world that is increasingly high tech, routinely impersonal and frustratingly anonymous, as more relationships are mediated through machines, it is more than necessary to become highly proficient and adept in engaging in personal relationships which manifest the entire range of interpersonal skills.

In a world where risks abound, where there are so many unplanned, unexpected and unforeseen circumstances that can derail efforts, an indomitable spirit that is not deterred by setbacks, not discouraged by mistakes and refuses to be crushed by disappointment is the sine qua non for success.

In a globalizing world dominated by virtual reality, mesmerised by the obscene presented as reality and distracted by celebrity, stability depends on having persons who are firmly centred in their Jamaican and Caribbean identity and convinced of the unique contribution that Caribbean civilisation is destined to make concerning the common humanity of all human kind.

The Call on Calabar

All Calabar students and old boys know the repeated phrase of the School Song: "the Call of Calabar." Allow me a slight variation to the School Song. Given the scenario sketched concerning the tides of the times, at the beginning of the twenty-first century, and the location of Jamaica and the Caribbean in the geopolitical waters, there will certainly be a need for men of brave endeavours, educated with the attributes of the heart, habits of the mind and disposition of spirit outlined. What situations will occasion the need to call on Calabar?

- Crises where people have lost their nerves, where conflicting views contend and uncertainly prevails thereby demanding calm, courageous and decisive leadership

- Conditions where confusion reigns and the need is clear-headed thinking based on sound application of tested principles, empirical evidence and corroboration with common sense

- Settings in which the conventional and traditional are no longer fruitful thus requiring the need for creative ideas, the adoption of imaginative approaches and new paths to be taken

- Environments that cronies, hangers-on and insiders can't handle but require persons of proven competence, capabilities and expertise

- Circumstances requiring persons who can be trusted to be faithful to the tasks and positions assigned and be depended upon not to abuse the power or the office or the resources entrusted.

In these situations, whether near or far, men of Calabar must answer the call: *Here Sir, Here Sir.* The call of Calabar is to serve others in building community and to serve God by serving others.

St. Hugh's High School, Kingston, Jamaica. Established in 1899.

Chapter 9

Anglican Deaconesses Advancing Girls Education: St. Hugh's, a Success Story of the Twentieth Century

◇

ST HUGHS HIGH SCHOOL AT 100
June, 1999

◇

Mr. Chairman and members of the Board, Mrs. Yvette Smith and members of staff, Dr. Inez Carnegie and Mrs. Marcia Stewart past principals, students and past students, invited guests, ladies and gentlemen, congratulations St. Hugh's High School for Girls for reaching this centenary landmark. I am fully aware that stating a lady's age is a very sensitive matter, however, a century is a landmark greeted with public celebration in cricket and even more so in the life of a school. In inviting me to deliver this Centenary Lecture you have accorded me a great honour that is deeply personal and for which I have no words to express gratitude.

My maternal grandmother, the late Louise Minna Dahl, nee Aldred, is one of the dearest persons to me in life. She, above all others, first saw in me what I did not see in myself. Louise Aldred was one of the early students of Deaconess Home School in the first decade of the twentieth century. She told me a lot of stories about her days at Deaconess Home School and about Archbishop Enos Nuttall while my eyes were still at my knees. I wish that I had the gift of total recall. I will come back to two of those stories. However, to think that, me, her grandson could be chosen to deliver this anniversary lecture at my grandmothers' alma mater, blows my mind. My prayer is that

God will give me the wisdom to do justice to the occasion and in so doing to honour St. Hugh's and my grandmother.

Antecedents of the Deaconess Movement

The 1830s was a time of great ferment in England. Not only was there the Abolition Movement for the emancipation of slaves but also the Oxford Movement to reinstate lost Christian traditions in the Anglican Church. The main tenet of the Oxford Movement was that there were three branches to the universal Catholic Church: the Orthodox Church, the Roman Catholic Church and the Anglican Church. The leaders of this movement were High Churchmen with roots in Oxford University. The Movement fizzled out by the mid-1850s, largely because of opposition from evangelical Low Churchmen who accused them of trying to 'Romanize' the Anglican Church and the fact that several of the Movement leaders converted to Roman Catholicism. However, three of the matters advocated by the Oxford Movement survived its demise: (i) Greater emphasis on the Eucharist, (ii) more use of vestments, and (iii) an order of religious women.

The Protestant Church was slow to develop any equivalent organisation to the orders of religious women of the Roman Catholic Church, which had such a record of Christian service especially to those in need. The Lutheran Church in Germany was the first to restore a deaconess order at Kaiserswerth in 1836. The difference between the Catholic orders was that the Lutheran deaconess took no lifelong binding vow. She could keep her surname, and was under the supervision and answerable to the male clergy, not a Mother Superior. Deaconesses lived together for reasons of work and not of vow. In 1861, the Bishop of London established a deaconess order, in the Anglican Church, following the pattern of the German Lutherans. The industrial revolution had created numerous slums that challenged the church to provide pastoral services. By the end of the 1870s over 700 women had joined the order.

The Anglican Church of Australia in 1885 was the first to introduce the Deaconess Order outside of England, followed by Canada and Jamaica in 1890. If the Protestant and Anglican Churches were slow in organising women in Christian ministry, the Jamaican church was swift to follow the English practice. Whether it is bane or blessing, Jamaica is never slow in adopting and adapting developments in Metropolitan countries, but not always for the same reason.

Leading the move to introduce the Deaconess Order in the Diocese of Jamaica was Bishop Enos Nuttall. He came to Jamaica in 1862 as an unordained Methodist missionary. He soon became a leading figure in the establishment of a Methodist High School. On the advice of the Jamaica Synod, proposed to the Methodist Missionary Society, in 1864, that this school should be the foundation for the establishment of theological education for Methodist ministers. He was soundly and swiftly put down for youthful exuberance. Seeing very limited prospects to implement his ideas he left the Methodist Church and joined the Anglican Church. He was ordained as a priest in 1866 and consecrated at Bishop of Jamaica in 1880 at the age of 38 years.

The Anglican Church in Jamaica was dis-established in 1870 as part of the reforms implemented by Governor John Peter Grant in the aftermath of the enquiry into the Morant Bay Rebellion. It was Bishop Nuttall who set the Church on a self-supporting foundation following its dis-establishment. He put in motion the training of local clergy through a theological college. He engaged in ecumenical efforts with other denominations. He became a leading force in education and health. With the benefit of hindsight, the young Nuttall was blessed with discernment. The Methodist Church had been a champion of the causes of Mulattoes and Blacks in Jamaica for over 80 years but the weight of its good works had become a burden on the Missionary Society. The Anglican State Church, aligned with the planter elite was about to be disconnected from the State. This necessitated a change in its orientation not only to the powerful but also to the general polity. The two denominations were on different trajectories. Nuttall opted out of the inertia of success and into the dynamism demanded for change.

Allow me a slight diversion in order to note a distinctive feature of Jamaica as a result of the history of the Church. Jamaica does not have a white church, a black church or a brown church. People of all races and shades of colour are members of all Christian Denomination in the country. This is because white missionaries and clergy of all denominations at some time in the past took up the causes of the Brown, Black and Indian segments of the society in substantial and substantive ways. For example, Moravians did so from the middle of the eighteenth century. Baptists and Methodists from the closing decades of the eighteenth century. Anglicans did so from the closing decades of the nineteenth century.

Sister Isabel and Sister Kate Vick arrived in Kingston in 1890, in response to Bishop Enos Nuttall's invitation to establish the Deaconess Order in the Diocese of Jamaica. They did not come to provide mainly pastoral care for poor people in the urban slums of Kingston. On a side note, Kingston has always had slums. Bishop Nuttall's vision for the Deaconess Order was work in education and health. This legendary Bishop was the leading figure in the founding of the Shortwood Teachers College in 1885 and the first chairman of the Board of the College. He was well aware of the difficulties in finding suitably qualified young women to fill the places available at the college. His answer was greater provision of education for girls of all races. In other words, Bishop Nuttall was adopting an innovation designed to address issues related to urbanization and the industrial revolution in Europe and adapting it immediately to address issues related to gender and race in Jamaica.

Names are important. Hence, having established who the principal agents were in founding the Deaconess Home School, now named the St. Hugh's High School for Girls, it is necessary to make a slight detour to set the background to connect the name of the school that was founded in 1899 with its current name. The change of name was no accident.

In 1886, Elizabeth Wordsworth, great grandniece of the great English Poet William Wordsworth, established St. Hugh's Hall for women who could not afford the fees charged by St. Margaret's Hall which housed women attending classes at Oxford University. She established it as an Anglican Hall and named it in honour of a thirteenth century ancestor of her father, St. Hugh of Avalon. Elizabeth Wordsworth's father was the Bishop of Lincoln. The first principal of the hall, Anne Moberly, was also the daughter of an Anglican Bishop. Ms. Moberly was determined that the Hall would become a college in its own right instead of being simply a hostel. As a result of a gift from Clara Mordan in 1913, St. Hugh's Hall was greatly expanded by a new building that allowed it to accommodate 64 women in 1916.

Women's Halls at Oxford, including St. Hugh's, were not officially recognised as colleges until 1909. Women students at Oxford only began to receive degrees of Oxford in 1920. Prior to that, they only received certificates from the male colleges attesting to the courses they had taken and the standards that they had achieved. Having gained college status and women students now earning degrees of Oxford, St. Hugh's College was the Anglican women's college at the University. Indeed, the vast majority of the early students were Anglicans with many of them being the daughters of Anglican clergymen. In the 1920s, enrolment at St. Hugh's college further expanded to more than 100 women as new buildings were added.

The Deaconess Order
Advancing Womens' and Girls' Education

The principal mandate of the Anglican Deaconess Order included caring for the poor and the sick; the education of the young; religious instruction of the neglected; and moral reformation. Under Bishop Nuttall's direction, the Deaconess Home was not only a location of the headquarters of the Order, and the residence at which many deaconesses lived, but it was the centre for organising the work of the Jamaican Diocese among women and girls. Public health was also a major challenge at the time.

Life expectancy in Jamaica in the last decade of the nineteenth century was about 39 years and infant mortality was in the region of 200 deaths per 1000 live births. Seventy-five percent of babies born did not make it to their first birthday. One of the first institutions established by Bishop Nuttall and the Deaconesses was a Christian Nursing Home in 1893. In 1908, Archbishop Nuttall and the Council of the Deacon Home established a fee-paying Nursing Hostel on East Street. The Hostel offered nursing care as well as formal training for nurses. It did so in conjunction with the Kingston Public Hospital. Indeed, the Nursing Hostel was the first place to offer 'proper' training for nurses in Jamaica. Sister Adelaide, a trained and experienced nurse from London was responsible for both the Hostel and training for nurses. A good case can be made that the Deaconess Order was a pioneer in nursing education in the colony and that Deaconess Home became a focal point of health education in the early decades of the twentieth century. This Lecture is not the place, nor does it permit the scope, for addressing the vision of Bishop Nuttall in bringing the Deaconess Order to Jamaica and making nursing and health education one of its principal foci. Suffice it to say, that it is a fitting tribute that Nuttall Hospital was built and named in his honour but the work of the Deaconess Order, and of Deaconess Home, is still to be fully documented and appropriately honoured.

Consistent with the vision of Bishop Nuttall, the Deaconess Order established girls' schools across the island. They were called Deaconess Home Schools. Twelve such schools were established. I have only been able to identify the location of eleven. These were at the Deaconess Home on Hanover Street and at St. Luke's in Kingston; in Port Antonio, in Portland; in Port Maria, Richmond and Highgate in St. Mary; St. Ann's Bay and Brown's Town in St. Ann, Falmouth in Trelawny; Montego Bay in St. James and Spanish Town in St. Catherine. The school in Spanish Town was established in 1897 as the lead school, named the Cathedral High School for Girls. In Montego Bay the Home School became the St. Helena High School for Girls.

In celebrating the 100th Anniversary of St. Hugh's High School for Girls, we are reaching back to the Deaconess Home School established at Deaconess Home in Kingston in 1899. Deaconess Home no longer exists. The Deaconess Order still exists in the Anglican Church. Indeed, Deaconesses Sybil Morris, Patricia Johnson and Judith Daniels recently made history when they were ordained as Deacons in 1994 and as priests of the Anglican Church in 1996. However, this triumph seems more related to the re-instatement of the Deaconess Order by Bishop Percival Gibson than to continuous operation of the Order from its inception by Bishop Nuttall. I am very aware that I could be wrong here. My only plea is that the history of the Anglican Deaconess Order in Jamaica is still to be written.

From the information available to me, it would appear that St. Hugh's High School for Girls is the only institution established in the first era of the Anglican Deaconess Order, and as a result of the strategic vision of Archbishop Enos Nuttall, that has survived as a distinct institution over the course of the twentieth century and will survive into the twenty-first century.

Of the twelve Deaconess Home Schools for Girls that were founded by the Deaconess Order and the Anglican Church, I have only been able to trace the fate of three: St. Hugh's, Cathedral High and St. Helena. It is not clear if there was any relationship between the Deaconess Home School in Brown's Town and St. Hilda's Diocesan High School for Girls founded in 1905 in that town. The word 'Diocesan' in its name seems to indicate a new and different institution, rather than an upgrading of the Deaconess Home School.

Cathedral High operated for close to 57 years. In 1954, Cathedral High School for Girls was merged with Beckford and Smith's Boys School to form the co-educational St. Jago High School, the latter being founded in 1744. St.

Helena was closed during the Depression in 1935. Because St. Helena was the only girls' school in Montego Bay, the Government built the Montego Bay High School for Girls which opened in 1935 and took over the students who previously attended St. Helena High School for Girls. The fate of the other nine Deaconess Home Schools is a research project still to be undertaken.

The Experiment of the Deaconess Home School at Hanover Street

Sister Madeline Thomas, who was responsible for the Teaching Branch of the Order, organised the founding of a school, in 1899, on the premises of Deaconess Home. It would appear that the Bishop and she decided to make this school somewhat different. It was to provide something more than just practical training for girls. The school was first modelled as a 'finishing school' for middle class girls. The official statement was that Deaconess Home School was a place for 'respectable' young ladies to gain training in areas of critical importance. In addition to the foundation subjects, the curriculum included home economics, home nursing and handicraft. This was the era in which middle class ladies did not work. Their sphere was in the home, to ensure that it was well run, healthy and industrious. The school started with Miss L. McDougall as Head Teacher and a student body of 24 students including boarders, who lived at Deaconess Home. There was a preparatory branch for students aged five to nine years. Boys could attend the preparatory branch.

My grandmother attended Deaconess Home School for Girls shortly after it was founded. She was a day student, transported to school by horse and buggy. Her father was a successful businessman, a committed Anglican, a church warden and representative to Synod. One of the stories my grandmother told me, was that, at that time, Amy Jacques, later to become the second wife of Marcus Garvey, National Hero; a lady who she referred to only as Mrs. Shackleford and herself were the only three black girls in the school. This is consistent with the official records which states that Bishop Nuttall's vision was committed to provide education for girls of all races.

Another story that my grandmother told me was that, in one of her years at Deaconess Home School, she had come first in the class. Archbishop was in attendance at the prize giving. She and the girl who came second, who was white, were called up to receive their prizes. The lady handing out the prizes crossed her hands, so that she would receive the prize given for second place. The Archbishop saw this, and whispered 'un-cross your hands Miss'. I heard this story long before I read that Archbishop Nuttall stated intention was to provide education for girls of all races. Clearly his public statements and his private actions were consistent.

My grandmother also told me that there were lots of rules about what young ladies should do and not do. A lady should never shout. I grew up with my grandmother. I cannot remember her ever shouting at anybody. Another rule was when sitting on a chair a lady should not lean it on its two hind legs.

One day in class she leaned her chair. The teacher shouted: 'Do not lean your chair Louise Aldred'.

'Do not shout at me Miss', my grandmother replied.

She was immediately suspended and a recommendation was made for her expulsion for insubordination and unladylike conduct. The case was referred to Bishop Nuttall who ruled against her expulsion. The teacher resigned in protest against the deterioration of standards set for the school. My grandmother said that Bishop Nuttall was a fair and just man who did not see race. She and the teacher were both wrong.

Amy Jacques-Garvey was an author, journalist, activist and Garveyite who did more than anybody else to promote and keep alive the views and work of Marcus Garvey. We would do well to explore the contribution that her schooling at the Deaconess Home School for Girls contributed to the person she turned out to be. Certainly, she is one of the most, if not the most, outstanding past student of the school.

Having taken a peep through history into Deaconess Home School, I have come to understand my grandmother's actions through another lens. Throughout her life she was always a lady who conducted herself with great dignity. She was a committed Christian who held strong but quietly expressed views on social issues and was a life-long Garveyite. Indeed, she left the Anglican Church and joined the Salvation Army because she felt she could serve God and her social conscience best.

However, what has intrigued me most is what my grandmother learned in that unique subject on the curriculum called 'home nursing'. Did that subject contribute to her considerable knowledge of home remedies, good nutrition and the curative properties of many Jamaican herbs? One of the very deep agonies of her life was that she had five sons and one daughter but only one son and her daughter, my mother, survived beyond three years and lived to become adults. The deaths of four infants was something she rarely spoke about, and then with great pain.

On the other hand, her daughter brought up eleven children and all of us are adults and still alive. Yes, over the period of three generations in Jamaica, in the twentieth century, public health has improved to virtually eliminating such contagious deceases as malaria and typhoid; vaccination of children has become more comprehensive and widespread; and there is a better supply of potable and clean water.

We are sometimes tempted to think of secondary education only in terms of subjects in external examinations, forgetting its wider impact. Did the work of Deacon Home make a significant contribution to public health in Jamaica? Life expectancy is currently 75 years, almost double that of the previous century. Infant mortality is under 30 per 1000 births. Reference to my family history is anecdotal. However, there is some empirical evidence that shows that the education of girls and women is a factor improving infant mortality and life expectancy. I think it is reasonable to entertain the hypothesis that the work of the Deaconess Order in nursing and girls' education, in the first decades of the twentieth century, contributed to Jamaica's current standing in the world where it has high income country life expectancy, financed by middle-income country resources.

From Deaconess Home School to St. Hugh's High School

The experiment with the 'finishing school' soon evolved as a few girls were prepared for the Cambridge Examinations. In 1913, the school became the Deaconess Home High School. In 1920, the Government through the Jamaica Schools Commission, introduced support for high schools through a grant-in-aid scheme. The school was renamed Deaconess High School for Girls and became a grant-aided Grade 2 high school in 1927. Deaconess Madeline Thomas, the midwife of the founding of Deaconess Home School in 1899, and who had been instrumental in its development even after the death of Archbishop Nuttall in 1916, returned to England in 1927. If when they left she thought that the school was then on a secure path, she was right. She died in 1928. It is right and proper to remember Deaconess Madeline Thomas of Bristol, England in the celebration of the 100th Anniversary of St. Hugh's High School for Girls.

For reasons not immediately clear, the Jamaica Schools Commission requested that the newly grant-aided school should change its name. Miss Evelyn Stopford was appointed Headmistress in 1926. She was a graduate of St. Hugh's College, Oxford. One is not sure what part she played, however, in 1928, the school was officially renamed the St. Hugh's High School for Girls.

The Oxford Movement was a factor in the creation of the Anglican Deaconess Order. St. Hugh's College was the Anglican Women's College, at Oxford University. The School and the College were Anglican institutions. Both were on similar trajectories of recognition and growth. The former had achieved grant-aided status as a high school. The latter then offered Oxford degrees and was growing. To link the Jamaican Anglican Girls High School with the Anglican Women's College at Oxford through a common name could have been symbolic, intending to inspire Jamaican girls to aim to be Oxford educated women. Ms. Stopford, the recent graduate of Oxford College and Headmistress of the High School could have been complicit in promoting such thinking.

The Critical Question

Why did Deaconess Home School at Hanover Street survive and has prospered? The answer seems to be related to the combination of at least six factors:

1. **The location of the School at Deaconess Home**, the headquarters of the Deaconess Order, gave the school an edge in status and accessibility to the best teachers. Further, boarding facilities at the school allowed it to cater to students from across the country as well as from other countries such as Panama, where some Jamaicans who went to work sent their children back to Jamaica for schooling.

2. **The location in Kingston, which kept growing at least for the first eight decades of the twentieth century,** created greater demand for school places. While Kingston became a commercial centre, after the 1692 earthquake destroyed Port Royal, it only became the capital of Jamaica in 1872. This necessitated the transfer of the seat of Government for Spanish Town to Kingston. Cathedral High School for Girls was established at a time when Spanish Town was declining in importance and population. The school was grant-aided in 1921

as a Grade 2 High School but was merged with Beckford and Smith in 1954 in order to enhance the survival of both schools. Deaconess Home School was founded when Kingston was growing because of its new status as well as increasing in population.

3. **The increase in the Government's support for institutional provision for secondary education for girls** in the first half of twentieth century. Basically, churches established the girls' schools which Government then assisted with their operational expenses. At the end of the nineteenth century there were seven boys' high schools, two girls' high schools and three co-educational schools under the Jamaica Schools Commission. Among the private high schools there were two boys' high schools, five girls' high schools including, Cathedral High, and five co-educational high schools. In other words, the Government assisted schools were mostly boys' schools. The private schools were mostly girls' schools. All were small schools. At independence in 1962, the grant-aided schools were seven boys' schools; fifteen girls' schools; and 24 co-educational high schools; all of medium size.

4. **The expansion of secondary education in Jamaica throughout the twentieth century**. In 1899-1900, total enrolment in all public and private high schools was 1372: 714 boys and 658 girls. By 1911, total enrolment had increased to 1544. The 1911 Census showed the population 10 to 19 years to be 178,106. This would mean that of the 12 to 18 population just about one percent attended high school. The 1943 Census showed that the Jamaican population had increased by approximately 50 per cent from the start of the twentieth century. During this period several private high schools, including St. Hugh's, had become grant aided. Total enrolment in grant-aided high schools was 3,637: 1696 boys and 1941 girls.

By 1984-1985, total enrolment of high schools was 55,256: 22,775 boys and 32,681 girls. Deaconess Home School started with 24 girls in 1899. Deaconess High School had 90 girls when it was grant-aided in 1927. St. Hugh's High School had 225 students in 1946 and 1451 girls in 1984-1985, which is just less than its current enrolment of approximately 1500.

5. **The resilience and resourcefulness of the Deaconess Order and the Anglican Church** in keeping the school alive in its first twenty-years and the school's responsiveness to challenges and developments in secondary education over the last 75 years. The great earthquake of 1907 destroyed Deaconess Home and with it the School. The Deaconesses had to be relocated to a house on Charles Street. They kept the school going in these less than optimal circumstances. The school evolved into a high school as some girls were prepared for the Cambridge Junior and Senior Examinations. It would appear that the school was separate from the residence of the Deaconesses when it was relocated on East Street as the Deaconess Home High School. Its shift in focus and its growth allowed the school to satisfy the criteria to be a grand-aided high school when that scheme was introduced in 1920. Reference to a few of the clauses that qualified schools to be grant aided is instructive.

Such schools should 'provide a progressive course of general study suitable for pupils of the age range 12 to 17 years'; should have an adequate proportion of students who remain in school for at least four years; and should not be for private profit or farmed out to the headmaster or headmistress. To be a Grade 2 school, it should have at least 25 students in regular attendance and at least 20 percent being educated to the standard of the Junior Cambridge examination. Relocation of the school from its cramped premises on East Street to spacious property on Leinster Road in 1940 consolidated the school's capacity to grow and advance as a high school.

In 1943 the school became a Grade 1 high school. In 1946, Glory Robertson won the Jamaica Scholarship for Girls, which at that time was based on the Senior Cambridge examination. The consolidation was complete. St. Hugh's had become a worthy contender with the best of girls' high schools. Mrs. Rita Landale was appointed Headmistress in 1940 and led the initial development at Leinster Road. She retired in 1962. For its first 62 years, the school was headed by a headmistress of English ancestry. Its first principal of Jamaican birth was Dr. Inez Carnegie in 1962. Since then the leadership has been Jamaican. Mrs. Marcia Stewart in 1987 became the first principal who had been a student of the school. The schools greatest physical development and increase in enrolment has taken placed under Jamaican leadership.

6. **A visionary clergyman who was able to get church women in succeeding generations to embrace his vision as their own**. Without Archbishop Enos Nuttall there would have been no St. Hugh's. Advancing girls' education through Girl's schools were part of his strategy to address a glaring deficit of his time. Sister Madeline not only embraced the vision but followed through with practical measures until the school was Grant-aided.

However, being grant-aided did not guarantee the schools survival. St. Helena was granted aided in 1928 but did not survive but ceased to exist in 1935. Montego Bay High which replaced St. Helena is still in existence. Government support is an important but not sufficient condition for survival. The fact that Headmistress Miss Stopford, resigned and returned to England in 1931, probably out of frustration with the limitations of the school-site at East Street compared with her aspirations for the school, would suggest that the future of St. Hugh's even with Government support for its operation was not a foregone conclusion. Mrs. Lindale's stewardship and leadership of the school for 22 years safely deposited the school in the hands of Jamaican leadership. However, we should not forget that it was the vision of an Englishman and a succession of English women who established the school and brought it to that point. Since 1962, the school has not only had committed but also competent leadership that brought the school to the point at which its beginnings appear quaint.

Girls Education a Success Story of the Twentieth Century

There was a full debate in the Legislative Council, in 1891, on the question of the virtues of female teachers and of recruiting females to be trained as teachers. The Superintendent of Schools, Thomas Capper, explained that the Department of Education had great difficulty in finding women with the appropriate level of education to be trained as teachers. One member of the Council retorted that women did not previously have the opportunity to be trained as teachers in the past. Therefore, the women had not prepared themselves for the opportunities then provided as a result of the establishment of Shortwood, but now given such opportunity they would qualify themselves.

Subsequently, when the Superintendent reported to the Council that many places at Shortwood were not filled and that many students had failed to meet the standard, one member of the Council insisted that if these first sets of women students failed then they should continue to recruit women to be trained as teachers until they started to succeed. The observations of these two members of the Legislative Council in the 1890s characterized the views of those holding power at that time. First, women had been denied educational opportunity which they should then be given. Second, the policy should be pursued until it succeeded.

In my books, 'Marginalisation of the Black Male and Men at Risk, I have written quite extensively on the reasons for the policy and its implication for peasantry men of African ancestry. I am not about to recite them here. Instead, one hundred years later, let us recognise and learn from its success. There can be no question that the provision of secondary and tertiary education opportunities, and the performance of women given those opportunities, has been one of the success stories of the twentieth century. Girls now outperform boys in the Common Entrance Examination at the end of primary schooling. They outperform boys in the CXC and 'A' Level examinations at the end of secondary education. Women outnumber men in colleges and the University of the West Indies. The only areas in which boys and men continue to hold an advance are in some technical subjects, Physics, Mathematics and Engineering.

The success of this policy, to correct the traditional injustice of denying women equal opportunities to education beyond the primary level, was addressed not only by rhetoric but by changes in the structural provision of tertiary and secondary education. In 1899 when Deaconess Home School was founded, two colleges training male teachers were closed. The result was that for the first half of the twentieth century there were three colleges preparing female teachers and only one college training male teachers. Then again, additional girls' high schools were founded. In 1899 there were five girls' high schools, public and private: Immaculate, Alpha, Westwood, Hampton and Wolmer's Girls. By 1962, there were 10 additional girls' schools but only two boys' schools. Thirteen additional high schools had been founded but one closed and two were merged to create co-ed high schools. The Anglican Church had founded six of the thirteen: Cathedral, St. Hugh's, St. Helena's, St. Hilda's, Bishop Gibson and Queens; and of these six, the first three had been the results of the vision of Archbishop Nuttall and the pioneering work of the Deaconess Order.

There are three observations that seem to scream out from this brief review of the century of which St. Hugh's was part of a sustained and successful policy to provide girls and women with increased access to secondary education. They are:

1. A significant increase in the provision of girls' schools that changed the structure of opportunity, allowing girls to have increased access to secondary education.

2. A partnership between the Church and the State, through the Jamaica school Commission, involving religious men and women that executed the policy.

3. Perseverance with this policy over several decades, despite setbacks and difficulties, which ensured its success.

I am constrained to say that from research I have done this pattern is not peculiar to Jamaica. Other examples include: The creation of the common school movement in the United States in the nineteenth century and in the Freedmen movement in the South following the Civil War. However, the scope of this Lecture does not allow for further discussions of the connections.

Conclusion: Looking to the Future

The 1990s have several points of similarity to the 1890s. A mere listing is possible here:

- Both decades have been periods of economic recession

- The 1890s was preceded by two decades of significant reform and expansion of elementary education while the 1990s was preceded by three decades of significant reform and expansion of secondary education

- Both decades had reversals related to educational policies in the preceding decades. In the 1890s, several elementary schools were closed and in 1899 educational expenditure was capped at no more than 10 percent of the budget of the Government. In the 1990s, tuition fees for public secondary schools was re-introduced and boarding grants at the tertiary level were discontinued

- During the 1890s, there was great concern about the under-performance of women in teachers college while in the 1990s there is great concern about the under-performance of boys at all levels of the school system.

This evening we celebrate the success of the measures taken to address the under-performance of women at teachers' college and the lack of access of girls to secondary education. Specifically we celebrated the success of St. Hugh's High School for Girls within this framework and have identified several persons, particularly in the early years, who have been critical to that success. The question is, what of the future? The broad contours of the answer reside in this celebration of the past. It is the deep commitment of persons of conscience and faith to address the real issues that limit other people's lives. It is vision and strategic thinking about the structural factors that need to be changed and then taking action consistent with the vision and strategy. It is about mobilising other similarly committed persons to embrace the vision and work to implement the strategy. It is about staying the course, despite difficulties. The evidence is that God blesses such efforts.

The institution of St. Hugh's High School for Girls has triumphed over the past twentieth century, notwithstanding all the adversities, disappointments and setbacks that came along the way. To do the same in the twenty-first century it must be inspired to follow the same course.

The Anglican Church, and indeed all Christian Denominations, needs to take up the challenge of doing for boys in the twenty-first century what they did for girls in the twentieth century. Healthy human society requires the wholeness of both genders.

~

Chapter 10

Honouring the Past: Building for the Future

~

SHORTWOOD OLD STUDENTS ASSOCIATION 85TH ANNIVERSARY

May, 2011

~

Master of Ceremonies Winston Wright and Mrs. Wright, Mrs. Elaine Foster-Allen Principal and Mr. Allen, Dr. and Mrs. Christopher Clarke and members of the staff of the College, Dr. Beverly McKenzie, President, Executive and Members of the Shortwood Old Students Association, Mr. and Mrs. Vivian Crawford and other specially invited quests, anniversaries are special. Eighty-five years is a long time for any association and 126 years for any college. The Shortwood Old Students' Association (SOSA), therefore, has much to celebrate and I am honoured to be asked to be the Guest Speaker at this Banquet. Allow me to apologize for my wife who contemplated being here tonight but as you know both her and our daughter live abroad, and our daughter is sitting exams next week, so it was not practical for her to come home this weekend. I am delighted, however, that my granddaughter, Gabriel is here with me.

You boldly chose May 21, 2011 for this banquet. It is after 6.00 pm and we are still here. We have either been left behind, or are in heaven, or this is yet another calculation of the end of the world that has proven false. Let us stick to the words of our Lord, "No man knows the hour".

Seeing that Shortwood, until very recently, has been a women's college, but you still keep 'old students' within the name of this alumnae association,

Shortwood Teachers College administrative building which was constructed in 1940, after fire destroyed the old one in 1939.

©*The Gleaner Company Ltd.*

I am advised to stay away from any notion of old girls. But, because I belong to the Calabar Old Boys Association, and have joined the ranks of the retired, allow me to share with you some stories sent to me recently by my good friend Reverend Dr. Gerry Gallimore about the future that awaits me.

A man said to his friend, "I am 83 and now all I have are aches and pains. You are about my age, how do you feel"?

His friend replied, "Like a new born baby!"

"What?" said the 83 year-old, "like a new born baby?" "Yes" said his friend, "No teeth, no hair and I think that I have just wet my pants."

An 88-year-old man had been deaf for a long time. However, as a result of new technology, his doctor had fitted him with devices inside his ears which could restore his hearing. A month later he went back to his doctor for a check-up. Following tests, his doctor told him that the devices were working perfectly. The man confirmed that he was hearing as well as ever. So the doctor said to him, "I suppose your family must be delighted that you are hearing again". The old man answered, "I have not told them yet, but I have changed my will three times during the month."

A 90-year-old man announced to his friend that he was getting married. So his friend asked, "Do I know her?"

"No," he said.

"Is she good looking?"

"Not really."

"Can she cook?"

"Not too good," was the reply."

"Does she have money?"

"As broke as a church mouse," said the old man.

"Is she good in the sack?"

"I would not know," came the reply.

"Then why are you marrying her?"

"She can still drive," was the explanation.

There is a fundamental difference between age of individuals and institutions. Among individuals old age is indicative of decline and deterioration. Among institutions, age is a sign of vigor and vitality. This is because institutions connect individuals within and across generations. Institutions pool the collective talents of individuals within generations and link these with preceding and subsequent generations. Eighty-five years indicate that the Shortwood Old Students' Association has survived several generations and is yet set to survive many more. It is this cross-generational element that gives institutions their vitality and uniqueness. Accept therefore my heartiest congratulations on reaching this milestone.

Your theme "Honouring the Past: Building for the Future", requires a backward look and a forward peek into the future. Since hindsight is always clearer than foresight, the former is easier than the latter. However, if in looking back we can accurately identify what is worth honouring, that is, what explains the vitality of Shortwood, then we should have a better basis on which to plan the future or prophesy what is to come.

Honouring the Past

Shortwood's founding in the nineteenth century, places it in the period when women's place and role in society began to change fundamentally from what these had been historically. The ideal of true womanhood that had been bequeathed from antiquity, was marriage and motherhood, and if that was not achieved, spinsterhood, with both being crowned by patriarchal dominance whether by father or uncle, husband or brother.

Industrialization at the beginning of the nineteenth century expanded employment opportunities and demanded higher-levels of literacy and numeracy, therefore expansion of elementary education. As dominant groups within Western Europe and North America sought to retain their hegemony in society, and as their men moved up to take the expanded opportunities, the argument developed among their middle and upper classes that teaching, at the elementary level, was woman's true profession. Teaching elementary school was but an extension of the care and instruction given in homes. However, it would not be mothers who would perform this role but single women, before marriage.

Colleges to train women teachers were founded in the middle to late nineteenth century. Many of these had previously been finishing schools. Women, in these times, were not admitted to most institutions of higher learning. Admission to these women's colleges in North America and Western Europe, therefore, was restricted to young single women of families that could afford to pay their fees.

Consistent with Jamaican history and pattern, Shortwood's founding was contemporaneous with the founding of similar institutions in the Western world. In honouring Shortwood's past we must recognise that Shortwood was part of the advance of women's education worldwide. In that regard, Shortwood shares a similar context with Bethlehem, founded in 1860, and St. Joseph's in 1897, but with two important differences. Shortwood was founded by the Government and not a religious denomination. Bethlehem was founded to train teachers for infant schools. Shortwood was founded to train elementary school teachers, which up to that time was a predominantly male occupation. St. Joseph's then followed the Shortwood precedent.

The point that must not be missed is that the predecessor and peer colleges in Western Europe and North America were established to train white middle and upper class women as elementary school teachers. Shortwood was established to train Black women, mainly from peasant backgrounds. This difference has to be understood in the context of the imperatives driving the founding of teacher training colleges for women in Jamaica. These were not industrialization or urbanization. Rather, it was emancipation and the creation of an elementary school system serving the descendants of the slaves, the Morant Bay Rebellion and the emerging intention to reduce the number of black men teaching in elementary school system.

To underscore the fact that the intention of the Government in founding of the Jamaica Female Training College, later renamed Shortwood, was not inspired by the same imperatives as in North America and Europe. The institution in its early years included two programmes: one to train elementary school teachers and the other to train domestic servants. Incredible as this may seem, it was possible to move from one programme to the other. I notice that this fact of the history of the College is treated in a tangential manner on the College's website by references only to curriculum options. I take this to mean that this is a delicate matter. However, if we overlook this fact of Shortwood's founding we will miss a most essential distinction of the College.

In 1880, Thomas Capper, Superintendent of Schools, proposed the idea of a college for training women teachers of quality. The history of Jamaican and Caribbean education is punctuated with adoptions and adaptations of Western developments in education. However, the funds to implement this forward-looking idea came with strings attached from the planter- minded Legislative Council. A common complaint among the elite was that there was a shortage of good household help. Capper's lofty vision was therefore tied with the planters' view of women of African ancestry, hence the dual programme options.

Two views of Black women were embedded in the founding of Shortwood. Only one has prevailed. The fact that the programme to train helpers died and the programme to train teachers survived and has flourished, is not to the credit of the Government provider but rather to the vision, ambitions, aspirations and abilities of participants; those who ran the College, those who taught the courses and those who offered themselves as students. The community that formed the College viewed themselves differently from the governing oligarchy that provided the funds for its operation. In this regard, Shortwood's founding and success cannot be separated from the transformation of the roles and the rise of Black women in Jamaica.

The most marginalised persons in modern Jamaica were slave women of African ancestry. They were triply marginalised: first as people of African ancestry, second as slaves and third as women. Emancipation freed them but its aftermath consigned them to being mainly poor rural peasants. Their overall marginal status remained unchanged in the free society. The unsung heroines of Jamaica are poor black women residing mainly in rural Jamaica. No group has been more resolute to change their lot, and that of their children, more resourceful in fighting against the enormous odds that confronted them, more resilient in recovering from setbacks along the way and have made sacrifices for their families and communities than poor Black women of this era—the era between emancipation and independence. That their daughters now occupy positions of power and prominence, leadership and influence, professional and technical competence in every sphere and field of endeavour in Jamaica, the Caribbean and across the world is testimony to the triumph of their indomitable spirit.

No history of this triumph can omit the symbol, significance and success of Shortwood Teachers College. As would be expected of any institution, set up to give opportunity to a disadvantaged group, at first it was difficult to find qualified females for the teacher training programme. This was a problem discussed in the Legislative Council up to 1900. To its credit, the Legislative Council persisted despite this difficulty. Then it took about two decades more before their performance matched that of their male counterparts.

Allow me to make the connection between the founding of the College in 1885 and the founding of the Shortwood Old Students' Association in 1926. At that time, the pension regulations provided for full pension after 40 years of service. Teachers qualified to enter teaching through the pupil teacher system. By the 1920s, some of the first graduates of the College would have reached retirement age or had retired recently. More importantly, by 1926 the problem of recruiting qualified women had long been solved. The graduates of the College were matching the standards of their male peers at the Mico. In a nutshell, the founding of SOSA 85 years ago came at a time when the graduates had confronted and confounded the negative stereotypes of their race and gender, had demonstrated their competence beyond any question and had developed the confidence to assert the permanence of the College in the teacher education landscape. Indeed, Shortwood had become the premier college offering tertiary education to females in the country.

In honouring the past there are six features of Shortwood, therefore, that we must celebrate:

1. Shortwood from its founding has been on the frontiers of educational development and has never languished in any backwaters in education.

2. It is not what Government provided that has been critical in charting the history of the College but what the participants have done with that provision.

3. The focus of the College has been setting new horizons for its students and therefore it has never been the apologists of, or pandered to or patronized any race, class, gender, region or religion. Instead the College has always demanded, insisted and assisted its students to meet the highest standards thus equipping its graduates to be the equal of any circumstances that they may face in the world.

4. The College has always inspired its students and graduates to balance personal advancement with service to others and to community.

5. The College has always produced dignified ladies regardless of the social prejudices or stereotypes that prevailed in any era.

6. Graduates of Shortwood have excelled not only in the classroom but in every field that they have chosen to pursue. In addition to teaching, their contribution to the building of Jamaica is beyond estimation.

Building for the Future

The circumstances of Shortwood, the Shortwood Old Students Association, Jamaica, the Caribbean and the world in 2011 are substantially different from the world at the time of the anniversaries celebrated in 1910, 1926, 1935, 1960, 1976 and even 1985.

The economic transformation is vast. It is no longer an abundance of raw materials, capital and cheap labour that produce wealth. Knowledge, technology, ideas, invention, innovation and imagination are key factors in wealth creation. This opens up great opportunities for material progress for those who possess content, invent new products and services, and captivate and inspire attention by their imaginations, regardless of their station at birth. At the same time, the prospects of marginalisation is always present although manifested in different guises.

The Western world, of which Jamaica and the Caribbean have been a part, is now in decline as significant portions of their middle classes have slipped into genteel poverty in suburbia. Listen to CNN or JNN and you will get vivid examples of such decline. China, India, Brazil, Russia, South Korea and other South East Asia countries are on the rise as major segments of their poor are becoming middle class, with the tastes and desires for comfort that accompany such rise. At the same time that pundits speak of convergence in lifestyles between the so-called developed and developing worlds, whether in the East or in the West, wealth and power are being concentrated into fewer and fewer hands. The implications for young people are enormous.

The political differences are fundamental. The issues are no longer government by descent, colonialism, nationalism, and political sovereignty but democracy, republicanism, regionalism, global competition between states and multinational corporations being more powerful than many sovereign states. Young people now do well to succeed their parents, much less exceed them, as was common in their parents' and grandparents' generations leading to great unrest and dislocation among the world's youths.

The technological changes are mind-boggling. Global telecommunications is instantaneous. Presidents and generals can now order military action and watch their soldiers execute it live. Surgery by laser is becoming commonplace, cutting recovery time by a half or more. Most gadgets are now smart. Cell phones are being used by great grandmothers. Laboratories are now experiments with machines that look like desktop printers that in a few years will allow for mass customization, making many factories obsolete.

The educational landscape is almost beyond recognition. Early childhood, primary, and secondary education are universal. Colleges and universities cannot enroll all the qualified applicants that apply for admission each year. Secondary school leavers with solid CSEC passes and college and university graduates find it very difficult to obtain jobs. This fierce competition for available jobs results in the escalation of the education credentials that employers now invoke on new entrants. In these circumstances succeeding in school and university is being delinked from upward social mobility as social connections often prove more important than academic qualifications. Further, the gender situation has been reversed. The problem now is to find qualified young men to enter colleges. Then again, girls and women are outperforming boys and men at all levels of the education system and in some disciplines.

There can be no question that contemporary circumstances are complex and daunting, but no more so than the circumstances at Shortwood's founding in 1885 or at other critical periods in its history. There are still negative stereotypes of the ruling elites to be confronted and confounded. Government provision is still linked to the past rather than on the world that is unfolding. Marginalised groups are still struggling desperately against the social and economic odds of their circumstances. The temptation to look out only for one's self rather than be concerned about the common good, still remains.

The future is constructed by the choices and exertions that we make in the present. Any institution that has found ways to overcome and prosper over a period of 126 years, and past students association of 85 years, have developed strategies, insights and coping skills that situate them in good positions to continue to cope with the present and flourish in the future. As a male outsider, allow me to suggest that the features that we honour and celebrate are distinctive of Shortwood. It is these features that have allowed the College and Association to survive the past and prosper in the present and are the bases for building for the future.

What then should the Shortwood community, college and Old Students, and the Old Students Association embrace as you seek to build for the future? The answer is simple, Shortwood is distinctive. My charge to you therefore is to continue to:

1. Reside on the frontier of educational development as the College seeks to respond to current imperatives and future needs of the Jamaican and Caribbean societies. Avoid being limited to your past.

2. Utilise the provision of Government by doing that which is consistent with the aspirations, ambitions, abilities and aptitudes of staff and students. Strenuously and shrewdly avoid being confined to, and constrained by the stated intentions of Government policy strings.

3. Focus on the horizons to which Jamaican and Caribbean people must aspire and achieve. Avoid being prejudiced by the stereotypes associated with the backgrounds from which students come.

4. Challenge students to be as concerned with and committed to personal gain as well as to the common good; to individual advancement as well as to the progress of community and country. Warn them of the emptiness of the life lived only to get and not to give; to receive benefits from the sacrifices of others but never to make any sacrifice for others.

5. Resolve to cultivate and foster the values of civility, dignity, integrity and an indomitable spirit. Avoid crudeness, crassness, vulgarity and hopelessness even if these are evident in high places.

6. Insist that graduates uphold and uplift the name of Shortwood by their conduct, character and competency in whatever spheres, fields and places they live their lives. Resist the temptation to be or do less.

God bless and keep the Shortwood Old Students Association and Shortwood College.

Chapter 11

The Rescue Mission in Kingston

~

FIRST MISSIONARY CHURCH 80TH ANNIVERSARY

September, 2008

~

Introduction

You have bestowed on me a great honour to be the guest speaker at this banquet celebrating the 80th Anniversary of the founding of the First Missionary Church, located on East Street, Kingston. This sense of honour comes from two sources. To begin with I am Baptist, and therefore of a different denomination, an outsider so to speak. Surely there are many insiders who would have coveted this privilege and a vast number of outsiders from who you could have chosen. To be the chosen outsider is a great honour. Second, I have known, respected and admired your pastor, Reverend Peter Spencer and his wife, for a very long time. It is accurate to say that we have grown up in the evangelical Christian community together. The opportunity to celebrate with this precious couple, in the area of their ministry, is a great privilege, indeed.

As I understand it, the teachings of the Missionary Church Association are not far from those of the Baptists. Your Association has Anabaptist roots. You believe in the four-fold gospel of Jesus as Saviour, Sanctifier, Healer and Soon-Coming King. You encourage a Keswikian orientation concerning the deeper life in Christ. You practice baptism by emersion and you maintain a

First Missionary Church, Kingston Jamaica.
Established in 1928.

missionary focus. But the links between us go further than being evangelical in doctrine and includes wholesome fellowship between our brethren.

The links even have some quaint elements to it. As you no doubt know, Bethel Baptist Church was founded by a Southern Baptist Missionary in 1954. After he left the Bethel Church, he decided to join the Jamaica Baptist Union. Some members of this young Bethel Church were not comfortable with this decision on the grounds that the Jamaica Baptist Union was part of the Baptist World Alliance, which had relations of which they did not approve. So several of those members left Bethel and joined the young Grace Missionary Church. This led to close relationships between the early members of both churches.

As a member of the Bethel Baptist Church for 52 years, I think that I can congratulate you on the occasion of your 80th Anniversary, not only on behalf of my family and myself, but also on behalf of the Bethel Baptist Church. We labour in the same vineyard and for the same Master. Eighty years of faithful witness in the city of Kingston is grounds for joyous celebrations.

Kingston

Kingston is the capital city of Jamaica but this was not always so. The first capital of Jamaica was Spanish Town. However, as you know, when the English captured Jamaica, Port Royal was built as the commercial centre. The city of Port Royal was destroyed by the devastating earthquake which struck at 11.43 am on June 7, 1692. Half of Port Royal sunk and remains to this day a sunken treasure. Over 5,000 people died as a result of the earthquake and tsunami which followed. To that date, Port Royal was the home port of many pirates and buccaneers and had a reputation of wealth and wildness. Port Royal was said to be one of the wickedest cities on earth at that time.

In July 1692, many survivors of the Port Royal earthquake were relocated to a makeshift refugee camp on the seafront, on Colonel Barry's Hog Crawle, which was just across the harbour. Prior to this, the area now called Kingston was an agricultural area mainly engaged in livestock rearing, particularly cattle, which was a popular enterprise on the Liguanea Plains. Indeed, the area now known as the Corporate Area had many pens, now renamed towns: Jones Pen, Vineyard Pen, Admiral Pen, Trench Pen, Rae Pen, Campbell Pen, Slipe Pen, Allman Pen, and others. Colonel Barry's hog crawle indicates that the good Colonel was involved in rearing pigs.

A more permanent provision for the refugees from Port Royal came about with the purchase of 200 acres of land from an absentee landlord, Sir William Beeston. I am sure that you immediately recognise that the landmarks of this early settlement of Kingston are preserved for posterity in the names of Barry and Beeston Streets, just one and two blocks down East Street on which your church is located. The Government allowed refugees, from Port Royal, to buy land on the seafront but no more than one lot each and no more land than they had in Port Royal. This marked the birth of Kingston. East Street on the East, West Street on the West, North Street on the North and Harbour Street on the seafront, marked the boundaries of the small town that grew from this sad beginning. First Missionary Church is now located on what was the original eastern boundary of Kingston.

Calamity and scandal marked the birth of Kingston. The absentee landlord, Sir William Beeston, returned to Jamaica as Governor. He realised that the land he previously owned had become much more valuable. He conveniently discovered that the instrument of transfer was not legal, hence parcels sold had to be acquired directly from him. By dubious means, he acquired additional lands on the waterfront, which considerably increased his holdings. When this came to light there was a huge public scandal.

Kingston inherited from Port Royal much of the commercial and economic activity related to trade and naval warfare, which were previously located at Port Royal, just across the Harbour. Further, Kingston's location made it easier to be connected by land to the rest of the island. Kingston therefore, grew very rapidly and became the largest town in Jamaica, and home to many merchants.

Kingston also inherited from Port Royal the licentious lifestyle, punctuated with violence, of which Port Royal was renowned, and for which many port towns and cities are known. The carousing of sailors in port, including the drinking, prostitution and sporadic violent brawls, along with similar behaviour of the town's people, soon earned Kingston the reputation of a 'wicked' place, just like Port Royal.

The Governor signed an Act, passed by the Assembly in 1755, to transfer the capital from Spanish Town to Kingston. However, he soon rescinded the Act based on pressure arising from fears expressed that such a transfer could corrupt the morals of the assemblymen. Probably the real fear was that Kingston would provide assemblymen greater latitude than Spanish Town.

In 1802, by legislation, Kingston was elevated to being a city. The Vestry of the Parish of Kingston was replaced by a Common Council with Aldermen who elected the Mayor of the City, also chairman of the Common Council. Kingston then became both a Parish and a City. Kingston was a cosmopolitan city with residents from many places. Indeed, its theatre often put on plays in Spanish for the entertainment of its Spanish speaking residents. Following the Haitian revolution, Kingston also had many residents who had fled Haiti.

In 1872, Kingston became the capital of Jamaica and the seat of the colonial government, despite the fact that nothing had changed in its lifestyle. Commerce trumped whatever fears existed about the corruption of morals, or perhaps the realization that assemblymen had already succumbed, even without the enticements of Kingston.

Kingston was born out of calamity but has had its own share of calamities. Since its birth, Kingston has had to deal with natural disasters beginning with great hurricane damage in 1784, a big fire in 1843, cholera epidemic in 1850, another great fire in 1862 and then the great earthquake and fire of 1907. Unlike Port Royal, so far Kingston has recovered from all its disasters and benefitted from those experiences. For example, since 1907, Jamaica has had very strict building codes. It should be noted that the Plantain Garden Fault Line runs between Puerta Prince, Haiti, and Kingston/Port Royal. Every hundred years, or so, a major earthquake seems to occurs on this fault line, alternating between Puerta Prince and Kingston/Port Royal.

Then there was the Roaring 20s, which not only captioned life in the United States but also in Kingston. I am from a Kingston family with Port Royal connections. My maternal grandfather was from Port Royal and my maternal grandmother and paternal grandfather were Kingstonians. Only my maternal grandmother is from 'the country', Manchester. Further, my maternal grandmother's father and my paternal grandfather's father were Kingstonians. So I am at least fourth generation Kingstonian. My maternal grandmother tells me that Kingston in the 1920s was a real hotspot. A popular dance at that time was the *Ochi Cuchi*. My grandmother told me that it was not uncommon for party revelers to dance in the nude. She told me that after a while the police started to raid some of these parties, with the attendant embarrassment of several very prominent persons were seen running from such premises, sans clothes or with clothes in their hands.

This is the context in which the First Missionary Church was established. Kingston is a city born out of calamity, and with episodes of calamities of its own. It has long been the centre of commerce and more recently the centre of government. Corruption and scandal, crime and violence, carousing and licentious living, and congestion due to population growth have all punctuated its colourful history. These are the contours that have fashioned and formed the founding and work of your church.

The Missionary Association

I am no authority on the history of your denomination. What I know is largely drawn from David B. Clark's "History of the Missionary Church Alliance" recorded in his book, "Origin and Growth of the Missionary Church Association in Jamaica" and from the Anniversary Magazines of the church. From these sources, the precursors of the Missionary Church Association made their first entrance in Jamaica in 1870 in Devon, Manchester. The first venture out of Devon was in 1905 with the establishment of the church at Coley Mountain, also in Manchester. From this Manchester beginning, other churches were established in the neighbouring parishes of Clarendon and St. Elizabeth. In the beginning, the denomination followed the policy that no church should be planted in any community where another church existed. Evangelism is to be directed to "unreached areas". So Kingston with its many churches fell outside of this policy. Indeed, this policy of the denomination was labeled the "McClare Doctrine" since Reverend George McClare, missionary and Chairman of the Executive Council, was responsible for implementing it.

Passing mention must be made concerning the connection that developed between the Missionary Church Association (MCA) and the Keswick Movement. Two Clark brothers, John and William, started the Keswick Convention in Mandeville in 1902. John eventually became a Baptist Minister in the United States. William, a lawyer and later Resident Magistrate remained in Jamaica. He became a member of the Devon Church; as a result of the family involvement in both the MCA and Keswick, he forged a strong fraternal relationship between the denomination and the Keswick movement.

Rescue Mission in Kingston

The subject of our celebration this evening is the founding of this church, First Missionary Church, in Kingston, eighty years ago. This was the denomination's first venture in Kingston. What I find intriguing is that the genesis of this venture resided in a burden that Reverend George McClare, exponent of the policy, had, of only planting churches in 'unreached areas.'

David Clarke, in his book, explains the genesis of the start of the work in Kingston in terms of the concern that Reverend McClare had for the underprivileged of the city. So, beginning in 1920, he gathered a number of willing workers and started the work at 55 East Street as a 'Life Line Mission' which became known as the "Hole in the Wall". Reverend McClare had no intention of starting a church, it was a 'Rescue Mission'. Through an arrangement with the Hanover Street Baptist Church the baptismal facilities were used to baptize the many young people and adults who were converted. With a growing Sunday School, and an increasing number of young and adult believers, the 'Hole in the Wall' could not accommodate the Mission and was forced to change into an established church.

While accepting the explanation of Reverend David Clarke, two important factors need to be added and one observation needs to be made. One factor is the migration into Kingston of several members of the churches started in Manchester and Clarendon. Reverend McClare at that time was the pastor of the Devon Church as well as the Executive Chairman of the Missionary Alliance. He had much to do with the churches in Manchester and Clarendon. He would have known at least some of the church members who had migrated into Kingston. Certainly, some of these members of the Manchester and Clarendon churches must have been among the willing workers that he was able to so readily recruit.

The second factor is that at least some of these church members from the Manchester and Clarendon churches would have desired to continue to be a part of the Missionary Alliance, instead of becoming members of other denominations. It is not unlikely that some may even have made a Macedonian call to Reverend McClare.

The observation is that Reverend McClare was constrained by the policy only to plant churches in "unreached areas". Hence, the initiative to address the needs of the underprivileged of Kingston and to continue to keep contact and assist members of the denomination that had migrated to Kingston, could not be a church planting missionary venture. It was therefore captioned as a 'Rescue Mission' in Kingston as there were many in Kingston that needed to be rescued. Constrained by a policy of which he was the chief custodian but impelled by the needs of the city and members who had migrated to live within its borders the astute, but principled Reverend McClare, crafted an initiative that conformed to the policy while at the same time addressed the twin needs.

Consistent with this intended character of the mission, it was located in the heart of Kingston. By the 1920s, people had already begun the move to create suburbs of Kingston. For example, my maternal grandmother was born and grew up on West Street. By 1920, my great grandfather had moved the family home to Mountain View Ave. So while some were moving out of Kingston the 'Rescue Mission' was moving in. Many from the 'country' who came into Kingston were moving into places from which Kingstonians were moving out. They were moving into areas with many rum bars, several houses of ill repute and sporadic violence. Interestingly, those areas were close to the waterfront and to the very area in which Kingston was first established. The

'Rescue Mission' was located in the heart of the area in which Kingston was originally established.

An intriguing aspect that must not be missed as we reflect upon the founding of the First Missionary Church, is that the initiative from which it arose was not intended to create a church, but it did. The initiative was conceived in very modest terms. It was not a mission to rescue Kingston. It had no such grand intention or design. The intention was to serve people who needed help: whether to maintain or retain their dignity or to continue their connection with the denomination to which they belonged.

From Rescue Mission to Church

The question that must be asked and answered is, how did a 'Rescue Mission' started in 1920 become a church in 1928? There are two parts to the answer to the question. The first part is straight forward. The great success of the 'Rescue Mission' in Kingston forced the change in the policy of the denomination. The growing number of Kingstonian converts and former members of MCA churches in Manchester, Clarendon and St. Elizabeth who had migrated to Kingston, strongly desired that the Mission should become a church.

The second part to the answer is quite intriguing. The Life Line Mission, as it was first named, soon outgrew its 'Hole in the Wall' location on East Street. Directly on the opposite side of East Street, number 58, was the Jewish Synagogue, which had been built in 1884 when East Street was still a residential neighbourhood. The Congregation of Israel in 1928 was moving to its present location at 92 Duke Street and the premises at 58 East St. were up for sale. Reverend McClare and Judge William Clark made an offer to purchase 58 East Street. However, the offer was rejected based on the objections of some members of the Congregation who were against selling the property to a church. Undaunted, McClare and Clark engaged the services of a real estate agent who was able to conclude the purchase. The Synagogue was remodeled and opened as 'Memorial Tabernacle' in September 1928. The new place of worship, and church, was named in memory of Mrs Sarah McClare, wife of Reverend McClare, who had died three years earlier. Tonight, 80 years hence, we celebrate the establishment of 'Memorial Tabernacle', later renamed "First Missionary Church of Kingston".

The Church with the Character of a Rescue Mission

'Memorial Tabernacle' was moving in at the same time others were moving out of that area of Kingston. The new Church attracted even more believers from other denominations concerned about the underprivileged of Kingston. The evangelical outreach was highly successful. Each Tuesday night was 'Second Coming Meetings.' Leading Ministers of the Association frequently preached at the church. Members of the new church started to earn a reputation of trustworthiness, honesty and consistent Christian living. Several couples who had been living in faithful concubinage got married with assistance from the church. The Church reached out in practical ways to help people in the neighbourhood, including obtaining tickets for rationed kerosene oil, during the days of World War II.

As has been the history of practically all Denominations, stuff happens. A wave of Pentecostal expressions spread through several churches of the Association, including Memorial Tabernacle. Missionaries and prominent lay leaders took different positions. One position was that there were excessive emotional outbursts that detracted from worship. Missionaries and lay leaders of churches that took this position, took strong steps to discourage such outbursts. Another position was that such were manifestations of the work of the Holy Spirit. Reverend McClare took this latter position. Churches over which he exercised oversight, including 'Memorial Tabernacle', took no action, even in circumstances where services broke up in disorder. The headquarters in the United States declined to take any sides in the matter and allowed local churches to sort the situation out. Some members left and joined in with the Brethren under the leadership of the young Harold Wildish.

Reverend McClare died in January 1943. 'Memorial Tabernacle' went through several years of less than satisfactory measures to secure the services of a pastor on a long-term basis. Everyone thought that the solution had been found when a missionary, who had been a Southern Baptist, was appointed in 1951. He curbed the emotional exuberances, provided a settled programme of preaching and stabilized the church. However, it was soon discovered that he had other plans for the Church. He served the church with an ultimatum to leave the Alliance and become independent. The future of 'Memorial Tabernacle' was to be separated from its founding. The church members meeting in October 1952 to address the ultimatum ended in a four-way split of the church. One group left with the missionary. One group, the smallest faction remained as 'Memorial Tabernacle'. While the other two groups left to form other fellowships within the Missionary Alliance.

The Association Headquarters in Fort Wayne stepped in. One of its past presidents was sent to take over as pastor of Memorial Tabernacle. The church was repaired from the damage done by Hurricane Charlie. When the repaired chapel was re-dedicated in 1953, the physical renewal was also marked by the change of name to 'First Missionary Church of Kingston'. From this low point, 'First Missionary' has grown from strength to strength.

'First Missionary' has retained the character of the 'Rescue Mission'. The central traits of a rescue mission are redemption and hope, through being given a second chance. Indeed, the essence of the Gospel of Jesus Christ is redemption and hope. To that mission, 'First Missionary' has always been consistent and faithful. This church, in the heart of the City of Kingston, has always preached the Gospel; in season and out of season while at the same time providing care and opportunity for residents of this central section of Kingston.

However, 'First Missionary' has always understood that the Gospel and redemption encompasses the whole person. While salvation is by the Grace of God and faith alone in Jesus Christ. It is not as a result of the work, or works of man, salvation is unto good works by those who are saved. Goods works is mandatory by those who proclaim the Good News. It is in this context that we celebrate the fact that First Missionary has never lost its character as a Rescue Mission in the name of Christ.

Tonight we celebrate eighty years of faithful proclamation of the Gospel and the pursuit of practical holiness in the midst of licentious living, debauchery, crime, violence and wanton disregard for law. Throughout the history of the Christian Church there have been those who believe that Christians should withdraw from such circumstances. They should follow the path of holiness, in separation and seclusion, from the wretchedness of the human condition. 'First Missionary' was founded on the firm conviction that the ugliness of the human condition in Kingston, needed to be rescued by the preaching of the Gospel and by practical demonstration of the love of God by those who have been redeemed.

Tonight we celebrate the transformation of the lives of those who, through this Church, have come to a saving knowledge of Jesus, also those who have beneficiaries of the programmes and acts of practical holiness, some of whom may not as yet accept Jesus Christ and those who have been saved and have benefitted from the programmes and acts of Christian benevolence. Evidence of this comes from many who have moved up and out of downtown Kingston as a result of the work of the church. Also, many of whom have continued their membership and links with the church, and those who are now members of other churches in Kingston, especially those who have helped to start such other missions.

It has become popular to believe that downtown Kingston has only become socially and spiritually problematic in recent times. I hope that the brief sketch of the history of Kingston, previously outlined, would have set the record straight. The Missionary Alliance was moved to establish the rescue mission because of Kingston's history and therefore Kingston's need. The celebration tonight therefore, is about the successes of this mission over these past 80 years in rescuing persons, one by one, who were living in Kingston in need of the Gospel and a chance to succeed in life.

What has intrigued me is that the Mission Alliance did not establish the mission on East Street or establish the Church to rescue Kingston. There was no such great or grandiose purpose. The founding of the work was much more modest and focused. This seems to have sprung directly from one of the first principles of the founding of the Denomination worldwide. That principle is that the work of reaching the world for Christ is not the exclusive prerogative of any single Christian Denomination. By logical deduction, this principle would be applied to rescuing any City. The practical manifestation of this principle is ecumenical cooperation with other denominations in the city and working with civil organisations, which have within their mission measures directed at the public good. This principle would also translate into taking innovative and pioneering action that are not patented but can be used by others for the same purpose.

The work and witness of 'First Missionary' over these past eighty years have manifested both aspects of the principle. 'First Missionary' has worked collaboratively with several other churches, of other denominations in Kingston, to spread the Gospel and address the practical needs of the people of the Kingston inner-city. This has been particularly so with churches of other evangelical denominations in the area.

The church has also partnered with community organisations. For example, First Missionary was a founding member of the PACT (People's Action for Community Development) network which since 1996 has worked in the Kingston inner-city. 'First Missionary' has worked collaboratively with the Kingston Restoration Company (KRC) and with Addition Alert, its neighbour on East Street.

'First Missionary' has also taken pioneering and innovative action. For example, the church established 'Thatch House Ltd', which provides skills training to young people in the area in garment construction and livestock agriculture. Several young people have secured gainful employment through its programmes. The Counselling Clinic operated by the church has served not only church members but persons from the community as well.

In this regard, there is an observation that I need to make rather delicately. 'First Missionary' has been restored to great vitality and dynamism since the pastorate past from missionaries to native sons of the soil.

It would be a tremendous oversight, if at this 80th Anniversary, we did not recognise and salute the Reverend Peter Spencer and also the Reverend Garnet Roper, two pastors of 'First Missionary', of purely local vintage. This is as delicately as I can put it. Reverend Spencer belongs to the Class of 1964 of the Jamaica Theological Seminary, which is the first graduating class of that institution. He was called and ordained as pastor of 'First Missionary' in 1965. In 1971 he was elected President of the Association and continued as pastor of First Missionary until 1979, when he became the full-time President of the Association. Reverend Garnett Roper then became pastor in 1979 and continued until 1998, when Reverend Spence again took over as pastor until 2008, the eightieth anniversary. In other words, for 43 of the 80 years of the life of the church two outstanding Jamaican ministers of the Gospel have had oversight of 'First Missionary'.

Over this period, the denomination has grown significantly not only in membership but in the number of churches island-wide. But if we focus on the work started by the 'Life-Line Mission' in 1920, there can be no question that First Missionary has remained a rescue mission in Kingston despite the fact that the situation in the area in which the church is located has become direr in almost every respect. 'First Missionary', located on East Street, has remained an oasis of hope, spiritually; care, materially and opportunity, socio-economically.

The church has supported many, over several generations, who have, in addition to becoming faithful believers, have made socio-economic progress through upward social mobility and have held all kinds of positions in the society. Many have moved out of the area while still continuing to worship at and be members of the church. By maintaining connections, these members have been giving back to the community from which they came through the ministries of the church. The point that should not be missed is that as many have moved out based upon forms of success, others have moved in that need to be supported and served.

May God grant the First Missionary Church of Kingston the faith, grace, love, wisdom and faithfulness to continue to be a 'rescue mission' in Kingston!

Bethel Baptist Church, Kingston, Jamaica.
Established in 1954.

Chapter 12

God's Shepherds at Bethel

~

BETHEL BAPTIST CHURCH, HALF WAY TREE, 60TH ANNIVERSARY
June, 2014

~

Bethel Baptist Church at Half Way Tree is celebrating its 60th anniversary. Bethel does not place a lot of emphasis on reciting history, however, a diamond jubilee should have some small place for recalling the past. Over these 60 years three remarkable men of God, and their wives, have been God's shepherds. Each played different roles under the guidance of the Spirit. In thanksgiving to the Father for taking us thus far, it is only right to recognise the shepherds He has chosen to lead His flock at Bethel.

Reverend and Mrs. Charles McCollough: The Shepherds who Laid the Foundations

Reverend Dr. and Mrs. Charles McCollough founded the church in November 1954 with 15 members. The McColloughs were Southern Baptist Missionaries, from the Foreign Missions Board, Virginia, assigned to the Jamaica Baptist Union. Church planting was not in their official assignment but Reverend Dr. McCollough did so anyway. The members first worshipped at the Rainbow Club, which was almost opposite the Clock Tower at Half Way Tree. It quickly moved to a rented house at 6 Hope Road just about a stone's throw away.

Half Way Tree in 1954 was far different from today. Half Way Tree had always been the capital of St. Andrew. However, in 1954, Kingston and

Crossroads held sway and swing. Half Way Tree was on the edge of country. It had a Police Station, a Resident Magistrate's Court, an elementary school, two girls' high schools, a Library and three churches: Anglican, Catholic and Brethren. The University College of the West Indies at Mona, founded six years earlier, had less than 400 students and was totally residential. The College of Arts, Science and Technology, Mona Heights, Hope Pastures, Trafalgar Park, the Plazas on Constant Spring Road and New Kingston were not yet ideas. One great asset of Half Way Tree was that it had three bus routes running through it to Kingston. It took vision to see its future potential. Reverend McCollough gleaned that divine vision and saw that potential.

The new church was organised around a simple programme. Sunday School was the church in teaching, followed by Morning Worship. Training Union, at 5.45 pm, was the church in training followed at 7.00 pm by an evangelistic service. Wednesday night was Prayer Meeting and Bible Study. There was no Youth Fellowship. The church was mainly young people, especially young men. Training Union was the magnet. Like Sunday School, it was organised by age groups. On a rotating basis each Sunday evening, three or four members of each age group had to prepare and deliver 'Parts' based on Topics in a Quarterly Manual published by the Southern Baptist but which required local research. Discussion followed the delivery of 'Parts'. Training Union also included missionary and social activities in its mandate. It had the largest attendance of all the meetings of the church, as some members left to attend evening services at their own churches.

Very early in Reverend McCollough's efforts in founding Bethel there was a major division. Some founding members, for example, Mr. George Forbes, left and joined in the founding of Grace Missionary Church. The division was not acrimonious. Bethel Baptist and Grace Missionary have had very good relations since their founding.

Mr. and Mrs. William Edwards joined Bethel in 1956 and quickly emerged as leaders in the Church with little more than 30 members. Reverend and Mrs. McCollough completed their missionary assignment and left Bethel and Jamaica in 1957 hoping that the church they founded would survive.

Reverend and Mrs. William Edwards:
The Shepherds who Established the Infrastructure

Probably growing up in a Baptist Manse gave William Edwards an intuitive and practical understanding of what was involved in the operations of a church. The most urgent matter was the payment of the monthly rent for the premises. Payment each month was reported as an achievement. Most of the young people like Alfred Johnson, Jean Ellis, Isom Heron, and Anthony Allen were still in school and Oscar Barrett at Calabar Theological College. Others like Ken Christian, Gerry Gallimore, Karl James, and Ann Johnson had just taken up their first jobs. Mr. and Mrs. Edwards, Miss Olga Coke, Mr. Calvin Hunter, Mr. Horace Rousseau, Mr. Heron, Mrs. Joyce Allen and Miss Pat Reynolds, and a few other adults, were the only ones with stable jobs. Mr. Edwards led the church in securing a Moderator to give general oversight and to preside at Communion once per month. First Reverend Leslie Larwood, then Reverend J. A. Leo-Rhynie, both from East Queen Street Baptist, and later Reverend Luther Gibbs of Hanover Street Baptist, served in this capacity. Mr. Edwards preached, Mrs. Edwards sang, or both did duets, but the Church still had to rely on preachers and singers from other churches. The preachers came mainly from the Associated Gospel Assemblies, Baptist, Brethren, Congregationalist, Church of God, Disciples of Christ, Missionary Alliance and Methodist. Indeed, some of the young men of Bethel got their first opportunities to preach when invited speakers did not show up, which was not infrequent. Indeed, there was a just-in-case-the-preacher-did-not-show-up roster.

Mr. Edwards was a prime mover in convincing the church to join the Jamaica Baptist Union (JBU). This caused another division of the small church. Some members left because the JBU was a member of the World Council of Churches and the latter had affiliations of which they did not approve. This led to the incredible situation in which Ken Christian, aged 21, was Sunday School Superintendent; Gerry Gallimore, aged 19, was Church Secretary and Errol Miller, aged 18, was Training Union Director.

It is therefore, very understandable, that Mr. Edwards and Miss Coke suggested that as many members as could, should attend the Mandeville Keswick in July 1958. He drove down every night. A few members drove down or got rides some nights. Some on summer holidays and those who took leave from work, resided in the House Party at the Jamaica Bible School.

The effect on all who attended was profound. We all realised that deeper knowledge of the Word, consecration and a commitment to our Lord and Saviour was mandatory. What followed was the long-standing relationship between Bethel and Keswick.

William Edwards and Ken Christian were the first deacons ordained by Bethel. In 1961, after four years without a pastor, but unable to support a full-time minister, the church called Deacon Edwards to be pastor. A layman as pastor was not standard JBU practice. In his capacity as deacon, and then pastor, this son of the Baptist Manse led Bethel to:

- Secure the 6 Hope Road premises through an arrangement where the Jamaica Baptist Union purchased the property and Bethel paid rent for the house. Later, the property was sub-divided. Bethel purchased the lot, with entrance on Hope Road, and the JBU retained the lot with entrance on Suthermere Road for its proposed headquarters.

- Build the Chapel in 1964. This was financed mainly through a very soft-loan and easy repayment plan from the late Mr. Albert Karram, a businessman and member of the Associated Gospel Assemblies. Mr. Karram's main condition for this loan was that it be kept a strict secret by the pastor and deacons. He wanted no acknowledgment, private or public. History is revealing that the late Mr. Karram gave similar assistance to other churches, for example, Grace Missionary Church. Pastor Curtis Cole, also of the Associated Gospel Assemblies, was the contractor who built the chapel, charged no fee to the Church, but gave his services as a contribution to God's work at Bethel.

- Construct the Education Building and extend the Chapel in 1965. The Christian Education Centre was an innovation within the JBU.

- Create the emphasis on stewardship as the basis of financing God's work. As a result, Bethel has seldom engaged in outside fund raising but has relied on the faithful giving of members. While at Bethel, Pastor Edwards rose to become a high ranking Civil Servant at the Department of Income Tax. The church never paid him a salary as pastor.

Always supportive of her husband, the late Mrs. Mavis Edwards played many roles in the church, chief among which were in the music ministry and in the formation of the Women's Fellowship.

In 1969, Pastor Edwards informed the deacons and Church Council that it was time for Bethel to have a full-time pastor who had theological training. He had done as much as he was capable of doing for the growth of the church. Hence, he was resigning so that the church could continue to develop by the Grace of God. To demonstrate the character and heart of these shepherds, they accepted the call to be God's shepherds at the Tarrant Baptist Church. In a nutshell, the Edwards did it again. Only this time, Pastor Edward underwent theological training and was ordained Reverend William Edwards. William and Mavis Edwards are examples of believers who answered God's calls to serve, served and then moved on to continue to serve without any other concern but that they continue to be witnesses of their Lord and Saviour.

Reverend Dr. Burchell and Mrs. Taylor: The Shepherds who Built the Superstructure

Calling a pastor in 1970 constituted a new experience for Bethel. Reverend McCollough had founded the church. Pastor Edwards was called from within. Calling a pastor from outside was uncharted territory. Bethel was growing and thriving spiritually and materially. The cadre of young people of the latter half of the 1950s was now in their late twenties and early thirties. Many had become deacons and leaders in different areas and had developed strong personal friendships as they encouraged and supported each other in Christian living. However, the church had expanded to more than 300 members.

The church went into deep prayer and thought as it sought to find the Lord's will. A consensus emerged. Bethel needed a pastor who had a deep knowledge of the Word; lived the Word; could preach the Word and would continue to build the Lord's work. The Lord led the church to call Reverend and Mrs. Burchell Taylor in 1970. They accepted the call.

Interestingly, Reverend and Mrs. Burchell Taylor, and their young family, were of the same age group as the young people who had grown up with the church. However, Bethel then had among its members many adults of mature years. Probably, this was one of the greatest challenges that Reverend and Mrs. Taylor faced in their early ministry at the church. They could not become close friends of any segment of the membership. Neither could they pastor by command. This would have been resisted even resented. They had to measure and maintain that distance that would allow them to be recognised and respected as Shepherds of the entire membership: young old-timers and mature newcomers but at the same time, be in cordial fellowship with all. This they achieved with easy grace and maturity.

The greatness of God is manifested in that Bethel got from the Taylors exceedingly more than the consensus of the call. In a self-effacing manner, the Taylors have been examples of believers in word and deed. God has blessed them with sons who have followed in their parent's footsteps as believers. The Taylor family has lived the Word by the enabling of the Spirit and have inspired the entire body of believers at Bethel. Reverend Taylor continued to dig deeper into the Word not only through formal study which earned him the PhD in theology but by constant study and writing. Not surprisingly, through his preaching and teaching, Bethel has literally had Keswick every month. Moreover, Reverend Dr. Taylor has become one of the princes of preachers of the Caribbean, sought after internationally, and is a regular speaker at Keswick Conventions in several countries. The evangelistic and mission emphases that have marked Bethel from its founding, have gone to a higher-level through sponsorships of several missionary ventures and leadership in the JBU. Indeed, with the full support of Bethel, Reverend Dr. Taylor was the prime mover in restructuring the Jamaica Baptist Union Mission Agency, the holding of the first Missions Conference in 2003 and in its continued activities.

Reverend Dr. Taylor's way of shepherding the flock at Bethel, under God, is marked by three distinct characteristics:

First, is fierce passion which constantly lifts up Jesus Christ as Lord.

Second, is deep compassion for those who stumble spiritually, fall ill physically, are challenged financially, are grieved by the death of loved ones, and are disadvantaged socially.

Third, is an unobtrusive, even benign but deliberate way of allowing members to exercise the gifts of the Spirit given to them for the edification of the body of Christ at Bethel. In this regard, Mrs. Ann Taylor is a co-conspirator who sometimes intervenes in areas that needs pioneering or could do with temporary bolstering. In her usual quiet and unassuming persona, Mrs. Taylor has been a tower of strength in the church.

It is in this context that the growth in membership of the church to over 3000, and the expansion into multiplicity of ministries and activities at Bethel, since 1970, need to be understood. The growth in membership has necessitated two Sunday Morning worship services which sandwich Sunday School. It has required the appointment of Assistant Pastors to assist Reverend Dr. Taylor: first Reverend Stephen Jennings, then Reverend Michael Shim-Hue and more recently Reverend Norman Mills.

The current ministries and activities at Bethel are best listed without elaboration:

1. Several choirs; an ensemble and a steel band.

2. A drama group; a dance troupe; Teen Action which more or less has replaced Training Union; A Summer employment programme for young people; junior church on Sundays and Youth Fellowship on Friday nights.

3. House Prayer Fellowships.

4. Wednesday Night Bible Study.

5. Thursday night games evening.

6. A healing Ministry, pioneered by Dr. Anthony Allen, which includes a medical clinic and a pharmacy staffed by doctors, nurses, pharmacists and laboratory technicians, who provide medical services at reduced costs.

7. Twelve Birth-Month Groups with their own agenda.

8. Women's Federation with its own agenda and activities, including support for homes for adults and children and Basic schools, including in depressed communities in Kingston.

9. Men's Brotherhood with its own agenda and projects.

10. Social outreach which operates a soup kitchen and gives assistance through gifts of food, clothing, money, and medical assistance.

11. A Lay Institute which offers formal short courses on various topics and themes delivered on evenings and Saturdays.

12. An Advice Service operated by Counsellors and Attorneys-at-Law.

13. Missionary and evangelistic outreach which includes starting outreach projects or supporting churches in Jamaica and the Caribbean region.

14. HIV/AIDS outreach

15. Skills Training Institute

16. A Literacy and Continuing Education Programme.

17. A Thrift Cooperative Society

18. A Development Fund

One feature of Bethel over the years is the number of members who have entered the Christian ministry, and have served in various churches and organisations in Jamaica and across the world. Another feature is the number of missionary activities that have either resulted in the birth and growth of new Churches or the strengthening of churches that once struggled. Yet another feature is the number of members of Bethel who have come to prominence in the practice of their faith in their professions, in their public posts and various commitments.

Concluding Comment

Over the 60 years, Bethel has been blessed with remarkable shepherds who answered the call of God. Unseen and unknown are the burdens they bore, the struggles they went through, the doubts they had to overcome, and the disappointments they had to put behind them. But underneath were the everlasting arms that carried them as they led the body of Christ at Bethel. Reverend Dr. Burchell and Mrs. Taylor built the superstructure that exists at Bethel today on the infrastructure put in place by Reverend and Mrs. William Edwards who built on the foundations laid by Reverend Dr. and Mrs. McCollough.

A very gratifying feature has been the relationships between God's shepherds at Bethel. When the Chapel was officially opened in February 1964, Reverend and Mrs. Charles Collough were invited to the event and Reverend Dr. Charles McCollough opened the Main Door and spoke. The McColloughs saw for themselves that the foundation they had laid, had been built on, physically and spiritually. Reverend William Edwards, at 90 years old, is still a regular preacher at Bethel and is always present at special events. Reverend Edwards is a participant in the superstructure that the Reverend Dr. Burchell Taylor has constructed on the infrastructure that he was led to put in place. We salute these worthy servants of God for their significant service and for the challenging legacy they have left behind.

To God be the glory!

Chapter 13

Finding It Within Ourselves

JAMAICA TEACHERS' ASSOCIATION
50TH ANNIVERSARY LECTURE
May, 2014

Introduction

Words alone are not enough to express my feelings of privilege, honour and deep humility in being invited to deliver this 50th Anniversary Lecture of the Jamaica Teachers Association (JTA). Consider the following:

Upon completing university, I applied to Excelsior High School for a job as a science teacher. I can still remember the great anxiety and apprehension in waiting to hear from Mr. A Wesley Powell, then principal of Excelsior. At the interview, he had made it very clear that there were several other applicants for the job.

Shortly after joining the staff at Excelsior, I learned about a body called JETA (Joint Executives of Teachers Association) of which Mr. Powell was the chairman. The aim was to form a single association to represent teachers. I had little understanding of what this meant. I vaguely remember the Special Conference that was held in the Excelsior Auditorium in December 1963 which passed the Resolution to establish the Jamaica Teachers Association.

What I cannot forget is that every member of the staff of Excelsior High School had to be a financial member of the newly formed Jamaica Teachers Association. Thanks to Mr. Powell, I am a founding member of the JTA, by default.

Early in 1985, Mrs. Fay Saunders and a few other JTA leaders, approached me for permission to put my name forward in the nominating process for

Jamaica Teachers Association, Kingston. Established in 1964.

President of the Association. I cannot remember ever having a thought about running for any kind of elective office anywhere. Competitive politics is not in my DNA. They gave me reasons why I needed to serve the Association as President. My concern was the political process. They promised to take care of that. I considered the reasons given and agreed.

In 1987, while I was President of the JTA, there was a meeting of four people: the late Honourable Glen Owen, then Director of the Jamaica Chamber of Commerce and Past President of JTA; the late Miss Colleen Ho, Chairman of the Education Committee of the Jamaica Chamber of Commerce; Lt Colonel Woodburn Miller, Secretary General of JTA and myself. We met to consider ways in which our organisations could take practical steps to promote wider recognition of the work and worth of teachers, promote teaching as a career among young people, and inspire teachers-in-service to continue their arduous work and not to despair despite difficulties.

The Honourable Glen Owen proposed introducing "Teachers' Day" in Jamaica. "Teachers Day" was being celebrated worldwide in October each year. We accepted the idea of "Teachers Day". However, we suggested that "Teachers' Day" be the Wednesday of Education week, celebrated in Jamaica in the first week of May each year. Both sides agreed. Finally, it was agreed that the Jamaica Chamber of Commerce would be responsible for the implementation of the first Teachers Day on the Wednesday of Education Week in May 1988.

I am quite certain that Mr. Woodburn Miller would agree that none of us sitting around the table that day imagined that "Teachers Day" would be so rapidly and universally embraced across the country. This is eloquent testimony to the appreciation of the work and worth of the vast majority of teachers by most of the students and communities they serve. To the extent that the Association in 2013, decided to have the 50th Anniversary Lecture delivered in Education Week and invited me to deliver this Lecture just boggles my mind.

The point is that the work of teachers, in schools and communities, and that of the Association representing teachers collectively are inextricably part of the education process and enterprise. Also, education is about mobilising a people to conserve the essence of their civilisation while responding to dynamic imperatives of the present in order to construct the future that promises the greatest possibility of their survival and even prosperity. Teachers, education, civilisation and the future of a people are so intertwined that they are virtually impossible to separate. Hence, while it is important to celebrate the actual dates on which events occur, like April 24 when JTA was formally founded, it is equally important to make symbolic connections with the foundations of our social being. Hopefully, going forward, whenever JTA celebrates its anniversaries, part of that celebration will include an event in Education Week. We are still a young country in the process of becoming. It is critical for each generation to build on the insights, energies and sacrifices of those who went before. Rituals are important in promoting continuity of striving.

As I look back on life, it is becoming patently clear that foresight is limited; that unintended outcomes shape the future course of life as much as planned objectives; and therefore, we ought to be thankful and grateful when a vision becomes sustained reality. I had little understanding, but was present by default at the formation of the JTA, and later was co-opted to participate in the struggles and aspirations of the Association. I have been fortunate to live to see the vision of the unified teaching profession sustained for 50 years, I can only recite the words of songwriter, Thomas Chisholm:

> Great is thy faithfulness
>
> O God our father
>
> There is no shadow of turning with Thee
>
> Thou changeth not
>
> Thy compassions they fail not
>
> As Thou has been
>
> Thou forever will be.

The Context in Which JTA was Founded

It is necessary to set out briefly the broad contours of the context in which JTA was founded and in which it has operated for its first 50 years. Some notion of this context is essential to assess and appreciate the achievements of the Association which ought to be celebrated.

The education system that developed during the colonial era had deep social divisions as a result of its virtual apartheid structure. There was the elementary school/teachers college segment which served the mass of the population. Tuition was free. The most able and ambitious students of this segment of the system became pupil teachers, sat the Jamaica Local Examinations, First, Second and Third Year, which qualified them to enter teachers colleges. Also part of this segment was Kingston Technical School and six vocational training centres which offered vocational training to students in the 14 to 17 age range. Some would have been successful in the Jamaica Local Examinations. This segment of the system was also administered by the Department of Education led by a colonial director.

Then there was the preparatory school/high school segment of the system which catered mainly to the small middle classes. The teachers of this segment were mainly British expatriates, supported by some qualified and mostly unqualified past students of high schools. Preparatory school and high schools charged fees. This segment was administered by the Jamaica Schools Commission. By 1953, there were about 400 Code Scholarships which provided funding for elementary school students to attend high schools. Most of the elementary school students winning these scholarships were children of elementary school teachers or Ministers of Religion.

The Jamaica Union of Teachers representing elementary school teachers was the largest teachers' association. It was male lead but majority female in membership and who were predominantly of darker complexion. The Association of Teachers Training Staffs represented the staffs of teachers' colleges. The staff of teachers' colleges were British expatriate led, but the lecturers resembled teachers in elementary schools with females having a slight majority. The Association of Teachers of Technical Institutions represented teachers at Kingston Technical and the six vocational training centres—all converted to Technical High Schools in the 1950s. They were mainly male and resembled teachers in elementary schools. The Headmasters' and Headmistress' Association represented the heads of high Schools. They were mainly British expatriates with some Jamaicans and were just about evenly balanced by gender. The Assistant Masters and Assistant Mistresses' Association represented teachers of high schools. These teachers were mainly Jamaicans but with a mixture of British expatriates, West Indians mainly from Barbados and Guyana, with a slight male majority but generally younger than the other associations. The five teachers associations mirrored social divisions within the Jamaican society. They constituted five separate bargaining units operating within two governing bodies.

The catalyst for change was the introduction of Ministerial Government, including the creation of the Ministry of Education in 1953. Indeed, Ministerial Government by the elected representatives of the people was a consequence of constitutional reform ten years earlier which introduced adult suffrage and representative government. The Jamaica Schools Commission was abolished. The Department of Education was absorbed into the Ministry of Education.

The Ministry of Education became the focal point of the intended integration of the education system within the context of the rule of law and a democratic society. The options facing the five teachers' organisations were whether to bargain separately or collectively with the single entity: the

Ministry of Education/Ministry of Finance. By 1957 the five began to explore the collective option through the creation of the Joint Executives of Teachers Association (JETA). It took seven years to form a single teachers' organisation, the Jamaica Teachers Association. The history of this process still remains to be written, and most of the architects have died. Hopefully critical documents remain.

To add to this sketch, it must be pointed out that sociologically, elementary school teaching and high school teaching were two separate occupations. Elementary school teachers came from one social segment of the society and high school teachers from the other social segment. Heuristically, this difference was marked by differences in shades of skin colour but more so by mindsets.

In his autobiography, J.J. Mills, legendary Vice-Principal of the Mico, records that when he and Mr. A. Little, President of JUT, appeared before the Moyne Commission which investigated the state of affairs in the colony following the 1938 riots, they were asked their views on whether teachers for elementary schools should be recruited mainly from high schools students. They had to point out to the Commissioners that there was no interest from high schools and their students and there was great snobbery on the part of high schools towards elementary school teaching.

Mills went on to explain that elementary schools were not free from blame in 'the estrangement and mutual lack of understanding'. In other words, there was reservations and even resentment between the segregated sectors in education. The point here is that the social distinctions between elementary and secondary school teaching and teachers were not academic. They influenced thinking, behaviour and action.

These sociological differences were also marked with differences in remuneration for teachers. Elementary school teachers and high school teachers were paid differently. Elementary school teachers were paid lower salaries than high school teachers. However, male and female elementary school teachers were paid the same salaries. Among high school teachers, males were paid slightly higher salaries than female teachers. The staffs of teachers' colleges were paid somewhat similar salaries to high school teachers. Teachers in vocational training centres were slotted somewhere within the mix. University graduates were debarred from teaching in elementary schools in that no account was taken of their graduate status. In a nutshell, by the end of the colonial era, salary scales for teachers in the public system were shot through with inconsistencies, inequities, anomalies, and arbitrary determinations that were reflective of the general socio-economic structure of the Jamaican society.

The five teachers' organisations were proud of what they had been able to accomplish separately but they were open to the possibilities of what they could accomplish together. They were also acutely aware that the way teachers were represented, mirrored and matched the divisive patterns of the colonial era and that these patterns ought not to have been carried forward into the new emerging nation. The executives of these five teachers associations found it within themselves to come together and form JETA, from which the Jamaica Teachers Association was founded. The leadership of these five teachers' organisations decided to look beyond the past reservations, resentments, suspicions and stigmas to search for common ground and a shared destiny.

In celebrating any anniversary of the Jamaica Teachers Association we must always remember the late Honourable A. Wesley Powell, the late Mr. Benjamin Hawthorne, the late Mr. Desmond Gascoigne, Mrs. Fay Saunders and all the other leaders of JETA. Indeed, JTA should have in its annals, and on a Board somewhere, and online, the names of these visionary teacher leaders of JETA on whose work we have built.

Major Changes in the Teaching Profession in Jamaica Since 1964

To complete the context, it is necessary to briefly list major changes that have taken place in the Jamaican education system, since the JTA was founded, particularly those that related to teachers:

1. The teaching force in the public sector in Jamaica has almost doubled. This is because the primary education system expanded to achieve universal primary education. The secondary education system expanded from about five percent of the secondary age cohort to around 80 percent of the cohort. There are now more infant schools or infant departments in primary school. And tertiary education, in national institutions, has expanded from about two percent to close to 20 percent.

2. The teaching force has become significantly better qualified academically and professionally.

3. The teaching force has become Jamaicanised and self-sustaining. This is because the country has developed the indigenous capacity to educate and train teachers for all levels of the education system.

4. Jamaica has moved from being a net importer of teachers to a net exporter of teachers who meet international standards where-ever they have plied their trade.

Major Achievements of the JTA Over 50 Years

In the interest of time, allow me to simply give an annotated list of 10 major achievements of the JTA over its 50 years of existence that ought to be celebrated:

1. Through several reclassifications of the teaching service, JTA has worked and achieved a set of rational and sound principles that are systematically applied to the remuneration of teachers across the levels of the education system. These have replaced the arbitrary, inconsistent, inequitable system of remuneration that previously existed. All teachers at the infant, primary and secondary levels are paid in scales related to academic and professional qualifications and years of teaching experience. The tertiary level has been separated from the infant, primary and secondary levels, and remunerated at higher rates also based on academic and professional qualifications and teaching experience. The category of Principals has replaced head-teachers, headmasters and headmistresses. Principals are paid on the basis of size and complexity of their institutions within each level of the school system that they manage. Over the last five years, teachers' salaries are equated to 80 percent of the private sector market. As a result of this history, words and phrases such as anomaly, parity of pay, ability to pay and reclassification have become part of the lexicon of JTA Salary Negotiation Teams. These teams have become renowned for doing their homework in preparation for negotiation.

The results of this homework have sometime benefitted the entire public service and even the entire country. For example, in the mid-1980s when the Government was revising the income tax code and linking this revision to salary negotiations, the firm proposal was for a flat rate of 33 percent across the board for individuals and companies. It was JTA's homework that produced the evidence that showed proposed benefit to individuals would only apply to a select few and not the vast majority. The final result was that the 33 percent rate was retained for companies and the 25 percent flat rate was applied to individuals. These rates still apply today. Further, JTA has consistently negotiated leave arrangements which provide a cost-sharing basis between teachers and Government, for teachers to upgrade their qualifications and incentives for achieving higher than the minimum qualifications.

2. Maintaining and strengthening the unification of the teaching profession. While the JTA cannot claim to have achieved a perfectly unified Jamaican teaching profession, it can rightly claim to have kept the five aboriginal strands together, deepened the integration between them, vigorously defended teachers rights at all levels of the education system, successfully survived breakaway attempts, kept the organisation focused on serving the interests of teachers and created a framework of unity with diversity as interest groups operate within common bargaining units. This is a remarkable achievement since it is virtually impossible to satisfy the expectations of all groups, and a common tendency of some people to want to take up their marbles and breakaway if their expectations are not met. In addition, Jamaica has a very strong, highly decisive two-party political system that continuously seeks to co-opt prominent individuals and organisations to serve their ends. Because teachers are not civil servants, there are many JTA members who have joined political parties, become dedicated workers of major political parties and have run for political office representing political parties. That JTA has deliberately and consciously developed the discipline to protect the Association from being co-opted, from within and without, is more than noteworthy.

An incident that happened in 1980, one of the most fractious and acrimonious period of Jamaica's political history, illustrates the approach of the Association. At the Annual Conference that was held at Shortwood Teachers College in January 1980, as usual, the Minister of Education addressed the conference. The teacher selected by leadership of the Association to move the Vote of Thanks to the Minister was the Campaign Manager of the JLP candidate running against the Minister in his constituency. That teacher was given very strict instructions. He was reminded very explicitly that he was representing the JTA. He had to be gracious, magnanimous and objective in giving the Minister credit for attending the Conference and for his proposals to improve the lot of teachers. Further, a Vote of Thanks is not a proper place for critical comments. The teacher tried to decline the assignment but the leadership would not accept this. They maintained that he was the best person in the Association to give the Vote of Thanks to the Minister and to demonstrate that JTA separated the office of the Minister from partisan politics. The teacher in giving the Vote of Thanks on behalf of the Association was gracious, magnanimous and commended the Minister on several counts.

He concluded the Vote of Thanks by saying that the one thing that he could not guarantee was that the Minister would be there to implement his proposals since the Minister knew that he was working to unseat him. The conclusion was that the teacher had carried out the assignment honestly and with transparency. Keeping the Association focused of the interests of teachers, education and the common good of the nation has been key to maintaining the unification of the teaching profession. Further, resisting every attempt to co-opt the Association to serve some partisan political end has been central to ensuring the unity of the profession. These the Association has succeeded in doing over its 50 years.

3. Become one of the strongest unions in the country, not only in terms of paid membership but in respect of its participatory and interactive infrastructure, the depth and diversity allows teachers' voice and vote in the affairs of the Association. The Association is organised around a revolving presidency, a full-time national Secretariat providing several services, Parish organisations, district structure which

includes all teachers in all schools in a defined geographical area and a contact teacher in each of the more than 1000 schools in the country. In effect, JTA is a network with an intelligent hub which has the function of keeping the network operating smoothly and seamlessly through the Annual Conference, Quarterly General Council, Monthly Central Executive Meetings, Parish Meeting and District Meetings.

4. Maintaining the democratic form of governance. There are annual elections of officers at the District and Parish levels, that is, in 78 District Associations and fourteen Parish Associations. Every member of the Association is entitled to vote in the annual election of President Elect. Invariably there is a campaign for election to the Presidency in which candidates must present themselves to teachers across the country. Nominations for the President are from the Parish level in a fashion analogous to a primary system. As a result of consistently maintaining democratic governance, through annual elections, JTA has developed and maintained the largest pool of expertise in the conduct of elections in the country. This has been to the great benefit of the country as a whole.

In 2002, the Electoral Advisory Committee decided to recruit Election Day Workers to serve as Presiding Officers and Poll Clerks. Workers should meet and invite various organisations and institutions to meet quotas given to them, and these volunteers to be vetted by recognised political parties prior to being trained and employed on Election Day. It was teachers who more than doubled the quota given to JTA and who were nearly half of Election Day workers in the General Elections in 2002 and in subsequent Local and General Elections. In other words, teachers recruited through the JTA have contributed significantly to the improved experiences that voters have had in polling stations across the country over the last decade. Let there be no mistaking the fact that Jamaica has been able to maintain a stable democracy, through free and fair elections, have contributed greatly to the standing of the country in the world, to the pride of Jamaicans at home and abroad and has bought us time in seeking to resolve our economic problems. JTA can justly claim to have contributed meaningfully to this outcome.

5. Continued the development of some and created new institutions and services to promote the economic and social well-being of teachers. The Credit Union has prospered; the Publishing House has survived; while the Housing cooperation and Book Store have failed. However, new services have taken root: Educational Tours during vacation periods, the Travel and Wellness Club, accessing housing solutions through the Association and annual Investment Seminars which encourage teachers to invest especially in relation to retirement.

6. Consistently championing measures to improve the education system, some of which have become major policies, and planks of national and regional education. These include the development of early childhood education first taken up by the Institute of Education of University of the West Indies Wan Leer Foundation and latterly by the Government through the establishment of the Early Childhood Commission; the creation of the Caribbean Examination Council (CXC) to replace the Cambridge Exams; the integration of different types of Secondary Schools to create a single high school system; and the introduction of the Education Tax to assist with the financing of education.

7. Consistently championed the causes of vulnerable groups and institutions in the education system and society. The following are examples:

   • JTA in the 1970s, through its liaison Officer at the Ministry of Education, that did the ground work to define remote rural schools. This provided the objective criteria by which the Association successfully negotiated incentives for qualified teachers to be attracted to work in schools serving remote rural communities

   • JTA in the 1980s, successfully worked to reopen eight small schools serving remote rural communities that the Ministry had closed in seeking to comply with World Bank conditionalities, consequent upon IMF Agreements. These schools served very small communities with poor roads leading to them and even worst transportation. They were located at least four to five miles from the nearest alternative school. They were not important politically because they had small populations which voted evenly for the two major political parties. JTA, in addition to working on behalf of the 38 teachers who would be dismissed, worked tirelessly to reopen the schools although several of the teachers had found jobs elsewhere. In addition, with help from sponsors JTA launched and executed a project to improve the quality of education in small multi-grade schools serving these eight and other similar communities

- JTA worked tirelessly to reopen Moneague Teachers' College after it was closed in the mid-1980s. Initially, the JTA sought to take up the matter in the courts. However, out of fear of victimization, none of the lecturers that were dismissed was willing to volunteer to apply to the courts for redress, even with the full support of the Association. JTA therefore, had to turn to other levers of influence to secure the reopening of the College with a limited mandate. Today, the Moneague College operates to serve the tertiary education needs of sections of the North Coast of Jamaica and regions beyond.

8. Being a reliable and constructive partner of successive Governments, of different political parties, in the implementation of policies, projects and programmes designed to enhance and improve education in the country. JTA has always followed the principle that the elected Government of the people has a mandate to set education policies, whether or not, the Association agrees with these policies. If these policies are not sound they will fail under the weight of their own folly without any action by the Association. At the same time, JTA reserves the right to express its considered, and collective opinion on education policy and to protest policies that it considers inimical to the interests of teachers and of the education system. Accordingly, JTA has operated on two tracks with Government: one in interaction with the Minister and his advisors and the other in interaction with the Permanent Secretary and civil servants in the Ministry. The first addresses policy while the second deals with the implementation and normal operational matters between the Ministry and the Secretariat. Accordingly, the partnership is principled, multilayered and systematic.

9. Persistently providing and promoting professional development for teachers through the Professional Development Unit, Conferences, Seminars, Colloquia and Workshops.

10. Linked teachers in Jamaica with their colleagues regionally through the Caribbean Union of Teachers (CUT) and internationally first through the World Confederation of Organisations of the Teaching Profession (WCOTP) and latterly with its successor Education International (EI) which includes teachers' unions and associations with a total membership of over 30,000,000 worldwide. Outside the region, the JTA has maintained strong fraternal relations with the Canadian Teachers' Federation; the National Education Association and the American Federation of Teachers of the United States; and the Swedish Teachers Union. JTA hosted the Secretariat of the CUT between 1999 and 2013 and is a reliable participant in CUT activities across the Caribbean. In 1971, JTA hosted the Congress of the WCOTP which brought the world's teachers to our shores. JTA was part of the Working Group that developed the Commonwealth Teacher Recruitment Protocol approved by the Ministers of Education of the Commonwealth at their meeting in Lincolnshire, England in 2004. Dr. Adolf Cameron is currently the chairman of the Education International Task Force on Teacher Migration and Mobility.

Pleas and Cautions

All of these ten major achievements of the JTA in its first 50 years need to continue to guide the Association going forward. As one of those who have battled and proudly bear scars from some of those battles, allow me to make specific pleas and issue some cautions related to some of these areas of achievements:

a. Beware of harebrained proposals that seek to undermine or replace the sound rational principles for paying teachers that are systematically applied across the education system and that have been so painstakingly worked over these fifty years.

Education is not a business. Its reason for existence is not the bottom line of profit from the sale of goods and services. Hence, teachers cannot be paid on the same principles as salespersons. Education is about the mobilization of a people to consolidate its civilisation and construct their future. Some elements of these outcomes are intangible but critically important. The outcomes of education and schooling cannot be accurately measured only by students' scores in examinations set on a limited number of subjects. Education and schooling are about producing persons with talents, knowledge, imagination, critical thinking capacities; know-how skills in technical, visual arts, performing arts and sports; constructive citizens, community members, and responsible family members; persons of character, integrity and conscience; with the ability to learn and adjust to future developments not taught or anticipated in schools; who can recognise spin and misinformation and therefore are not gullible to the wiles of the powerful.

Anyone or group who claims to be able to link the personality, mastery of subject content and pedagogic performance of teachers to the listed outcomes in such a manner that would pay teachers on an equitable and fair basis is no different from the urban hustlers who sells country people public buildings, country ginnals who sell town people defective livestock, the proverbial American snake oil salesman and the lottery scammers who dupe elder people out of their life's savings.

Further, schools are social organisations and teaching is a social profession. The spectacular results of a class of Grade Six students, in a primary school, could be as much the product of the foundations laid by teachers in earlier grades than the teacher who taught them for the GSAT. The same is true for student performance in any subject in a secondary school. The fact is we do not know enough about the education processes to device pay systems based upon individual student and individual teacher performance.

Teachers' responsibility is to teach.

Students' obligation is to learn.

The obligation of parents is to present their children to school in a condition that they can learn.

The obligation of the state is to provide the environment and materials for learning.

There are ontological relationships between all of these actors. While there may be a few misguided persons who embark upon teaching to become rich, the vast majority enter teaching as a result of a love of children and adolescents, a love of learning and a desire to make a difference in the life of their students and the progress of their country. What they require in return is a respectable living standard. To be able to feed their families, own a home in their lifetime, send their children to school and university, own a car, and take periodic vacations. Within these parameters they make no equation between the work output with the students and the income earned from doing this job.

Their reason for joining the Association is to protect them from exploitation from those who would wish to violate their sense of dignity by preventing them from making two ends meet while demanding the ultimate in effort.

JTA must never betray that responsibility, fear any foe or back away from any fight related to the dignity of teachers.

b. Make sure to preserve and strengthen the interactive, participatory, democratic governance structure of the Association which renews itself continuously through the elective process. This is the best way to ensure that the Association remains faithful to its purpose and mission and of guarding against any faction or group using the Association to advance their own interests and agendas.

c. Strive to maintain the study leave arrangements that allow teachers to upgrade their mastery of academic content as well as pedagogy. All eyes these days are on the excellent achievement of Finland's education system. Finland has maintained very strong links between their universities and the training of teachers; invested heavily in the professional development of their teachers; paid their teachers well in comparison to other occupations; and over time, have been able to recruit their teachers from top performing graduates who desire to pursue careers in teaching.

In Jamaica, if you analyse the subject areas in which students at the secondary level are performing unsatisfactorily, you will find that many students are being taught by teachers who have not specialized in the teaching of the subjects they are teaching. Do not blame those teachers. They have volunteered or been conscripted to fill a breach. Do not blame the principals either, they had to find someone to put before the students. The source of the problem is that we do not have a sufficient number of persons with the required subject content and mastery of the pedagogy for teaching these subjects. These kinds of problems are not new. What happened in the past, is that systematic schemes were devised to remedy the problem and study leave granted to upgrade some of the teachers who were part of these schemes. The name, blame and shame approach that has become very common, from different quarters, does not solve the problem. JTA should use the outbursts from this approach to propose constructive solutions and then follow-up with the full weight of the Association to have these solutions implemented.

d. JTA proposed the *Education Tax* as a means of providing addition resources for the education. Successive Governments have not honoured the intentions of the JTA and the understandings on which the public accepted the introduction of the tax when it was proposed. Any analysis will show that the Education Tax has not been in addition to Government subvention for education prior to the introduction of the Tax. In effect the education tax has been swallowed up in debt repayment. This is why neither the IMF nor the World Bank, which set conditions with which the Government has to comply, have ever required Government to honour the intentions of the Education Tax.

The reason that JTA should never give up the fight to honour the intention of the Education Tax is that the greatest challenge facing education is stagnation. The education budget, over the last 30 years, has been for keeping the existing system running. There has been gross under- investment in the capital inputs needed to reform education adequately to prepare our people for the future. I will come back to his point.

e. JTA must continue to prevent being co-opted by any partisan political purpose, sectarian alliance, economic interest, and remain focused on the interest of country, education and teachers. This means no relent by the leadership with respect to internal vigilance and discipline in conducting the external affairs of the Association.

f. Over the second half of the twentieth century there has been greater and greater accumulation of wealth in fewer and fewer hands. As a result, corporations have become more powerful, nationally and internationally. Middle income countries and the middle classes are being put under increasing pressure, as more and more people are descending into the ranks of the working poor, as their salaries and wages stagnate and their pension rights are whittled away.

Unions have been the greatest champions of the rise of the middle classes. Not surprisingly, unions have increasingly become scapegoats of the rich and powerful. The reasons for these changes are structural and will not be abated in the short or even medium term. Teachers' unions represent an important segment of the middle classes. Therefore, they have not been immune from the assault on unions. Indeed, in some countries, as corporate interests have sought to have greater say in education policy, there have been outright action to break teachers' unions by blaming them for practically all that is wrong in school and society. International trends, especially those prominent in the United States, will eventually reach our shores. JTA needs to brace itself and prepare to meet this assault.

What of the Future?

When JTA was founded 50 years ago, it was as a result of the fact that teachers and their unions assessed the situation of the country and themselves within it, over a seven year period. They saw a divided profession; an emerging new sovereign nation; an education system taken over by the elected representatives of the people; a world re-ordering itself in the process of de-colonisation and a Cold War between two great ideologies that divided the world. What are the circumstances that JTA and country face in 2014?

A quick scan of the contemporary Jamaican situation can be briefly summarised as follows:

1. Jamaica has a largely unified, mostly qualified, teaching profession that constitutes one of the largest organised pools of talent and thinking power in the country.

2. The Jamaican nation is politically stable. However, the Jamaican economy is almost stagnant and depressed as a result of debt. The

state is compromised in several areas as a result of structural and physical violence. Crime is prevalent and only loosely restrained.

3. The Jamaican people are almost equally divided between those living inside and outside the country but declining relatively, as their prime-age population, 20 to 49 years, is now larger than the school age population, 5 to 19 years, but with large numbers of youths unemployed.

4. The education system is mostly integrated, and is a strength of the country, but it manifests wide disparities in outcomes and is deformed; having a very broad body of early childhood, primary and secondary education topped with a small head of tertiary education.

5. The world is globalizing and becoming multi-polar with the rise of new regional powers, with global reach in Europe, Asia, South America and Africa. The Caribbean has been marginal in the old geopolitics and is marginal in the emerging geopolitics. The region can be expected to be caught in the interstices of these competing powers, especially being located next door to the superpower, the United States.

6. The technological change sweeping the world is exponential, digital, innovative and pervasive, affecting almost every area of human endeavour with the result that science fiction has become reality in some areas.

7. Climate change is a reality in the world. Wild variation in weather patterns, more severe weather, and the melting of ice in the Arctic and Antarctic is predicted to lead to rising of sea levels. These all portend to major adjustments in the future human settlement patterns, including the island-nations of the Caribbean.

8. The world economy has now entered the era of 'winner take all' which creates huge income gaps between the superstars and peers of business in all areas, sports in all fields, music in all genres, visual arts of all forms, the performing arts in all disciplines, media in all areas and even in religion. The super-rich, or one percent, has increasingly accumulated a greater share of the wealth of the world.

9. While democracy has spread across the world, it is under stress, in some of the most unexpected places, including among its champions and strongest advocates.

10. Racism that some had declared dead, is alive and well in very sophisticated and subtle forms.

This list is by no means exhaustive but they are indicative of the imperatives with which the Jamaican nation, people and society, must contend. This quick scan is not meant to raise an alarm, create panic or predict any calamity. Jamaica is not going to disappear anytime soon. So no apocalypse is envisaged. History is replete with instances of peoples who chose to ignore or procrastinated when confronted with fundamental changes taking place in their times. Overtaken by those changes, the outcome is either that they no longer exist as a distinct society, or went into doldrums for decades or even centuries, or have remained in some esoteric niche outside the mainstream of civilisation.

This quick scan is not meant to suggest that we as a country, or teachers, try to develop some detailed super plan as a blueprint for action going into the future. The imperatives are far too complex, compounded and convoluted to adopt such an approach. As I indicated at the beginning, human foresight is very limited and invariably cannot anticipate the future in great detail.

JTA at its founding was not only concerned about teachers but of issues and challenges that faced the new nation. The contemporary imperatives facing the country, require: new thinking both logically and imaginatively; conserving and consolidating achievements that are critically important to future survival and prosperity; changes in behaviour, both personal and corporate, in order to respond to these imperatives; and frameworks for collective action in critical areas. JTA at 50 is in a position to play a leading role in the conversation and dialogue on these matters.

It is my view that there are four critical and strategic issues that the country needs to carefully, comprehensively and coherently consider. If we can achieve consensus and act collectively on these issues, the others will fall into place. These are democratic governance; embracing the technological revolution; youth as the future; and finding it within ourselves to make the moral choices in constructing the future. Allow me to expand briefly on each.

Democratic Governance

Perfect governance is a theocracy with the Sovereign Lord on the throne. He is sure to rule with perfect love, grace, righteousness, justice and mercy. This will happen in heaven. However, on earth, democratic governance, where the people are sovereign, is the best there is. There, sufficient history with rule by monarchs, warriors, priests and dictators to counsel against sovereign rule by individuals.

Democratic governance is an emerging strength of the country. However, we would be very mistaken to be sanguine and satisfied with present achievements.

At the core of democracy, there is a fundamental contradiction. Simply put, while the people are sovereign they cannot rule directly but must elect representatives to Parliament which then exercises the sovereign powers of the people. There is no higher body in a democracy than Parliament. However, acting within Constitutions, it is Parliament that establishes electoral law, provides the resources and creates the machinery for the conduct of elections. Incumbents in Parliament therefore, can legally and constitutionally enact laws, provide resources and direct the election machinery so as to ensure their re-election. In other words, elected representatives of the people can usurp the sovereign power of the people, thus becoming unaccountable to the people.

The danger of self-satisfaction with democratic governance can best be illustrated with respect to the United States, which has been a leader and champion of democracy in the world. Gerrymandering of Congressional districts is widely practiced in many states by both the Democratic and Republicans Parties, with the Republicans currently holding the advantage. Voter fraud is infinitesimal in the United States. The American people have a great record of participating in the electoral process according to law. Yet, using voter fraud as justification, Republicans, in some states, are imposing restrictions on voting, designed to affect electors who traditionally vote for the Democratic Party and skew the provision of resources to conduct elections to favour candidates of their own party. Some Republican Governors and Secretaries of State have tampered with Voters' Lists by mandating that electoral officials purge Voters List close to elections. Here is the fact. It is all legal and constitutional.

Gerrymandering is legal in the United States because the US Constitution stipulates that Congressional District boundaries are determined by the Senate and House of Representatives of each state, based on the results of the Census taken every ten years. Accordingly, the party in power in each state, at the time of the Census, gets to draw congressional district boundaries for their state and can do so to the advantage of their party. Likewise, the Senate, House and Governor of each state set electoral laws for the state. Further, the Governor and the Secretary of State of each state, who are partisans, determine the resources given to conduct elections, determine where those resources should be deployed and set the rules by which electoral officials determine such matters as the Voters List. Hence, election officials and voters acting according to law can do so in a system rigged for partisan advantage.

We often vilify and demonise our politicians and deny them credit for noble things that they have done. In the midst of the most violent and acrimonious period in Jamaica's political history, in the late 1970s, Prime Minister Michael Manley and Leader of the Opposition, Edward Seaga, agreed in principle to remove the determination of electoral boundaries and the conduct of elections from direct partisan political control. They appointed a team, three from each side, to work out a proposal. That team consisted of the late Hon. Hugh Shearer, Hon. Bruce Golding and Mr. Abe Daboub representing the JLP and the Hon. P. J. Patterson, the late Keble Munn and Dr. Paul Robertson representing the PNP. That bipartisan team presented the proposal that later formed the legislation passed by Parliament to create the Electoral Advisory Committee (EAC). As a result, gerrymandering of electoral boundaries has been eliminated in Jamaica. The electoral machinery, the compilation of the Voter's List and the conduct of elections has been placed outside of partisan political control. Jamaica now has a world class electoral system.

Having had turns with the 'winner take all' electoral system that the country inherited from the colonial era, and therefore knowing the extent to which that system could be, and had been abused, the leadership of the warring political parties and Parliament in the late 1970s found it within themselves to set the framework to chart a course for the common good of the country. However, just before anyone becomes ecstatic, know this. The essence of this Jamaican solution rests upon three main factors outside of the integrity, fidelity and competence of those in charge of the electoral processes.

These are:

1. The wisdom of the Governor General, the Prime Minister and the Leader of the Opposition in nominating and appointing the Members of the EAC, now the Electoral Commission.

2. The Convention that Parliament will only act on electoral matters placed before it, if those matters come as recommendations from the Electoral Commission.

3. The Convention that the party in power will never use its majority in Parliament to determine matters of boundaries and elections but will accept, without change, and act upon the unanimous recommendations of the Electoral Commission.

Note that wisdom cannot be legislated. However, since 1979, Governors General, Prime Ministers and Leaders of the Opposition, have been wise in their nominations and appointments to the EAC/ECJ. Note as well, that, Conventions are not laws. The Electoral Commission is subservient to Parliament. It cannot dictate to Parliament. Parliament is supreme. Hence, every time recommendations on boundaries, and electoral matters come before Parliament from other sources than the ECJ and every time the ECJ makes unanimous recommendations to Parliament the Conventions are put to the test. In other words, Parliament can at any time, now or in the future, legally and constitutionally choose to break these conventions by which Jamaica has advanced its democracy.

While Jamaican Parliamentarians must be commended for their actions since 1979, in taking boundaries, electoral laws and conduct out of partisan politics, we would be myopic not to see inertia and reluctance as well. The Interim Act which established the EAC in 1979, promised the formation of an Electoral Commission which would be included in the Constitution. The Electoral Commission did not come into being until December 2006. A report from the ECJ to include the Commission in the Constitution was submitted to Parliament in 2008 and approved by Parliament in 2010. The amendment to the Constitution is still to be tabled. The Commission made recommendations to Parliament on the Registration and Financing of Political Parties in 2010 which was approved by Parliament in 2011. Draft Legislation has been completed since the end of 2011 which are still to be tabled in the House. A similar story can be told with respect to Campaign

Financing. It is my considered opinion that there are some incumbents in Parliament, on both sides of the aisle, who would like to halt, if not reverse, the process of preventing incumbents from seeking to ensure their re-election.

JTA is not only a shining example of democratic governance but teachers are among the most knowledgeable about the electoral system and experts in conducting elections. To be explicit, there is a body of knowledge and successful practice with respect to democratic governance and elections that has been built up, at least over the last 35 years, in Jamaica that has not yet been systematized and is not taught in our secondary schools, colleges and universities. JTA is therefore in a unique position to lead teachers to further widen, strengthen and deepen democratic governance in the country by infusing and diffusing this body of knowledge and practices in the existing operation of schools, colleges and universities. For example, it is now almost customary in secondary schools for there to be elections for the students' council. Those elections could be conducted by students under the aegis of a body comparable to the ECJ and with candidates who have agents in polling stations organised by grade levels. This would give the opportunity, both to explain the philosophy to students and also to allow them to conduct the process based on that philosophy.

At all levels and in all spheres of our society, elected leaders need to be stewards of the power bequeath to them through elections. Stewardship in office is one of the outcomes of being truly accountable to the electorate, whoever the electors are.

The Technological Revolution

Two MIT researchers, Erik Brynjofsson and Andrew McAfee, published a book earlier this year titled *The Second Machine Age*. They argued that the world is at the inflection point of a revolution in technology comparable to the Industrial Revolution, the first machine age. There are three bases of their assertion.

The first is that for the same price, the power and speed of a microchip is following Moore's Law, that is, they are doubling every two years. The result of this exponential growth is that computer-related devices are becoming faster, smaller, lighter, more powerful, cheaper, and therefore more affordable.

The second is that everything is becoming digitized and can be inter-connected. The volume, velocity and variety of interconnections are exploding: for example, cameras, phones, computers, printers, sensors, GPS devices, tablets, and televisions can all be interconnected. Moreover, almost everybody on the planet can be part of a digital network. One feature of digital information is that it is non-rival, it is not used up within its use. Hence, digital information is costly to produce but very cheap to reproduce. Copies can fly around the globe in seconds, making huge amounts of information readily accessible.

The third is that digital information can be recombined. Each innovation is the building block for future innovations. Therefore, the innovative possibilities are endless, restricted only by the imagination of those engaged with any particular issue.

Among the first outputs of the second machine age are robots, taking over factory jobs, airline passengers being able to make reservations and check themselves unto flights, software that have literally replace some secretaries and clerks, all resulting in more jobs being done by machines. Also among the outputs are computers that can beat world champion grandmasters of chess, can drive cars, remotely control drones that can drop bombs, robots that can go around and inside buildings and allow remote viewing and hearing of all that is going on, and computers that can think, that is, real artificial intelligence. This has resulted in cochlear implants that can restore hearing to the deaf; retinal transplants that can restore sight to the blind and wheel chairs that can be controlled by thought. This is not science fiction. Recently the BBC carried a news clip of a thirty-nine year old woman, deaf from birth, who had received a cochlea transplant and was hearing for the first time. One of the things she said that fascinated her was that when you flicked a light switch it made a sound. She said that she did it about ten times just to be sure.

Brynjolfsson and McAfee make the point that while computers have been built to defeat the best chess players in the world, a moderate chess player working with a mid-range computer can easily defeat computers built to beat the best chess players in the world. In other words, moderately knowledgeable human beings working with computers of reasonable power can be superior to the best available artificial intelligence. The challenge of the future therefore, is to embrace the exponentially increasing power of the microchip making it much more affordable, the use of the connectivity of digital networks with their increasing volume, velocity and variety in order to engage in innovations that enhances organisations, improve communications, solve problems, improve productivity and do whatever we can imagine.

I am well aware of the strides that the Association has been making with the use of information and communication technology with respect to the website, the use of video-conferencing, the building of databases and in the live streaming of events, including this one. I am urging the Association to make significant investments in order to go faster and further in embracing the information revolution because it is not a fad but a fundamental change. It is predicted that by 2017, three years from now, smartphones will constitute approximately 70 percent of all mobile phones sold in the world.

Consider the following as objectives that the JTA will promote and seek to achieve within the next five years that:

a. All members of the Association, and trainee teachers, will own a smartphone or tablet or an Ipad with network connectivity and which will be the device of interaction within the life of the Association outside of face-to-face contact.

b. JTA will be a full-fledged member of the Jamaican REN and of the Caribbean Knowledge and Learning Network engaged in knowledge sharing, virtually, with its counterparts in the Caribbean Union of Teachers and other teachers' organisations worldwide.

c. The Association will have completed its efforts to build comprehensive up-to-date databases of its members which will provide real time data to be used in its decision-making in almost all areas of its operation

d. The JTA website will be the main portal and virtual hub of the Association replete with the full documentation of the Association's history and ongoing operations.

e. The Association will have built a virtual component of the Association that parallels its organisational structure of School, District, Parish, Council, Executive and Conference such that all members of the Association can communicate, participate and interact both horizontally and vertical within the organisation.

f. The virtual infrastructure built by the Association will facilitate the interests groups within the Association so that they become full-pledge communities of practices whether in subject areas such as the Teaching of English, Mathematics, the Sciences, Foreign Languages, Electricity and Electronics, the Performing Arts, Fashion Design or Administration and the different levels of education system or with respect to the application of ICT to the education enterprise etc.

g. The Association will have developed connections with Centres of Excellence of teaching and learning, within the Caribbean and worldwide, such that the expertise of those Centres and the knowledge generated from them, are readily and easily available to Jamaican teachers for consideration and dialogue with respect to their application into Jamaican classrooms.

h. That the Association will be close to completing a comprehensive database of Jamaican teachers in the Diaspora, including information on their location, expertise and teaching experience.

i. The Association will be engaged in cloud computing with respect to problem solving, canvassing opinion of teachers on a wide variety of topics, and holding referenda related to various aspects of its efforts to improve and enhance the conditions of service of teachers.

j. The live streaming of events on the JTA calendar will be a matter of routine.

Part of the idea informing this suggestion that the JTA should fully embrace the information revolution by urgently, and comprehensively applying the technology to itself is that such an explicit and overt exercise will mobilise teachers in utilizing the technology and will engage the Association in innovations that ultimately benefit their students.

Youth as our Future

Teachers work with young people. There is no more intractable and important problem facing the country than issues concerning our young people. Youth represents the future of any and all societies. Generally speaking, young people in the Western World are in trouble and mostly, not all, of their own making. They are coming into the world, and to maturity, during a period of downward economic trajectory, fundamental changes in technology where machines are taking over many functions and jobs previously done by people; and equally fundamental changes in structure of human society as it shifts from its patriarchal origins. Youth in countries such as China, Korea and Brazil, faces similar challenges but do so in the context of countries with an upward economic trajectory, occasioning greater hope or less hopelessness. Jamaica and the rest of the Caribbean has been part of the West for the last 500 years. Hence the issues related to youth are similar to several other countries of the West.

Like all major issues, those related to youth are not uniformly distributed. They affect more males than females, more from the lower than the middle and upper socio-economic groups, more of those living in remote rural areas and urban inner cities, than those in suburbs of cities and towns and more of some ethnic groups than others. Succinctly, the issues related to the young generation are connected with gender, class, race, and religion than with the other main axes of inequality and inequity in human social organisation and its history that is in matters related to social justice in human society.

Over the last 150 years, upward social mobility through education, has been the great hope of marginalised groups in society, including Jamaica. However, in the last 30 years this avenue of upward mobility has been closing at the very time that education opportunities especially at the secondary and tertiary levels have been expanding. The result has been threefold:

First, is the devaluation of educational credentials as higher-levels of credentials are required to obtain access to the same level of opportunity open to previous generations.

Second, is the de-linking of education and upward social mobility as many children are remaining in the same socio-economic circumstances as their parents, but having earned much higher education credentials. Indeed, some are even unemployed.

Third, many social problems previously occurring in society are now in schools, particularly secondary schools, based on the fact that a much larger proportion of the society of that age cohort are now in schools. Hence, violent incidents and matters related to sex are far more prevalent in schools than previously.

To add to the complexity, at least in Jamaica, the teaching profession has been the source of greater upward social mobility for many, especially as a result of the great expansion of schooling over the last 50 years. This pre-disposes some teachers and principals to be less sympathetic to the plight of some students of their social roots, especially those appearing not to be making the efforts or those engaged in antisocial behaviour, and therefore making it easier for them to join the ranks of gatekeepers of the status quo.

As the structural violence related to inequality increases in society, as access to upward social mobility become less likely through the legitimate channels such as education, as hopelessness increases in the segments of the society denied legitimate opportunities particularly among the young, sub-cultures that glorify and justify illegitimate channels, physical violence, prostitution and other antisocial activities can be expected to increase. The issues related to youth therefore are not simply about generation, or gender, or class, or residence. Rather it is about all of these and their inter-relationships.

While structural violence may be a sociological explanation of the rise of anti-social, destructive and sometimes amoral behaviour among youth; it is not a moral justification of such behaviour. Both the structural violence perpetrated and inflicted by those who hold power and advantage in areas of society and the physical, violent and destructive response are independently wrong and reprehensible. Each human being is responsible and accountable for the moral choices he or she makes, regardless of their position in society. Schools and teachers cannot be extricated from these issues, and their complexities, neither can they be neutral in views nor stance. Schools are obliged to adhere to moral behaviour on the part of all members of society irrespective of the social position.

There are many organisations, agencies, and institutions concerned and engaged in activities related to issues affecting youth. These include churches which belong to a wide range of denominations; numerous central and local government agencies; many non-governmental organisations; some service clubs; the security forces; grassroots community organisations including youth groups; several companies and corporations, several philanthropic foundations; as well as schools and colleges engaged in outreach and universities carrying out research. While diversity is rich, conversations with all of these entities with the objectives of coherence, cooperation, coordination and continuity, could be to the benefit of all. This is especially in light of the fact that conversations that do take place are often driven by the agenda of a specific group, or matters of current topics of interest, or some evidence that generates a sense of crisis or alarm.

JTA can make a seminal contribution by sponsoring a Task Force, with a secretariat, for say two years, charged with brokering a comprehensive framework agreement, after consultations with of all of the entities listed and drawing upon the best knowledge nationally, regionally and internationally and bringing its own wisdom to bear. This framework agreement should explicitly include practical and pro-active measures to link education to employment opportunities locally, regionally and internationally through partnerships between colleges, universities, corporations and various levels of governments.

Finding It within Ourselves to Make the Moral Choices

Data from all the recent Surveys of Living Conditions, poverty assessment studies, done over the last five years in the Commonwealth Caribbean, reveal a common pattern. The education gap is narrowing between the richest and the poorest quintiles in terms of literacy, years of primary, years of secondary education and credentials earned in secondary examinations while at the same time the income disparity is widening. It is only at the tertiary level of education that the richest quintile continue to hold significant advantages compared to the poorest quintile. In other words, as populations especially among youths are becoming more equalized, in terms of basic education, incomes are becoming more unequal. Within the Commonwealth Caribbean, this can be partially caused by Governments having much greater control over education policy than economic policy; the latter being subject to the twin influences of external influences and legacy advantages of economic elites. What is amazing in light of these data is that it has become cliché to assert that the answer to the economic stagnation and income inequality is more and better early childhood, primary and secondary education. Further, from current trends, it would appear that tertiary education will be increasingly outside the reach of the poor as a result of cost. What are being virtually ignored are the moral issues: past, present and future:

- Whether it is the 'winner take all' legacy of the social order of colonial history, or

- The 'winner take all' political system that incumbents in parliament are prone to practice, or

- The 'winner take all' trends of modern economy where those who run corporations pay themselves huge salaries compared to the rest of their employees, or

- The 'winner take all' in sports with superstars who are rewarded with huge pay packages, or

- The 'winner take all' Don-run inner-city gangs.

The 'winner take all' approach stretches the gap in material well-being between those in central control and the rest. In the USA, it is characterized by the label of the 1% against the rest. 'Winner take all', in whatever area of human activities becomes the *modus operandi*, and it breeds selfishness, greed, self-aggrandizement, delusions of grandeur, notions of superiority, ingratitude, contempt, arrogance and even idolatry. Among the so-called 'winners' who invariably come to believe in their right to dominate, to rule, to be beyond question or even law. All 'winner take all' systems involve exploitation, most inflict oppression, all leave in their wake misery, frustration, despair, disillusionment, and depression among the vast majority, the so-called 'losers', and all engender resentment and resistance, even if this is muted. Among the so-called 'losers' 'winner take all' engenders fatalism, self-doubt, a paucity of spirit, a lack of will to strive, division, destructive behaviour, resignation to the status quo which traps them to the mindset that this is the way things are, and will ever continue to be.

There is no immunity for schools, unions, churches, and community organisations' from becoming 'winner take all' entities. Indeed, it becomes relatively easy in an ethos where 'winner take all' is spreading. It only takes one set of incumbents to set the precedent of running the school or the union or the church for their own benefit and for subsequent incumbents to follow the precedent, using it as justification. But this is not inevitable if some find it in themselves to reject the concept of 'winner take all'.

Having said so much about the importance of embracing technological revolution, let me immediately say that technology can be and is being used for the common good as well as for 'winner take all'. Here is a Jamaican example of the latter: Montego Bay was the first area of the country in which computers were given to secondary schools, in the late 1980s early 1990s, to promote computer literacy and proficiency. This was done in support of call centres that were established there. It was the first place that the new skill set was developed which required proficiency in the use of ICT; good speaking voices that gave the aura of comfort and competence; persons who could take instructions and carry them out to work on their own with little supervision; and who could achieve results in a timely manner satisfactory to clients. This is the same skills set that in the 2000s was the tool of the lottery scammers, and the association with white collar and violent crime and murder in that section of the country. It is outrageous enough for those who have mastered this new skill set to use it to dupe seniors in the United States out of their savings. It is even more outrageous that some have tried to justify these immoral acts on the grounds that Jamaicans have been hurt by the abuses of trust by Wall Street bankers. Hence the scamming is only payback since it has provided food for poor people in some communities. It is not good enough for youth to simply acquire new knowledge and skills of any kind without also being challenged explicitly with respect to the moral and ethical use of such knowledge and skills.

I sincerely hope that, despite the limitations of language, I have been able to establish that JTA exists today because teacher-leaders of different ethnicities, genders, generations, social backgrounds and nationalities, despite misgivings, past strained relations, different group loyalties, found it in themselves, in 1957, to make the moral choice to give up personal advantages in their respective associations, for the sake of unity among teachers which would serve the common good of the teaching profession in the emerging nation. I hope that I have been able to show you that in the late 1970s, despite great personal animosities, deep distrust, considerable acrimony and frightening violence in the street among party supporters, leaders of the two major political parties and their members in Parliament found it in themselves to make the moral choice, to give up the 'winner take all' electoral system, and to set up the electoral framework for the common good of the country.

The scope and time of this Lecture do not allow me to multiply Jamaican precedents where people, past and present, have found it in themselves to make the moral choice of rejecting 'winner take all' and have committed to the common good of community and country. There are sufficient Jamaican precedents to demonstrate that because 'winner take all' is spreading internationally, that Jamaica can do much better than go with the flow

The point is that noble choices made by previous generations can be overturned by the choices of succeeding generations. There is nothing automatic in either conserving progress made toward achieving the common good or continuing or reverting to 'winner take all' systems that only benefit a few to the disadvantage of the many. If progress toward the common good is to be sustained over time, then the first challenge is to exercise fidelity and be faithful to those choices made by those who went before and in whose footsteps we tread. This is why anniversaries cannot only be sentimental or ceremonial affairs. They must recite and repeat the meaning of the 'milestone'. The second is to expand the areas of progress by confronting and replacing legacy and new 'winner take all systems that will constrain the continued construction of civilised society.

Jamaica in 2014, is confronted by legacy 'winner take all' systems that continue the structural violence that has marked our society from its inception. Added to the legacy is the structural violence of 'winner take all' activities of the modern nouveau riche. The country is also confronted by the 'winner take all' activities of the Don-controlled communities. Trapped in the interstices are numerous good people whose silence is not agreement.

A group that is often maligned but certainly is among the most marginalised and victimized in the country yet constitutes the salt of the earth of our society are single mothers, mainly black. They have limited education, toil in low paying jobs, often doing very menial work. Their earnings are totally consumed in trying to make ends meet. Yet, daily they find it in themselves to do everything to keep their sons in school, and out of gangs, and to keep their daughters in school, and out of relationships that will get them pregnant. They make this sacrifice for one reason only: that their children will have a better life than they have had. We will become a more civilised and moral society when we do justice by these single mothers and their children.

I thank God for those primary school teachers, and principals, who not only teach their children to master the functional skills of basic education but who know their students well, and identify the children of these single mothers described above. These teachers find it in themselves each day to brave the dangers of violence in inner-city communities, or to accept the inconvenience of living and serving in remote rural communities. They encourage and inspire these students, helping them without charge and often at expense to themselves.

I give thanks for those secondary school teachers, and college lecturers, who in addition to teaching their subjects, engage with their students with respect to the values and the virtues that are essential to living constructive and meaningful lives as good human beings and responsible citizens, and then find it in themselves to be exemplars of these values and virtues.

My hope for the Jamaica Teachers Association, going forward, is that it will continue to inspire teachers to unite, and serve our children and adolescents, our nation and our people, the wider Caribbean and the world.

∼

Chapter 14

Enterprise in the Seminary: Profits Serving Prophets

≈

THE LAUNCH OF
THE UTCWI FOUNDATION
April, 1999

≈

Introduction

Mr. Chairman; Your Excellency, Sir Howard Cooke, Governor General; Minister of State, Phyllis Mitchell; President, Dr. Howard Gregory; Deputy President, Members of the Board, the Council, the staff, the students of the United Theological College of the West Indies, (UTCWI) Reverend Fathers and Reverend Mothers I am deeply honoured to be asked to be the guest speaker on this auspicious occasion. Over the life of the College, and my own professional life, the UTCWI has been very generous in inviting me to speak on some very important occasions. I have never really understood this generosity, but will not question it. I simply accept, and recognise how blessed and honoured I am to speak with you on such an evening as this.

I am also very conscious that I am in the presence of the best and most practiced exponents in the art of the spoken word, as well as the greatest critics of speeches: theologians in training. It is hardly possible to be more intimidated. I feel even more so as the circumstances of my life have not allowed me all the preparation I needed. I don't even have any jokes. The reason is that when you think of all the jokes that I have told about parsons, it is quite likely that I will tell some that you may have already heard. Further, there is something fundamentally wrong about stale jokes at the launch of something new.

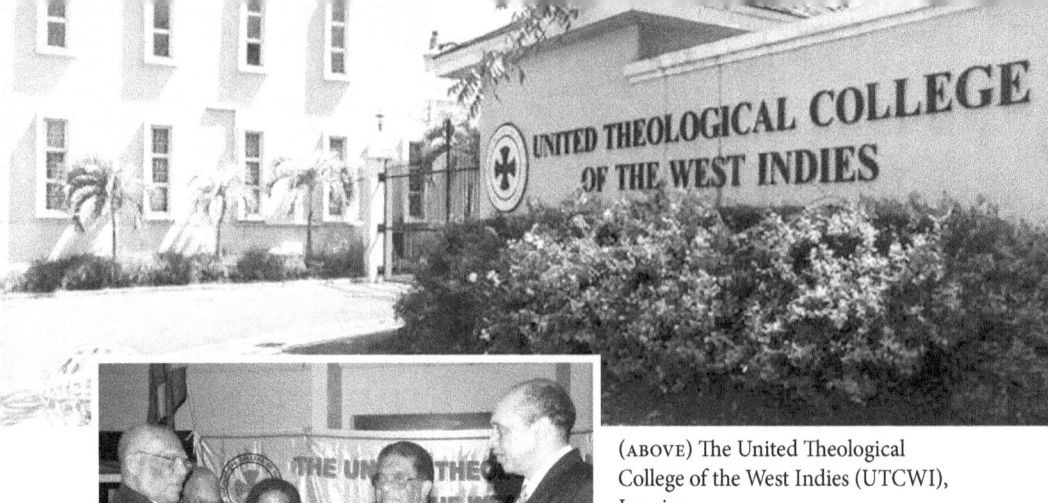

(ABOVE) The United Theological College of the West Indies (UTCWI), Jamaica.

(LEFT) At the April 1999 launch of the Foundation of the United Theological College of the West Indies (UTCWI) which was held at the University of the West Indies, Mona Campus are (L-R) Governor General, Sir Howard Cooke; Richard Nelson; Phyllis Mitchell; and Professor Errol Miller.

©The Gleaner Company Ltd.

However, allow me to share a family incident. You know my interesting family history. I started a bit early and I hope I am ending strong. I have three grandchildren who are older than my daughter and they are all under 10 years old. This summer the three grandkids were visiting from the US. They and my daughter were getting ready to go to Sunday school and church. The grandkids were returning shortly, hence, as an exception, I promised that on that Sunday evening I would take them to the cinema see "Star Wars". On getting ready to go to Sunday school, one of them reported feeling sick, and everybody got sick. We were around the breakfast table, so I said, "Look, anybody who is so sick that they can't go to Sunday school and church will not be well enough to go to "Star Wars" this evening." Whereupon my grandson shouted out, "I'm healed brother, I'm healed!"

On reflection, this illustrates the power of television, of modern communications. I don't think that when I was his age I would immediately shout out that often repeated phrase associated with healing. There was no doubt that he had heard the phrase on several instances of dramatic healing on television. This is the age of the emotive video clip, the compelling sound bite, and the dramatic newspaper headline; all designed to command attention. In this regard, probably the only memorable thing that I could do this evening; is to give you a caption to this occasion.

But before I do so, allow me a nostalgic moment. It is 25 years ago that I met Sir Howard for the first time on the 1st of April 1974. He and I joined the Ministry of Education on that day: he as Minister of Education and I as Permanent Secretary. I knew of him as a legendary teacher but had not met him before. Much has been said about Sir Howard. I am adding this as an absolute truth. In the time that I was his Permanent Secretary, I can tell you, Sir Howard never once practiced partisan politics, and never once asked me to do anything that was not absolutely above board. It was a pleasure to work with him. I can testify to his Christian character not from afar, but from the close dealings on the floor of the political process. One of the things that always amazed me about Sir Howard was how quickly he would grasp complex issues and how eloquent he was. As civil servants, we would work on cabinet submissions and other important documents for weeks, even months. Then we would brief him for an hour or two, sometime before he presented these documents to Cabinet or Parliament or on some important occasion. Then when you heard Sir Howard make these presentations, if you did not know, you could readily believe that he developed these ideas from scratch and wrote the documents himself. It was really a pleasure working with you Sir Howard, I hold you Sir in the highest regard.

Theological Education and Enterprise: A Novel Idea

We are gathered here this evening to launch the United Theological College of the West Indies Foundation: The UTCWI Foundation. My caption for this occasion is "Enterprise in the Seminary: Profits serving Prophets". It is this caption that gives focus to my thoughts about this very special occasion.

Theological Colleges, Seminaries, and academies represent the oldest forms of tertiary education in the world and in the Caribbean. Theological colleges have been the pioneers in the development of this level of education, and indeed of education itself. Indeed, contrary to common sense, education started from the top and moved down; and not from the bottom and moved up.

The President explained that it took six years to get from idea to this launch. It would seem that the theological community is not easy to convince on matters of innovation. The Mico was the first to establish a Foundation of a college or school in Jamaica. It was my honour to have led in its formation. The purpose is to enhance the Mico Community in its mission to prepare teachers. The late 1970s were 'socialist' times. Profits were not respectable, so without baptism, we called the excess of income over expenditure, "surplus". It took me three years to convince the Board of the Mico College to establish the Mico Foundation in 1980. The Mico Foundation is still going strong.

Recently, the Mico Foundation, under the leadership of its Principal, Mr. Renford Shirley, completed the construction of a 20,000 square foot, 3-story Library/Museum/Resource Centre. It did so without any gift or grant from any government or donation from any bilateral or multilateral donor agency. Most impressive is the fact that the Mico Foundation has not taken out any mortgage and does not owe any money for the construction of this major and massive building. This building has been constructed from the efforts and enterprise of the Mico community, spearheaded by its foundation. This is a mere 19 years after the establishment of the Foundation. There can be no doubt that the Mico Foundation has made the case for the concept of the foundation, of enterprise within the Tertiary Institutions, in Jamaica and the Caribbean.

Translated into this launch, enterprise in the seminary is definitely a new and novel idea. It speaks to the potential of generating profits that will serve prophets. It was to my great fortune that after graduating from the University of the West Indies, I was given my first job in teaching, by the Honourable A. Wesley Powell, of Excelsior. Mr. Powell saw in me potential that I did not know I had. He took me as a sort of protégé and taught me many lessons that have served me well in my professional career. He told me that as a young man in the 1930s and 1940s, a popular saying was "Here abideth these three: Colour, Class and Cash, but the greatest of the three is Cash." On this basis, he concluded that you could have the greatest educational ideas in the world, if you couldn't get the money to implement them, little would be accomplished.

In a pragmatic sense, it is necessary to generate income from more than just the traditional budgetary sources in order to: (i) explore new possibilities, (ii) engage with innovations that are required in education, and (iii) deliver a level and a quality that would not otherwise be possible. So there can be no question that additional income can always be deployed constructively in educational institutions. It is also true that there are limits to donations and gifts from the community of well-wishers of schools and colleges. While the idea of a foundation takes account of gifts and donations it goes beyond that. It also includes generating income from enterprise.

What is intriguing and interesting is this notion of income-generating enterprise being embraced at the very heart of theological education.

Theological education has long been supported by financial obligations bourn by churches and gifts from supporters and sympathizing individuals. Income earned from enterprise within the Seminary requires close examination.

The Temple as the Original Place of Economic Exchange

It is not published yet, but my latest book is titled: *The Prophet and the Virgin: the Masculine and Feminine Roots of Teaching*. I have spent time, consistently over the last 18 or 19 years, researching and writing this book. I am grateful to two fellowships from the Fulbright Foundation and a sabbatical year from the University of the West Indies which assisted me along the way. Because schooling came out of the education for priests, during the sabbatical, I spent more time in theological libraries than anywhere else. That book is my personal magnum opus. I am not sure how many will take the time to read it because it is painstaking in its build up. It is my attempt to understand myself as a teacher, the mission of teachers in society and what it means to educate and train teachers. Some of what I have learned from this exploration is germane to this launch, so pardon me in starting from a point which may appear remote.

Initially, small extended families, clans and lineages, lived in relative isolation. They practiced their own language, with their own culture, provided for their subsistence, and engaged in their own physical and spiritual defence. They were self-sufficient. As populations grew, there was the transition from nomadic to sedentary patterns of living. Settled living marked the dawn of civilisation as different clans and lineages began living in shared spaces, settling in villages, and engaged in growing crops and raising domesticated animals. As surpluses of products were generated in some clans and lineages, these products began to be exchanged by barter for surpluses generated by other clans and lineages.

The pattern was for each extended family, lineage or clan to provide for its own subsistence and survival which included food, shelter, mates, physical defence and ritual defence. However, the generation of surplus allowed for the emergence of the priesthood, the first non-manual occupation, as ritual defence became a specialized function. Priests assumed primacy over patriarchs of lineages, and clans, in performing this collective and cooperative function within temples. As such, temples became the first public space in the communities that were formed.

As economic exchange spread to more than between neighbours, economic exchanges were also made in temples. The issue of economic exchange, bartering with another lineage of another bloodline was no small matter. Such exchanges needed to be transacted in the temple so that they could be sanctioned by the Gods, witnessed by priests, and sealed by sacred vows. Economic exchanges needed to be manifestly ethical and sacred, given the fact that people who were increasingly engaged in such exchanges were not bonded by blood.

To bolster the fidelity of the temple and to demonstrate their integrity, priests developed a system of accounting. For example, in Sumerian civilisation, priests used clay tokens of different denominations to record the numbers of items stored or exchanged; and clay envelopes in which to secure tokens recording transactions. The clay envelopes were then sealed appropriately. Later, pictographs were engraved and baked on the surfaces of envelopes to indicate their contents.

Writing was invented in the temple by priests. This happened after the revolution in agricultural productivity with the invention of the wheel, the metal plough and the harnessing of animals with ploughs to engage in land preparation. With many, and more types of products being exchanged, markets in the temple expanded. Consequently, there was a need to strengthen, and give manifest evidence of their morality by the existing systems of counting, accounting and also by written documentation of transactions.

The point here is that from very early in the emergence of economic exchange in human civilisation, markets were located in temples as unrelated, and marginally-related clans and lineages came to live together and trade goods among themselves. Approval of the goods, witnessed by the priests, and vows made by the participants, made the transactions sacred. At least this was the assumption and expectation. Priests, probably as a result of bitter experiences, invented systems of counting, accounting and written documentation, not only to be accountable but also to clearly demonstrate the morality of their stewardship in the markets. In other words, every effort was made initially to ensure that markets were moral.

The Estrangement of the Temple from Markets

From this beginning, the history of the separation of markets from morality is still to be written. By the time of Jesus, markets located in the temple had been compromised. Given the audience to which I speak, I wish to indicate that I am being very careful in my next sentence:

An incident of Jesus taking physical action against people, engaged in economic exchange in the Temple in Jerusalem, is recorded in all four Gospels. This signifies, that what Jesus said, and did, were very significant.

All Gospels state that Jesus did not argue.

He acted.

His action showed his outrage.

The Gospels of Mathew, Mark and Luke are agreed on the reason for His outraged action:

> "My father's house is a house of prayer, but you have made it a den of thieves".

The contrast is clear. The temple is sacred. The trading, in money and doves, was being conducted immorally. This violated the sacredness of the temple. There was no need for argument. The action of Jesus in dismissing the moneychangers from the temple is often quoted as a physical act. However, it has to be understood not only as a physical act but as a symbolic point at which economic exchange had most decidedly lost contact with morality and ethics. The temple no longer provided the sacred foundation for the conduct of business.

Markets did leave temples.

Temples have continued to be sacred places. However, markets and business do not appear to have recovered from their moral lapse. Evidence of this currently is the oft-repeated cliché 'it is business' as an explanation for lack of conscience in some deals. This seems to indicate that morality, on the one hand, and business and markets on the other hand, are estranged. Some would say that markets and business appear to be largely amoral. They are geared to the bottom line of profit, however it may be achieved. People now speak with awe about market forces, and the invisible hand of the market, as if it was some mysterious mechanism to keep markets honest. However, just as I am grammatically challenged sometimes, and many who speak and write the English language perfectly are mathematically challenged, if the invisible hand of the market is made visible, the means of its manipulation would be exposed and its moral challenge revealed.

Against this background, when the seminary embraces enterprise, and establishes a foundation, capable of not only receiving gifts and donations, but also mandated to do business, it is natural to expect cautions and caveats. Such cautions and caveats are required whether the foundation is a limited liability company, for profit or not-for-profit. The only real distinction between these two forms of incorporation is that the 'not-for-profit' foundations do not share any of its surplus with the Government through the payment of taxes.

Being keenly aware that you are conscious of the differences between priests and prophets and that in the narrative of beginnings of the priesthood, temples and markets; I have omitted the seminary as an educational institution, before proceeding with cautions and caveats, allow me to return to the narrative of beginnings in order to specifically address the seminary as an educational institution with its own identity and mission. This is essential to the caption of this launch: "Enterprise in the Seminary: Profits Serving Prophets".

Invention of Schools to Train Scribes for the Palace

Writing was invented and the scribal art practiced in temples at least 1000 years before schools were created. Priests who practiced the scribal art apparently learned and passed on this skill and knowledge of writing and reading through some system of apprenticeship involving master scribes. I will follow the history of schooling as it was invented in Sumer, since Sumer claims primacy over Egypt in the invention of writing and schools.

Some prosperous villages clustered together to form ancient cities principally to protect their prosperity from raiding rivals. Accordingly, most ancient cities were protected by walls, had farmers who doubled as warriors, and appointed kings from among their most successful warriors. Kings acquired wealth. They imposed taxes to pay for the defence and administrative services of their city states. Palaces therefore came to need counting, accounting and documentation systems similar to those of temples. At first, scribes from the temples were recruited to administer these systems of the palace. However, kings soon desired their own scribes.

It is in this context that schools in city states of Sumer first arose. They were called the edubba. These first schools were sponsored by the palace but used the curriculum that had been developed in the temple for training scribes. These first schools were intended to provide personnel for public administration. They trained scribes in the art of writing, reading, and operations of the areas in which they would work. The classified and stored the clay tablets with their writing. They distributed written tablets. The edubba was a school, a library and a scriptorium in one. Teachers, librarians and publishers have common roots of origin as non-manual occupations.

Students entered as children and left as adults. Edubba provided instruction from the fundamentals to higher-level learning. Schools developed as a single-level institution that started with the fundamentals and concluded with occupational training of scribes. Schooling started from the top down and not the bottom up; as subsequently the academy providing scribal training was separated from the reading school, which taught the fundamentals. This two-tier system of schooling persisted, for more than 1500 years, before the intermediary level of secondary education emerged between the elementary level and the academy.

Prophets and the Need of Kings
to be Informed of the Future

As city states grew, and palaces expanded, kings extended their reach, scribes began to explore areas of knowledge and to develop areas of expertise that were of importance to kings. These included keeping kings and their courtiers, healthy and foretelling the future. Kings needed to make decisions in which some glimpse into the future gave them the advantage. From Biblical sources, we are mostly aware of expertise in the interpretation of dreams. Probably not so well known, but more widely used, was foretelling the future based upon examining the entrails of animals offered as sacrifice to the gods. Pardon this aside, but although modern methods of advising leaders of states, claim to be much more scientific, there is good reason to suspect that they have not altogether lost their ancient connection with tripe.

More to the point is that within the scribal occupation and training, a prophetic stream developed, whether in attempting to forecast the future, on whatever basis, or advocacy for constructing a future based upon belief systems. These beliefs spawned visions, values and virtues that were considered consistent with the perceived origin and claimed destiny of particular city states and their citizenry.

City states formed into kingdoms because of the dominance of the warrior class either in the defence or expansion of territory. It is a matter of debate, well beyond the scope of this address, as to whether priests co-opted kings, or warrior-kings co-opted priests. It is abundantly clear though, that warriors, kings, priests, and scribes/scholars were the most visible and important personages in the governance of ancient states. Wars produced warriors and kings. In the monotheistic religions of Judaism, Islam and Christianity it is the academy that produced priests and scribes/prophets.

There is a very rich, variegated and colourful history of the combinations and permutations of the relationships between kings, priests, scribes and prophets. Indeed, some kings became emperors, then chief priests, and elevated themselves to the status of gods; some priests became kings and emperors; dissident priests challenged the orthodoxy, were declared heretics and even executed, but today are great martyrs of the faith. But two traditions repeated themselves through the ages: prophets of the palace who told the king what he wanted to hear, not necessarily out of conviction, but more so out of dependence for material well-being and prophets of the people who confronted kings at great peril to themselves.

UTCWI and the Need for Profits in Training Prophets

It is against this history, that UTCWI now launches a foundation to engage in businesses that generate profits to support its mission to prepare prophets and priests for the Caribbean region. It is also against this history that we must take account of the cautions and caveats that must constrain the UTCWI Foundation.

In the first place, the UTCWI is owned by the participating denominations which have come together by ecumenical agreement for the purpose of preparing clergy. The Foundation is a corporate steward of the UTCWI. The Foundation does not own the College but is owned by the College. However, the UTCWI owner will give the Foundation access to its buildings and equipment, the talents and expertise of staff and students and the goodwill of the name, UTCWI, so that the Foundation can use these resources profitably and for the profits so generated to be employed in service of the mission of the UTCWI to educate and train prophets and priests for the Caribbean region.

The decision of the Board of the UTCWI to establish this Foundation clearly demonstrates its recognition of three important facts:

First, that the entrepreneurial potential of schools and colleges are grossly under-estimated and greatly underdeveloped. Classrooms, boarding accommodation and other resources often lie idle when they could be utilized. The gifts, talents and expertise of staff and students have economic value. There are unmet demands that can be supplied and unsolved problems waiting for enterprising solutions.

Second, that given scarce resources, and pressing needs, the denominations that form the College are hard-pressed to meet their obligations. Supplementary means have to be found to maintain and enhance the capital assets of the College as well as to meet felt needs have staff and students that are outside the statutory requirements.

Third, that such limited entrepreneurial actions that are taken, are ad hoc and mostly undertaken by individuals. Accordingly, as an act of responsibility in the management of the College, the Board needs to take a more systematic and corporate approach to entrepreneurship in order to maximize the gains that could be made.

Business is not inherently immoral or amoral. Many businesses are conducted ethically, at least for the most part. If profits can be generated morally, why then should there be any cautions or caveats to constrain the operations of the Foundation given the Board's sound, strategic decision to establish it? Is it prudent to burden and hamstring the Foundations with caveats and caution before it even begins to operate?

Mandatory Cautions and Caveats

The short answers are simple. First, single-minded focus on the bottom line of profit, which is then used as justification to make money by 'any means' possible, is not an option for a Foundation that serves theological education. The bottom line of profit by the 'any means' approach to business has earned for business, a moral taint which is not fatal to business but will certainly be fatal to theological education. Profits earned by morally tainted means will undoubtedly compromise, at least perceptually, the prophets and priests who benefit from their use. Business conducted by the Foundation must be manifestly moral in the means that are employed. Second, prophets and priests are by no means immune from being seduced by financial gain or being silenced in the exercise of their calling by dependence on the powerful or the desire to please the powerful. I am not sufficiently schooled in biblical interpretation to determine whether or not Levites doing duties in the temple were among the moneychangers or vendors of doves, or whether the priests in charge of the temple permitted money changing and dove vending. But what is abundantly clear, by the words and actions of Jesus, was that the corruption in the Court of the Gentiles had become systemic. It had become a den of thieves by commission or omission of the priesthood. It was not just that individual priests had become corrupted.

However, there is an even more profound danger to be avoided when church institutions become engaged in enterprise and entrepreneurial activities. Allow me to return to the act of Jesus in the Temple at Jerusalem. As some of you may be aware, I have done quite a bit of academic writing on the subject of marginalisation. I promise you only a small connection here. The people of God are commanded to bring their tithes and offerings into the storehouse. Then Scripture commands that the tithes should be used to address the needs of the widow, the orphan, the alien and the Levite. It is fairly straightforward to understand that widows, orphans and aliens were among the marginalised of ancient Hebrews. However, additional explanation is needed to establish why Levites were also marginalised.

I do not need to tell this audience that among the twelve tribes of Israel, the tribe of Levi was assigned responsibility to preside over the worship of

Jehovah in the Tent of Meeting/Tabernacle, and then in the temple, and to teach the Israelites the meaning of the sacrifices, ceremonies and anniversaries. Of the tribe of Levi, the direct descendants of Aaron, were the priests and the other members of the tribe, who were referred to as Levites. The Levites carried out various roles and functions in the temple, including being assistants to the priests, guards, musicians, scribes and teachers. When the Israelites entered the Promise Land and Joshua distributed the lands, the tribe of Levi was excluded from the distribution of land. The tribe of Levi was marginalised with respect to the major source of material wealth in ancient society because of the central spiritual role they were assigned to play in the worship of God in tabernacle and later the temple. In return, the other tribes were to pay tithe for the sustenance of the priests and the Levites.

The outer court, the Court of the Gentiles, was the only part of the temple to which strangers, aliens, could have access. Money changing and the purchasing of doves for sacrifice was a service to Jews who journeyed from afar to the temple and to Gentiles who came to worship Jehovah. The poor sacrificed doves. Surely the selling of doves at close to cost was a legitimate service. Probably, a small surplus could be justified. The abomination was that priests and Levites, deliberately marginalised in the pursuit of material wealth, and centralised in the worship of God in the temple, either permitted or participated, or both, in the exploitation of the poor, the Jews who were strangers to Jerusalem, the poor and alien Gentiles who had come to worship God. This was perversity compounded. It was wrong on several levels. Jesus could not abide it. It was beyond argument. Only decisive action would suffice.

God has called, separated and set aside those who are earthly representatives of His Kingdom. Those engaged in theological education are in training to perform central spiritual roles in the Kingdom of God. Part of their calling is the separation of the pursuit of mammon. While there is the responsibility to be good stewards of the physical and financial resources connected to this calling, the management of those resources must be manifestly moral at several different levels. The UTCWI Foundation must not offer services, do business and make investments that involve exploitation of the marginalised in society. God forbids this. It is an abomination. Profits derived by such mean have no place in the Seminary or in training prophets and priests.

I hope that I have clearly shown that the Board of UTCWI is prudent and responsible in establishing a Foundation to be a corporate steward of the resources that has been given to the College for the purpose of ministerial training. I hope that I have been abundantly clear that the Foundation in doing business, receiving and deploying gifts and donations must do so morally and ethically. This is an obligation to man, woman and God. Allow me to conclude with the main mission of the Foundation.

The Mission of the UTCWI Foundation

Background

From the beginning of the ancient city states, the sphere of work and influence of priests and prophet were not confined to temples. It was the temple that first provided priest/administrators for the palace. It was the temple that provided the curriculum for first academies created by the palace. Indeed, what is today regarded as classical and academic education first began as vocational training for priests. As I listened to Dr. Gregory report some of the comments made about new practices implemented at the College, it would seem that while some things change, many of the reactions to change remain the same. It is recorded that at first in the Jewish academies of Shammai and Hillel, students had to stand through their classes while they were taught Torah. Standing honoured the law. When in time students were allowed to sit, some teachers and scholars of the past were dismayed. They claimed that by allowing students to sit, the glory had departed from the teaching of Torah.

One substantive pattern that has remained down the centuries is that prophets have been of two basic types: (i) Prophets of the palace who told kings what they wanted to hear. They probably lived comfortably in the palace, or the glamour of being closely allied to power which seemed to silence prophetic utterance, or dull its edge; and (ii) Prophets independent from the palace who facilitated dependence on divine revelation, although it put the prophets of the Lord at great personal risk. Even kings realised this. For example, having heard from the prophets of his palace, King Zedekiah was very skeptical of the xenophobic political scenarios they had laid out to him. Zedekiah sent for Jeremiah, where in private audience, he asked Jeremiah, 'Is there any word from the Lord'?

Jeremiah, a prophet of the Lord, told Zedekiah what he needed to hear but did not want to know.

Looking Ahead to the Future

We build on these lessons from the past—of respect, and honour and truth. So now, we are at the end of the twentieth century; the dawn of the twenty-first century and a new millennium is at hand. Many people are speaking with euphoria about the prospects of the new century, especially in the area of technology. It is my practice to change out my computers every four or five years. I recently taught my little three-year old to use my old computer. I was watching her. She is extremely facile with the mouse in pointing and clicking but she has not yet learned to read. When the programme stops working and a message comes up on the screen, she comes to me for help. The message is usually 'This program has performed an illegal operation.' We are all very familiar with this message. I have taught her to click "OK". I now get fewer calls for help. Just think of the possibilities where technology empowers us with new methods of learning and new ways of working. It's mind-boggling.

However, look beyond technological inventions and innovations. We are living at a time of increasing economic polarization. The rich countries are becoming richer and the poor countries are becoming poorer. The rich in the rich countries, and the rich in the poor countries are becoming richer. Alternatively, the poor in the rich countries and the poor in the poor countries are becoming poorer. Economic polarization is being compounded between and within countries.

Paradoxically, the call is for social inclusion.

Everybody is to be included socially when large numbers are being excluded economically. It is social equality in the context of deepening economic polarization.

What purpose should theological education serve in these times?

Surely it cannot be to get people to accept the contradiction and to behave themselves. The church cannot simply be an instrument by which to pacify people who are being excluded and exploited. At the same time, the anti-imperialist posture and experiment of the 1970s failed.

"Is there no word from the Lord?"

Pardon my layman's understanding of identifying who is the prophet. In that understanding, the prophet is not only somebody who barks at those who strays from the straight and narrow way, but in essence, the prophet of the people and of the Lord, has always had a vision of a people and of a society. That vision has always been cast in noble terms, in terms that recognise the best in human potential and human society and the ideal of God's intention of His creation. Invariably, prophets of the people have always been confronted by the fact that small, marginalised people have little chance against the powers of the world if they contest with those powers on the terms of military and economic might.

We can take a look, as an example, at the small nation called Israel, located between the powers of western Mediterranean and the powers of North Africa. On one side were the Assyrians, the Babylonians, the Persians, the Greeks and the Romans and on the other side were the Egyptians. In fact, the reason why David is celebrated in his victory over Goliath is that it was one of the few occasions that David won. On most of the other occasions, Goliath won. Israel was beaten up and oppressed by every major power: Assyria, Babylon, Medes and Persians, Greece and Rome. But it was the prophets, not kings that formulated the basis of Israel's survival. "Not by might, nor by power but by my spirit."

Prophecy and spirituality must take account of time and place. For example, the School of the Prophet in the Caribbean cannot only be a school about scribal arts: classical and academic learning. Neither can prophets be a-historical and a-sociological. The United Theological College of the West Indies has to be about prophetic vision, destiny and spirit applied to the Caribbean in these modern times. God is spirit. His Holy Spirit is with us. I am speaking therefore, of the spirit that needs to be engendered in us, by His Grace, and nurtured by those who are called to be leaders of His people, here in this place, at this time. It is:

A spirit that will not be run over by the powerful.

A spirit that will not be crushed by might.

A spirit that will not be disillusioned by difficult circumstances.

A spirit that does not require sufficiency as a condition for success.

This is an indomitable spirit marked by the will to creatively, and constructively, confront the circumstances of the time and to emerge in ways that demonstrate:

God enables the marginalised—if they do His Will, obey His Word and walk in His Way.

I believe that there is something unique about us in the Caribbean. I believe as a people we have a unique destiny to fulfil. The following anecdote is only one way that demonstrates how we are perceived: The former Vice Chancellor of the University of the West Indies, Sir Alister McIntyre, worked with the United Nations for close to 25 years, and he tells the story that at a farewell function, held in his honour, someone said to him:

"You know we can always recognise a person from the Caribbean".

Sir Alister replied, "Oh yes, how?"

The person then said, 'Well in the United Nations system, the Africans speak to the Africans, the Asians speak to the Asians, the Europeans speak to the Europeans, the Latin Americans speak to the Latin Americans but Caribbean people talk to everybody!"

There is a sense in which we have come to understand, in the most fundamental way, the common humanity of all of humankind. This understanding resides in the spiritual, not the material.

The materialist dream put forward by communism and by capitalism is fast becoming not only a dream deferred but a dream denied to the vast majority of people in the world. Wealth and power are being concentrated in fewer and fewer hands. The fact that Moscow has bought into the market does not mean that capitalism has triumphed. It only means that communism is collapsing first. As these two materialistic systems stagger to their collapse, in several parts of the world, there is a return to historical divisions and the ancient enmities.

We in the Caribbean have gone too far down the road of understanding the common humanity of all of human kind to turn back. We have a destiny to continue on the road, recognising that we are all God's children, now located in this region, with a destiny to construct a new civilisation and society based on the common humanity of human kind.

The founding fathers of the United States, for all their limitations in owning slaves and suppressing women, had a glimpse of this new civilisation and society, despite the contradictions of their own lives. Indeed, they had a prophetic vision of a people:

"We hold these things to be self-evident that all people are created equal and have the right to life, liberty and the pursuit of happiness".

Currently, in the United States, this prophetic vision of the founding fathers has been translated into a materialistic dream of a two-story colonial, a three car garage, and a four martini lunch. Tragically, we in the Caribbean seem to be embracing the American materialist dream and not the spiritual vision of the founding fathers of America. This is at the same time that the global political economy is denying the means of realization of this materialistic dream, mostly to young people and particularly to young men from disadvantaged groups.

The profits of this Foundation must be deployed to prepare prophets who will help us hear the Word from the Lord as it speaks to destiny, repentance and justice. I do not need to spell out what repentance means with respect to man's relationship to God. However, some elaboration is needed with respect to what social repentance means in the Caribbean.

Caribbean societies were not established on foundations of any noble vision of people or society. Caribbean colonies were colonies of exploitation. The goal was for a few to make it rich even at the expense of the many. At first, the many were British bond-servants who were quickly outnumbered by African slaves.

Unmindful imitation of the past and continuation of the status quo perpetuates the exploitative foundations of our societies. Social repentance is needed among those who hold power and command major resources. These endowments cannot be mainly for their benefit and for their relatives and clients. Power must be exercised and resources used for the common good of community. Social repentance is needed among those who are co-opted by the powerful, and the rich, to administer and manage public and private bureaucracies. It is also needed among the rebels who seek to overthrow current incumbents not to change the system but so that they will be in power and own the major resources. The message of prophets has to be directed and delivered to the potentates, moguls, bureaucrats and don-men in our societies. The mission is conversion from exploitation of the many to the common good of all.

For reasons of historical accuracy, and with reference to the denominations that own the United Theological College of the West Indies, it must be said that the mission of social repentance alongside spiritual reference begun nearly 250 years ago with the arrival of Moravian missionaries in the West Indies—the first arrivals among the non-conformist denominations. In nineteenth century Jamaica, the Baptists and Methodists were the spearheads. It cannot be overlooked that there were always a few dissident Anglican priests and Presbyterian ministers engaged in the mission. Indeed, after the disestablishment of the Anglican Church in 1870 their activities came to the forefront especially in education and health.

The call therefore, is not to commence the mission of social justice but rather to continue that mission in contemporary times. In this regard, let me point out that social injustice is institutionalized in the institutions that serve the mass of Caribbean populations. It is manifest in public primary school systems; public hospitals and health clinics; the jails of police stations; resident magistrate courts; and in polling stations. The manifestations are in infrastructure and relationships in which there are overtones of social class and undertones of race and colour. It is with the added complication that this behaviour, once characteristic of white racists, are observed among blacks, browns and Indians. Herein lies the great challenge in the preparation of prophets for these times. The weekly cries for 'Justice', heard across the region, underscore the stark reality and urgency of the challenge. The profits of the Foundation must be deployed to prepare prophets for words and actions of spiritual and social redemption.

Finally, the profits of the Foundation must help the College to show mercy within the College community. Two imperatives that drove me to engage in entrepreneurial activities as the Principal of The Mico were debt, that the College owed, and the need to show mercy. The debt of the College was related to the fact that Government subvention covered nine months but the College expenses for such things as utilities were for 12 months. Two examples of showing mercy should suffice:

1. The College employed just over 200 ancillary workers, half of whom were temporarily employed. When the College went to break at Christmas, Easter and summer they had no work therefore, the workers got no pay. This was a real hardship to these employees.

2. Tragedies occur in the lives of people within the College community that demand more than sympathy. Taking up collections to assist is less than desirable.

The College addressed these challenges

First, the College had hostels with boarding accommodation of 520 beds. Operating the hostels as hotels during the vacation periods produced a triple result. It allowed the College to balance its annual budget; provided the temporary workers with employment during times that they were previously laid off and gave the permanent workers some extra income; and it generated surplus.

In the meetings with representatives of the academic, administrative and ancillary staffs to discuss how the surpluses generate by this and other ventures should be deployed to help employees of the College it was agreed to establish a revolving loan scheme for each category of staff where it was possible to borrow between one to three month's pay, interest free, to be paid back in one year, through salary deduction. Having left the Mico for several years now, I am told that in the more than 25 years since those schemes have been established there has not been a single default. The staff has seen to that.

The ancillary staff wanted to improve their education through taking classes in the Evening College. It was agreed to use part of surpluses either to provide the courses at no cost or with a substantial subsidy. Some wanted courses to assist them to help their children with home works, others to learn particular skills, and still others to obtain formal credentials like the GCE 'O' Levels. What no one foresaw was the transformation in relationships that would occur when ancillary workers entered the classroom as students and the academic staff taught them. There was new respect all-round. I still remember the General Assembly at the beginning of one College year when among the first year students was a young groundsman, who had obtained his 'O' Levels, and was admitted to the College. It is one of the General Assemblies that almost everyone attended. Some staff members, of all categories, wept.

Showing mercy is not sentimental expression. Mercy helps people to overcome hardships; to recover from tragedies with dignity; to maintain respect in their families; and to seize opportunities of upward mobility. Mercy is caring in practical and meaningful ways. May the profits made by the

Foundation allow UTCWI to care for and show mercy to members of the College community who help to prepare prophets for ministry within the Caribbean.

God bless the United Theological College of the West Indies Foundation as it seeks to generate profits to support prophets in training for their mission in the region.

❧

President of South Africa, Thabo Mbeki receives the Keys to the City of Kingston from Mayor of Kingston, Councillor Marie Atkins, as Town Clerk, Errol Greene looks on.

Chapter 15

An Introduction to Kingston

~

PRESENTATION OF
THE KEYS OF THE CITY OF KINGSTON
TO PRESIDENT THABO MBEKI
June, 2003

~

President Thabo Mbeki, President of South Africa; Mayor, Marie Atkins, Mayor-Elect, Senator Desmond McKenzie; Mrs. Portia Simpson-Miller, Minister of Local Government; specially invited guests, ladies and gentlemen, I am more than conscious of the signal honour that has been bestowed on me to give the main address at this ceremony, this afternoon. At the same time, this great privilege has left me in a deep quandary.

What can I say to a man who has succeeded the giant Nelson Mandela, and is not considered a midget even by his most ardent detractors.

What can I say to the Leader of the African National Congress, which fought and triumphed over one of the most oppressive and heinous systems of oppression the world has seen—Apartheid.

What can I say to a leader who, in victory, has not embarked upon revenge and retribution, but rather, has started the journey down the road of reconciliation.

What can I say to the Leader of a nation that has had the moral courage to seek reconciliation through truth, truth not only from the oppressors with respect to what they did but also from the oppressed in terms of what they did to resist the oppression.

For you, Mr. President, in continuing to lead your country down the road of reconciliation through truth, has not only given the world an example of African civilisation at its best, but has demonstrated by deeds the Biblical injunction: "You shall know the truth and the truth shall set you free". Thus the way is opened to build South Africa on a moral and social foundation different from its Apartheid past.

Jamaica, the first country to impose sanctions on the Apartheid government of South Africa, salutes you and your people, for choosing a different path from the vengeance and recrimination that is so rampant in our world.

Mr. President, your Worship the Mayor, Madam Minister, Ladies and Gentlemen, fortunately my search has revealed one small subject on which I can address our illustrious and esteemed visitor. It is Kingston. I am a Kingstonian. So are my parents and three of my four grandparents. I can trace Kingstonian ancestry going back five generations. Sir, most of the residents of this great city, are people whose roots are elsewhere, hence their love and loyalty belong to some other place. In these circumstances I feel obliged to share with you my love for my city called Kingston.

As you can see, Kingston exists in continuous embrace of a semi-circle of hills and mountains. You can't see it from here but I can assure you that Kingston is kissed daily by the Caribbean Sea. Indeed, this City boasts one of the best natural deep water harbours in the world.

I doubt if you will be here long enough to see the full moon as its rises over the hills on the eastern side of the City, but I can tell you that the Mona Moon, as it is called, is as enchanting as it is beguiling. Couples, young and old, have exchanged endearments in the serene brightness of its night light.

I hope that you will be here long enough to look, from the shoreline, at clouds flirting with the majestic peaks of yonder Blue Mountain. Also, that you will be taken up to any of the surrounding hills to see some of the breathtaking views of the Liguanea plains as it slopes gently down to the sea; especially at nights.

I am sure that you have been briefed on the violence that sometimes erupts on the streets of Kingston and sometimes in its homes. I must agree that the beauty of Kingston's physical appointment is sometimes defaced by brutality of the violence that far too often occurs. We Kingstonians are pained by this defacement and take no comfort from the fact that such defacement is common in many other cities around the world, whose physical appointment is no match to that of Kingston. Like these other cities, we, in Kingston search to find the source of the alienation, especially of our young men, and by so doing, attempt to bring them back into harmony with their society and surroundings.

While violence in Kingston is highly publicised, one of its best kept secrets is the range and diversity of the creative expressions of its citizens. You have to go to cities three or four times the size of Kingston to find plays, concerts, exhibitions, festivals, dancehall sessions and shows that cater to such widely divergent tastes and styles. The point is that violence does not define the character of Kingston. The character of Kingston resides in its vibrancy and vitality. Life, not death, is the hallmark of this City. It is its vim, vigour and vivacity that capture and captivate those of us who live in and love this City.

Mr. President, Kingston comes with all of the contradictions and paradoxes of human existence. Kingston comes with beauty and brutality, magnificence and misery, violence and vitality, triumph and tragedy all accruing at the same time. It is this dynamic nature that allows Kingston to successfully host:

- The World Junior Games, last year June
- The World Netball Tournament in a few weeks
- Commonwealth Ministers meetings
- World title fights in boxing
- Conferences and conventions, too numerous to count or mention.

To accommodate:

- The Mona Campus of the University of the West Indies
- The University of Technology
- The Office of the renowned Reggae Boys
- Sabina Park, one of the celebrated venues of Test Cricket
- The Headquarters of the Seabed Authority
- One of the largest trans-shipment ports of the Eastern seaboard.

Kingston is not configured or packaged for outsiders. While it is a very friendly city and welcomes visitors, Kingston expects visitors to become part of the inside experience. Accordingly, Kingston practices authentic Jamaica culture and does not water it down for the sake of convenience. The conversations in its plays, its comedies, its exhibitions, its festivals, its music and its forums are about its challenges and contradictions. And yet, we have found that these conversations have attracted international audiences and have had global appeal as Kingston's offsprings, for example, the likes of Marley and Shaggy, traverse the global stage.

Allow me to point out a unique feature of Kingston and Jamaica, by making one small comparison with your great country. It was my privilege to visit South Africa on one occasion. After just a few days, I became very conscious that I was coloured and was reminded of that by various acknowledgements on a daily basis. The only comparable experience I have had was when I studied in the United States, where, on that overwhelming white campus, all black persons acknowledged each other every time their paths crossed, whether they knew them or not. In those circumstances I understood myself to be black.

Becoming curious, I checked the population statistics and found that of the various groups categorised by colour, whites and blacks were each both much larger than coloureds. This contrasts sharply with Jamaican history, in that Blacks were always the vast majority followed by coloureds, with whites being the smallest group. I draw this contrast to make this observation. Historically in Jamaica, and more so in Kingston, white and black were not immutable categories. It was possible to become white or black, through what the geneticists call, backcrosses, and we label as 'interracial mating'.

The historical outcome of this ethos is that no matter how society in Kingston is divided by day, it is integrated in bed at night. In this city, there are marriages and liaisons between Arabs and Jews, Chinese and Indians, Blacks and Whites, and Browns with everybody. The result is the kind of milieu that will drive any strict adherents of eugenics into permanent confusion.

Mr. President, welcome to the City of Kingston. With key or no key, we invite you to be one of us, for we have always felt one with you and your people.

Chapter 16

The Role of Higher Education in Nation Building: The Case of the Dame of COB and Queen's College

~

THE INAUGURAL DR. KEVA BETHEL MEMORIAL LECTURE
August, 2012

~

Master of Ceremonies, Dr. Gail Saunders, protocol has been established and is hereby observed. The President and Faculty of the College of the Bahamas (COB), and members of the Bethel and Eldon families could have chosen from a host of eminent persons, the individual to deliver this first in the series of Distinguished Lectures in honour of the late Dr. Keva Bethel. Therefore, I feel deeply honoured and privileged, beyond measure, that I should be given this incredible opportunity. First occasions are always special. The first in the Lecture series to honour Dr. Bethel is extra special. My prayer is for the wisdom and words to match this very special occasion.

I wish to assure you that I will address the topic assigned: "The Role of Higher Education in Nation Building", but not as an abstract thesis. The approach taken is that of a concrete demonstration of the role of higher education in nation building by way of the life, labours and legacy of Dr. Keva Marie Bethel. I wish to illustrate from the life of Dr. Keva Bethel that 'the role of higher education in nation building' is a generational matter that includes more than policy prescriptions of Governments and institutions.

Dr. Keva M. Bethel. 1935 - 2011

Titles of honour in the Caribbean are not inherited. They are not based on bloodline. Titles of honour in the Caribbean are bequeathed by the sovereign or the people, based on character, calibre and career after account is taken of the depth, breath and length of quality service given to communities and countries. It is social elevation rooted in esteem for the individual. The bias in bequeathing the highest honours in the Caribbean is towards careers with character given in the fields of politics and business. The careers in education are often given less recognition. Fully cognizant of the fact that I have no authority so to do, but constrained and impelled by conscience, on behalf of the education community of the Bahamas and the Caribbean, I wish to nominate posthumously, Dr. Keva Marie Bethel, nee Eldon, Companion of the Order of St. Michael and St. George (CMG) to be the Dame of COB and Queen's College. In celebrating her life's work, we the educators wish to elevate her to the realm of royalty in the pantheon of Caribbean educators. What follows are arguments and some of the evidence to support this nomination:

I wish to present and explore the work and worth of Dr. Keva Marie Bethel in relation to family, Queen's College, the College of the Bahamas, as a nation builder and as a good human being. Probably the only one of these categories that may not appear to be self-evident is that of family. Yet to tell the story of the role of higher education in nation building by reference to the life and labours of Dr. Keva Bethel, and indeed her brother Bishop Michael Eldon, with only casual reference to their parents, Sidney and Rowena Eldon, would be an act of omission, leading to prosecution on the charge of negligence, with possible conviction, in the court of academic competence. Indeed, understanding the family background unlocks the door of understanding to numerous aspects of Dr. Bethel's life and work in higher education. The basic requirements of meaningful assessment of social phenomena are relevant history, incontrovertible facts and an appropriate conceptual scheme. I crave your indulgence as I try to satisfy these requirements.

A Woman from a Quintessential Bahamian Family

The genealogy of the Eldon family encompasses the tap roots of modern Bahamian society. The Eldons trace their ancestry back to 1648, and the founding of the Bahamas with the arrival of Captain William Sayle and the Eleutheran Adventurers from Bermuda. The Eldons admit to the fact that there was some mixing between the early Eldons from Bermuda with the Lucayans, who lived on Eleuthera, and who were the first settlers of the Bahamian islands. The Eldons therefore, have been all shades of Caribbean pigmentocracy; ranging from dark to very fair complexion. However, in Bahamian social classification, Keva's branch of the Eldons have always carried the label of being a coloured family, since the meaning of this designation across the Caribbean has never resided solely in complexion.

Having been present at the founding of the Bahamas on Eleuthera in the seventeenth century, in the mid-nineteenth century, some Eldons moved to Nassau; as New Providence became the new frontier of Bahamian development. The first Eldon in New Providence was Charles Eldon, a sign painter. He married a Sweeting who was from a white family from Abaco but who was born in Long Island. This opens the possibility that the Eldon line may have contributions from a Loyalist lineage.

When Sidney Alexander Eldon married Rowena Beatrice Hill, this completed in the Eldon line the kaleidoscope of ancestry that is quintessentially Bahamian. The Hills were from a coloured family from the Eastern Caribbean islands of Grenada and Tobago. Rowena's grandfather was from Grenada but was appointed Colonial Secretary in Tobago. He died young and his widow joined other members of her family who had migrated to New Providence. Her children married Bahamians. Apparently they were fair-skinned but not fair enough. When her eldest daughter married a white Bahamian his family disowned him and cut all ties, because he had married a coloured woman. The point is that the Eldons, as a coloured family, have always enjoyed some of the benefits and suffered from the vicissitudes of this social ascription. For example, several occupations, including the Anglican priesthood, were not open to coloured men in the Bahamas in the nineteenth and early twentieth century.

One of the lesser known facts is that marginality is neither a social pathology nor a fatal condition. It is a social fact common to all societies and to peoples of all times. Marginality is a product of inequality, on whatever basis. The critical issue is how marginality is perceived and tackled. The record shows that Sidney and Rowena, and his brother Alfred were determined to rise from their marginality and to overcome the social stigma of their ascription. It is their decision, not to be victims of their social circumstance but to be victors, which is the foundation upon which we laud the life and work of their daughter, Keva.

Sidney, and his brother Alfred, made full use of the benefit of being able to obtain posts in the civil service of the Bahamas in the first half of the twentieth century. Alfred rose to the position of Postmaster General. Sidney became Controller of Customs, and after retirement from that post in the early 1950s was appointed Member of the Legislative Council and on a number of occasions acted as Governor. In colonial Bahamas, Postmaster

General and Controller of Customs were two of the highest positions that any Bahamian could attain: white, coloured or black.

When Michael was born in August1931, and Keva in August 1935, this marginal branch of the Eldon family was on the rise. Alfred had desired to be a scholar but that was beyond the means of his family at the time. Sidney was a self-taught man of letters. His early ambition was to be a priest but being coloured did not permit the realization of this ambition. Nevertheless, this did not dim his Christian devotion. Over the years, at St. Mary the Virgin Anglican Church, he was chorister, cantor, catechist and vestryman. Rowena, otherwise called Winnie, wanted to be an accountant and was interested in politics. However, such pursuits were not possible for women of those times. However, not to be outdone, Rowena engaged in business activities and became involved in charitable works. She became the first President of the Bahamas Red Cross Society. If the men could overcome and triumph over the circumstances and the treatment of coloured families, so could she. Rowena Eldon nee Hill was renowned for her love of, and service to people. Most significantly, Sidney and Rowena were intent on giving their children the formal education they did not get.

It is evident that Michael and Keva were highly influenced by the authenticity of the strivings of their parents, the rock solid security that they provided and their practical Christianity. All the evidence suggest that brother and sister were highly impacted by the ethos of their home in terms of the habits of the mind, the disposition of spirit, the choices of the heart, the outlook on life and the commitment to service, displayed by their parents. Michael became the priest his father could not have been by reason of social exclusion. And what a priest and bishop he was!

Keva grew up and married Edward Clement Bethel in April, 1962. In so doing, Keva became surrounded, in the intimate circle of family, by men of incredible achievement in the colonial and post-independence eras of Bahamian history.

She was daughter of Sidney who had risen from relative marginality to the top of the civil service, appointed to the Legislative Council and Acting Governor on occasions. He was made a Member of the British Empire by the Queen.

She was niece of Alfred, the Postmaster General. She was sister of Michael: iconic Anglican priest who rose to become the first Bahamian Bishop of the

Diocese of Nassau and the Bahamas, with responsibility for the Turks and Caicos Islands. Bishop Eldon was revered by the Anglican community and beloved by people of all walks of life. She was wife of Clement: music prodigy, the pioneer ethnomusicologist of the Bahamas, outstanding composer and arranger of Bahamian folk music, and legendary director of folk operas and pageants, including the Independence Pageant in 1973.

Although Keva Bethel lived her life surrounded by these men of her immediate family who were of such considerable statute, and to whom she was deeply devoted, she was not overshadowed by them. This is because, by her work she grew in stature, in her chosen field of education, to a height of being on par with them. The sun of achievement shun directly from above on her as it did on these male members, leaving no shadow on any of them but rather amazement that such brilliance and exemplary service could come from a single family over two generations. What is particularly special about Keva is that in this constellation of Bahamian stars, she was female at a time when women's ability to succeed in areas traditionally held by men, was extremely limited.

But the story of Keva Bethel and family cannot end with her roles and relationships as daughter, niece, sister and wife without taking into account of her role as mother. Information is that Clement, though a great father, was genuinely baffled about how to relate with children before they could hold a conversation. Further, he was a night person and not given to waking early. The chore of taking the children to school could not be undertaken by him. Keva had to fill these gaps. Then again Clement died at the early age of 49 in 1987. While the children were already grown, Keva again had to fill the gap as the surviving parent of young adults.

Information is that Keva was very fair in dealing with both Nicolette, Nico, and Edward. She had no favourites. She displayed great patience and was incredibly warm and loving. She expected both of them to do well and gave no material reward when they did well in school. Allow me to say to Nico and Eddie when Keva and I met socially we often spoke of our children. I must tell you that she was extremely pleased with and proud of both of you. This was not just in terms of your achievements but equally in terms of the persons whom you have become. My sense is that, like her brother, she fully accepted and embraced the values, views and virtues of her parents. In her lifetime she had lived by these verities, and with Clement, did their best to pass them unto you both. To see you embrace these values and virtues, make life choices consistent with them, continue the great work of your father and pursue careers in her chosen field of education was deeply satisfying to her. In this regard, she had a sense of fulfilment equal to that of any of her accomplishments.

Keva Marie Bethel was a loving, loyal and faithful wife. She was ever so happy to be Clement's wife. She served his interests with joy. When Clement declared Sunday evenings "Indian Nights", she dutifully prepared full Indian dinners to give the occasions some feeling of authenticity. When he became critically ill she took leave to be with him as they sought medical treatment in Canada. She was also the ultimate sister that any brother could have. She was the original member of Michael's congregation as he played church as a child. Her dedication to him during the six years of his terminal illness, exceeded exceptional. That she died on the day of his funeral is symbolic of the degree and depth of the filial bonds they shared in life. After her mother died in 1995, she became the matriarch of the Eldon and Bethel families.

I wish to posit that it is royal to honour and revere the sacrifices of our forebearers, to build on the legacy that they bequeath to us by the strivings and accomplishments in our own time, to be loyal to our spouses and siblings and to pass on to our children the verities of individual enterprise and service to community. Keva Marie Bethel, nee Eldon, succeeded at all of these.

Forgive me for this postscript on the Eldon family. Keva had the fair complexion of her parents. Michael was of dark complexion. To use the terminology of Caribbean pigmentocracy, Keva was Brown and Michael was Black. This is not an uncommon occurrence in coloured families across the world, and sometimes is not without its own tensions within and outside families. In that remarkable speech Keva gave in 2009, of her vision for the Bahamas, she said: "I should, moreover, like to see a society in which my grandson and all others are comfortable in their own skins (of whatever shade those may be) and never have to feel apologetic or defensive about any aspect of their heritage."

Queen's College and Dr. Keva Bethel

From the founding of Queen's College (QC) in 1890, members of the mainstream Eldon family had gone to QC. Sydney and Rowena Eldon determined to ensure that their children, Michael and Keva, would go to QC as well, notwithstanding the strain on the family's treasury. Michael blazed a trail of brilliance in academic accomplishments and even developed some reputation as a sprinter. In 1947, Michael Eldon graduated from QC, placed first in the Cambridge School Certificate Examinations and was head boy of the school. Keva entered QC in 1941 and followed the trail of her brother's academic brilliance with nonchalant ease. She made no attempt to match his athletic exertions. He had conquered the Cambridge School Certificate at age 16. She did so at age 15. She graduated in 1950, was head girl and won the prestigious Parkinson Prize for Progress. She remained at QC for another year to take Latin which was a matriculation requirement of English Universities, but was not a subject on the regular curriculum.

Michael had entered Cambridge University in 1949 and read theology at St. Catherine's College, from which he graduated with First Class Honours. To the Eldons, Keva would take a similar path. However, the family treasury needed some respite. So in 1951 Keva took a job with Barclay's Bank, the only employment she ever had outside of education. Being advised that Cambridge had only two women's colleges and that competition for admission was fierce, in 1953 Rowena and Keva sailed for England on the HMS Queen Elizabeth to enroll Keva at Kirby Lodge, a school specializing in preparing young women for entry to Cambridge by way of the Higher School Certificate. This gambit proved successful in that Keva obtained her Higher School Certificate and had offers from women's colleges at both Cambridge and Oxford. Keva chose Girton College, Cambridge from which she graduated with BA Honours in Modern Languages in 1959 and MA in 1963.

It is almost impossible to appreciate the farsightedness of the sacrifices made by Sidney and Rowena Eldon in providing higher education to their children in the 1950s, particularly for their daughter. At that time, the career prospects were extremely limited for highly educated Bahamian men and even more so for educated Bahamian women. Sidney and Rowena had to contend with many naysayers who questioned the wisdom of their sacrifice. It is to the great credit of Queen's College that it was a partner in such perspicacity in the foundation it gave to both Michael and Keva.

Looking back, with the benefit of hindsight, Keva left Queen's in 1951, the same year that Mary Ingraham and Mabel Walker led the first petition for women suffrage in the Bahamas. Further, Keva's graduation from Cambridge in 1959 coincided with the march on Parliament and militant presentation made by Dame Doris Johnson on the subject of equal rights for women. In other words, the decision by Sidney and Rowena Eldon to give their daughter the same higher educational opportunities as their son, meant that young Keva Eldon was not only competent and capable but qualified to give proof in practice to what Mary Ingraham, Mabel Walker, Doris Johnson, Georgina Symonette, Eugenia Lockhard and Albetha Isaac were advocating in principle about Bahamian womanhood. In a nutshell, without collusion, parents with foresight, forward-looking Queen's College and advocates for gender reform in Bahamian society, acted in concert with mutual benefit to all and to the country.

Keva was always grateful for the educational foundations that she received at QC. She loved QC. Allow me a personal comment here. Keva and I were professional colleagues for close to thirty years and morphed into being really good friends for at least 20 years. One of the things that baffled me over the first few years was her absolute devotion to her brother, the Anglican Bishop, who had such a passion for education, and her commitment to QC, a Methodist school. That she was a QC old girl partially helped to resolve my silent puzzlement. However, the matter was not fully resolved until as friends, we shared views on education, talked about children, identified promising young Bahamian educators and how best to guide them. Then it became clear that she served on the Board of QC and on its Staffing Committee for close to thirty years not only for reasons of gratitude, or for being a QC old girl, but her desire to ensure that QC, even with its great reputation, kept pace with the changes demanded by the rapid developing Bahamian nation while at the same time being firmly anchored in the unchanging core values and virtues that had served her generation so well.

Just over four years ago, I informed Keva that my wife was being transferred to Nassau and sought her advice about schooling for our daughter, who was of secondary school age, there was little discussion about the school that my daughter would attend. Obviously it would be QC. Having absolute confidence in Keva's advice, that was that.

Dr. Keva Marie Bethel was inducted into the Queen's College Hall of Fame in January 2011. Of the four inductees so far she is the only female. At her passing, the QC community celebrated her life in a manner that indicated that the love she had for QC was truly reciprocated by the institution. These provide tangible evidence that Queen's College regards Dr. Keva Marie Bethel as a Dame.

The College of the Bahamas and Dr. Keva Bethel

Historically, Commonwealth Caribbean education has had an unusual deformity. It has become characterized by a broad base of early childhood, primary and secondary education on which a pin head of higher education sits. This deformity has its genesis is the reluctance of the colonial authorities to develop local talent that could challenge or compete with them. Unlike Latin America and North America where college education was introduced not long after the establishment of their education systems, in the Commonwealth Caribbean there was a lag of over one hundred years before the first college, Codrington in Barbados, was established in 1745. Then it took another 100 years before other small theological colleges were established. Between the 1830s and 1948 there were only a few small theological colleges, about 10 small teachers' colleges, a few small technical training centres and one Imperial College of Tropical Agriculture in the entire Commonwealth Caribbean.

The post-World War II movement to political independence put the issue of higher education firmly on the agenda of national development, resulting in the establishment of the University College of the West Indies in 1948 as a regional institution. As countries moved to independence, national colleges were established in the larger countries starting with the College of Arts, Science and Technology, CAST, in Jamaica in 1958, the University of Guyana in 1963 and the Barbados Community College in 1968.

Bahamas became independent in 1973. Impelled by the imperatives of a rapidly growing tourist industry and the need to develop local talent, the Government immediately created the College of the Bahamas (COB) by Act of Parliament at the end of 1974. COB was formed from the amalgamation of The Bahamas Teachers College, the San Salvador Teachers College, the C. R. Walker Technical Training College and the Sixth Form of the Government High School. This Bahamian strategy, of amalgamating small single discipline institutions into a large multidisciplinary college, was later followed by nearly all the smaller countries of the Commonwealth Caribbean.

Archdeacon Michael Eldon was elected Bishop of the Diocese by acclaim in 1972. To place the governance of this pioneer college beyond controversy, the Government appointed Bishop Eldon, acknowledged scholar and trailblazing priest, as the founding Chairman of the Council of COB in 1975. He held this position of Chairman for the first twenty years of the College.

Keva Bethel came to COB, en passant, as the French would say. She came with the passing of the Sixth Form from Government High School to COB in September 1975, when the college first opened its door to the public. Keva was the Deputy Headmistress of the Government High School, and Head of Modern Languages. She was part of the amalgamation, prescribed in the Act. The Eldon brother and sister were present on the ground floor of the establishment of higher education in the Bahamas, but came independently by separate routes.

Dr. Bethel was not the first principal of the College of the Bahamas. That distinction rightly belongs to Dr. John Knowles, a noted Bahamian scholar. He was principal from 1975 to 1977. Dr. Kazim Bacchus, noted Guyanese scholar, followed Dr. Knowles as principal between 1977 and 1979. Dr. Bacchus was followed by another distinguished Guyanese scholar, Dr. Jacob Bynoe, who was principal between 1979 and 1982. In 1982, Dr. Bethel became the fourth principal of COB. She had risen from the ranks. In 1975 she was first appointed Chairperson of the Humanities Division, the division that included the transferred Sixth Form. In 1977, she became the Dean of Academic Affairs. In 1979, she was appointed Vice Principal. Having moved into the College, and up the ranks, Keva further qualified herself by acquiring the PhD in Educational Administration from the University of Alberta.

When Dr. Bynoe left in 1982 for a post in Antigua, Dr. Bethel was appointed principal of COB. She served as Principal from 1982 to 1995 and President from 1995 to 1998, when she retired. The question to be asked and answered is how have the names Dr. Keva Bethel and the College of the Bahamas become so intricately and inextricably linked?

There are at least three parts to the answer to this question. The first is tied to mathematics. COB has been operational for 37 years. There were three principals in the eight years before Dr. Bethel was appointed. There have been four presidents in the fourteen years since her retirement. Dr. Bethel has been the only principal/president so far whose tenure has exceeded one term. She served for 16 years. These calculations would suggest that from its inception, the leadership of the College has proved to be a high risk challenge to all who have been brave enough to accept the appointment of principal/president.

A possible cynical explanation is that her brother was the Chairman of the Council for 12 of those 16 years. The simple answer is family connection. However, there is no evidence that the Lord Bishop had to protect his little sister from any charges laid against her, or rescued her from situations that she was unable to handle or of any public expressions of dissatisfaction or disgruntlement with her leadership. To the contrary on demitting office she was given the honourable title of President Emerita and accorded the position of Scholar in Residence. Indeed, a strong case can be made that it is the Eldon children, over those twelve years, who placed the College firmly on the higher education map of the Bahamas and the Caribbean.

This leads to the second element of the answer, the essential nature of colleges and universities and Keva's family background. It is often overlooked that colleges and universities are institutions with constellations of stars in different orbits. Students are stars catapulted into the orbit of the college by their achievements at the secondary level. Faculty members are stars put into another orbit within the constellation, principally by virtue of accomplishments at the tertiary level. The administrators in the registry, bursary, library and maintenance are stars in their own orbits based upon specialized competencies. National and State colleges and universities must also interact with stars in the political directorate and stars in the civil service. All colleges and universities, state and private, must also contend with stars of the press and public. In this universe of stars, the principal/president of the College, must not only be a star but a special star. The Principal/President must be the sun/star, which keeps the other stars in their respective orbits by contending and coping with their gravitational forces. Once orbits begin to overlap in a college, clashes and crashes are almost inevitable. While the metaphor of chemistry is often applied to personal relationships, that of physics is more appropriate for colleges and universities.

Growing up with, and living in, a constellation of stars in her family, and being a star herself, provided Keva with the kind of preparation needed to succeed in a college. Having learned by osmosis to deal with a star father, a star uncle, a star mother, a star brother, a star husband and rising star children, Keva diffused this knowledge in her dealings with the different constellations of stars at the College of The Bahamas. This allowed her to effectively communicate the vision of the College, stated on paper, in such a personal and persuasive manner that all stars came to an understanding of what should be accomplished in their orbit and the implications for the entire constellation. To change the metaphor, Keva Bethel succeeded in communicating effectively with the different constituencies of the College community with the result that they embraced a common vision of the College and their diverse roles in its development.

Lofty language was used in the Act of Parliament of 1974 that established the College. Its mission was to provide 'an institutional focus for the intellectual sovereignty of the country". The Ministry of Education interpreted that mission in a most inclusive manner: 'to meet every important need of The Bahamas'. On becoming the fourth Principal, Dr. Bethel graciously acknowledged the work done by her predecessors, faculty, staff, students, council and government. Her Message on the Tenth Anniversary of the College in 1985 provides eloquent testimony of her recognition of, respect for and resolve to continue to build on what had been achieved. At the same time, the interview published in the Nassau Guardian, just prior to her official installation as Principal on December 1, 1983, and other documents, give clear evidence of the clinical analysis she had done to determine the tasks that needed to be undertaken in moving COB forward in her time:

- Students needed better career guidance with respect to several occupations and better explanation of the opportunities open to persons possessing the skills acquired for those occupations.
- Better facilities were required for students outside of class-time.
- The library needed to be upgraded to international standards.
- The science labs had to be upgraded if the desired standards were to be achieved.
- The College had to collaborate with the University of the West Indies (UWI), and other universities in gaining further international recognition for programmes particularly in the areas of hospitality and tourism.
- The College had to address the educational needs of the Family Islands, beginning in Grand Bahama.
- The College had started with a two-year Associate Degrees but had move to four-year Bachelor Degrees and university status; after careful consideration of the priorities of the society and realities of resources: human, material and financial.
- The basis for charging students fees had to move from fees charged per semester, to fees charged per credit if the college was to be financially sustainable.

- In moving to meet all the demands on the College, the pitfall that would be avoided was that of offering "Mickey Mouse" courses.

- In all it did, the College had to maintain a Bahamian sense of culture and intellectual initiative.

Dr. Bethel's approach could be summarised as gracious and generous acknowledgement of the work of those whom she succeeded; adherence to the broad goals set for the College; hard-head and hard-nosed analyses of the tasks to be undertaken in her time; assignments of tasks to different constituencies of the College and mobilization and motivation of these constituencies to accomplish these tasks.

The ability to mobilise and motivate people to implement the critical tasks identified by sound analysis is the touch-stone of leadership. It is the final step in translating plans on paper to physical plant in the ground; of transforming organisational procedures into improved efficiency; of ensuring that persons to whom responsibilities are delegated perform their tasks; of gaining credibility; and of winning public confidence.

For most of the 16 years that Dr. Bethel was Principal/President I had a front seat in watching her strive to put COB firmly on the higher education map: nationally, regionally and internationally. In my mind's eye, I can still see her demeanour as she engaged all stakeholders and actors: diminutive, dignified, driven but disarming, diplomatic but never deceptive. Dr. Bethel worked with single-minded purpose with the students, faculty, administrative staff, political directorate, civil service, community and regional and international institutions to make COB serve the further education needs of the Bahamas and to put the College irrevocably on the road to university status:

- Buildings were erected that transformed the campus.

- Programmes were introduced that widened and deepened the areas of preparation offered.

- The College spread its tentacles and impacted the entire Bahamas.

- The College progressed to offer degree programmes and formed alliances with universities on all sides of the Atlantic.

- Graduates were produced who commanded recognition and respect at the workplace and at institutions internationally.

- Bahamians of all walks of life came to embrace the College of Bahamas and became proud of it.

Impelled by this progress, in 1995 the Government repealed the Act of 1974 and replaced it with the Act of 1995 which gave the College degree granting powers and autonomous status. Dr. Keva Bethel became its first President. In the process of providing leadership for these accomplishments, the College of the Bahamas and Dr. Keva Bethel became synonymous.

Today the College of the Bahamas pays its own tribute to Dr. Keva Bethel. A tribute truly worthy of a Dame.

Dr. Keva Bethel:
The Nation Builder and Caribbean Personality

I have always been willing to concede that "It is better in the Bahamas" provided that 'it' is clearly defined. However, when it comes to scholarship, the general assumption across the Caribbean is that excellence resides outside the region. Scholars who decide to live and work inside the Caribbean always run the risk of being regarded as second class. Keva Bethel could have pursued a stellar career in higher education anywhere in the world and be acclaimed in the Bahamas for it. To Keva Bethel, however, the risk of being regarded as second class was of little importance compared to the consequences of not applying her scholarship to nation building in her native land. As she said in that memorial speech in 2009 on "A Vision for the Bahamas of the Future":

> ….education has to be understood in its broadest sense: the process that occurs in all settings from the time we are born and that teaching involves not only words but actions, as the latter reveal what we truly value.

Consistent with her view of education and teaching, Keva not only taught courses, administered institutions, wrote academic papers, made numerous pronouncements but acted in substantive ways outside of her official positions. She was:

- Soloist, chorister and honorary President of the Renaissance Singers
- President of the Girl Guides' Association

- Chairman of the Screening Committee of the Lyford Cay Scholarship Awards

- Member of numerous Committees and Boards in The Bahamas including the National Arts Committee; The Bahamas Government Scholarship Advisory Committee; The National Women's Advisory Committee; The Women's Forum of the Bahamas, the International Women's Forum; Board of Trustees of the Governor General's Youth Award, the Bahamas Hotel Training Advisory Board, The Board of Directors of the Bahamian Field Station; The Board of Directors of Cable Bahamas; The Board of Directors of Doctors Hospital; the Board of Directors of Bahamas Supermarkets; the Board of the Finance Corporation of The Bahamas; the Board of Governors of Queen's College, The Primary Student of the Year Association, the Kappa Alpha Sorority; the Blue Ribbon Panel of the Cacique Awards and the All Bahamas Merit Scholarships and The Bahamas Teachers' Union.

She served on numerous Caribbean and Hemispheric bodies including:

- The Council of the Association of Caribbean Tertiary Level Institutions

- The Joint Board of Teacher Education of the University of the West Indies

- The Association of Supervision and Curriculum Development

- The Board of Non-Campus Countries and Distance Education, University of the West Indies, and

- The Inter-American Committee on Education of the Organisation of American States (OAS).

She was appointed to serve on several task forces and committees mandated to address very important issues. These included:

- The Committee of Experts established by the CARICOM Heads of Government to review the System of Legal Education in the Caribbean

- The University of the West Indies Strategy Committee

- The Team to Review the Faculty of Education of the University of the West Indies

- The Chancellor's Commission to review the Governance of the University of the West Indies, and

- Chairman of the National Task Force on Education appointed by the Prime Minister of The Bahamas in 1993.

The scope of this Lecture only allows for the mere listing of these engagements but leaves virtually no room for discussion of their significance and importance. However, it would be a grave omission not to elaborate, even briefly, on the work of the National Task Force on Education. The implementation of the recommendations of the Task Force has laid the foundation of Bahamian education in the first two decades of the twenty-first century.

The National Task Force on Education was commissioned in March 1993 to evaluate the public educational system of the Bahamas and to make recommendations for its reform. Its composition comprised 47 individuals from the public and private sector, eight ex-officio members from various Ministries, and three deputy chairmen: Archdeacon William Thompson, Mr. Charles Saunders and Mr. Vincent Ferguson, and the secretary. It worked through eight subcommittees, held 22 town meetings in New Providence and 22 meetings in 14 family islands. The Task Force produced its final report, "Education: A Preparation for Life" in January 1994.

The following have emanated from its recommendations:

- The revision of the Education Act in 1996

- The reorganisation of the Ministry of Education (MOE), and its relationship with the Department of Education, the computerization of its systems, revision of its budgetary systems and the allocation of a budget for the development of professional staff at all levels

- The establishment of school districts in New Providence with District Superintendents and the upgrading of the District Education Officers in the Family Islands to District Superintendents

- The establishment of school boards, elected by parents, to assist with the management of schools in New Providence and Grand Bahama School boards were given budgets to assist with the efficiency, and rapid response to challenges and required to account annually to the MOE for the expenditure of funds

- The implementation of The Teacher Cadet Core as a means of selecting and retaining more teachers in the educational system
- The revision of the College of The Bahamas Act in 1995
- Improvement in the salary scales of teachers including increased allowances for master and senior teachers
- The establishment of the National Parent Teachers Association with local chapters
- The incorporation of teachers' aids
- The establishment of a National Board of Teaching Standards
- Appointment of a National Education Advisory Council, which would be responsible for the advising of the minister on all matters related to education
- The restoration of the Bahamas Junior Certificate examination
- The National Accreditation and Equivalency Council of The Bahamas in 2006
- Established a Public Information Unit of the Ministry, which has developed into a Communications Section, responsible for disseminating information on education to the public.

As a postscript, note that the new Free National Movement Government had established the National Task Force on Education in 1993. The previous Progressive Liberal Party Government had left behind the Master Plan for Post-Secondary Education. Under the prudent leadership of Dr. Bethel, the National Task Force on Education considered and adopted several of the recommendations of the Master Plan, thus ensuring bipartisan consensus on several matters.

Dr. Keva Bethel: The Person

Volumes remain to be written on the accomplishments of Dr. Keva Marie Bethel and her impact in her time. Hopefully, in subsequent Anniversary Lectures and publications, this gap will be filled. Allow me therefore to conclude with some reference to Keva Bethel, the person that we all knew. She was gracious, gentle, generous but never glory-seeking. She attributed her accomplishments to the example, and sacrifices of her parents, the trailblazing path set by her brother which she felt obliged to follow and the encouragement and support of her husband. Yes, she was self-effacing but at the same time, undertook whatever task that was set for her with the work ethic and expectation to succeed. She was not a high maintenance person. To the contrary she made every attempt to put others at ease and to care for them.

It is said that during her tenure at Government High School she was the disciplinarian in the school. Boys feared her. Fearing Keva is difficult to understand given the fact that she was petite, polite, patient and pleasant in almost all circumstances. Fear and this persona seem to be at odds. The key to unlocking this conundrum resides in the different sources of fear. Some teachers drive the 'fear of god' into their students because of the draconian measures they often employ. Crossing such teachers result in an 'end of the world' experience. Others are so miserable that students positively fear the nagging and, therefore to spare such, they comply. To fail such teachers is to hear about it for the rest of your life. Still other teachers are so charismatic that they mesmerise their students into learning and behaving through a combination of eloquence, humour, almost magical presentations and eccentric mannerisms. Failing such teachers, runs the risk of great ridicule. Yet, other teachers communicate such high expectations to their students, who in turn hold these teachers in such great regard, that they are finessed into learning and behaving, without even realizing it. Failing such teachers, results in unending pangs of conscience. How in the world could I have done that? Keva belonged to this latter category. Her students and colleagues feared letting her down. In such cases, she would say little if anything at all. However, in that silence the offender would feel so small that their greatest wish was for a hole in the ground to appear, into which they could crawl. The only saving grace was that she would reach out to pick you up before you had crawled fully into it.

Information is that there were a few occasions when Keva was not so calm and controlled at home. However, the matter that really got her going was selfishness by drivers on the road. Sometimes she swore at their behaviour, although none of what she said would have brought her before courts. I offer these kinks in her usually calm and civilised demeanour as proof that she was truly human.

Keva confessed to having few personal ambitions. Her great ambitions were to be a good daughter, wife and mother, a teacher by profession and to live a quiet life. She was undoubtedly a great daughter, an exceptional sister, an exemplary wife, a superb mother and an iconic educator. But, the quiet life eluded her. Most likely this was because of her lack of other ambitions. Driving personal ambitions are often great hindrances in serving others and in seeking to advance community and country. They cause self to get in the way of service to community. Her dedication to service, above self, made her trustworthy, reliable, dependable and greatly sought after. Her life was therefore busy, but never boisterous nor banal.

Keva found joy and great satisfaction in the simple pleasures of life. She loved singing and playing the piano. She loved gardening and collecting plants but laughingly concluded that she had a 'brown thumb' which killed the plants. She had far greater success with small animals. She always had pets: cats and dogs. At different times she had birds, fish and rabbits. She was afraid of heights and hated crowds. She maintained that being short did not allow her any enjoyment in a crowd. Consequently, only duty compelled her to attend events involving large crowds.

Anthropologists maintain that Lucayans were peaceful and peace loving people. They were gentle and generous. They enjoyed the simple pleasures of life, including singing and dancing. They reared small animals. Culture runs deep in any society. Cultural retentions are often not readily recognised because they are so embedded in the fabric of relationships. One hypothesis worth exploring is that Keva Maria Bethel, nee Eldon may have been more Lucayan that any of us may have imagined.

Concluding Comment

Hopefully, in making the case for Dr. Keva Marie Bethel to be Dame of the COB and Queen's College, I have demonstrated that the role of higher education in nation building is not abstract or academic. Rather, it is the outcome of concrete decisions and sacrifices made by individuals across generations. Nations are built over generations. Were it not for the decisions and sacrifices made by Sidney and Rowena Eldon to give their children, Michael and Keva, the higher education they lacked, the contributions of the latter to nation building would quite likely not occur. Further, the role of higher education in nation building is not a prescription or a recipe. Rather, it is the product of individuals with diverse talents and with different personalities, who cohere in pursuit of the common good. Then again, it is the result of exemplary leadership with minimal personal ambition but maximum motivation to advance the people who comprise the nation. Such leadership is infectious and inspiring.

Declaration

A common formulation recited at University graduations is for the chancellor to declare: "By the authority vested in me by…I hereby confer". This is not a graduation. The College of the Bahamas does not yet have a chancellor. In the Bahamas I have no authority that has been vested in me. Nonetheless, on the wealth of evidence available to me and constrained by conscience, I hereby declare Dr. Keva Marie Bethel, "Dame of COB and Queen's College", posthumously.

~

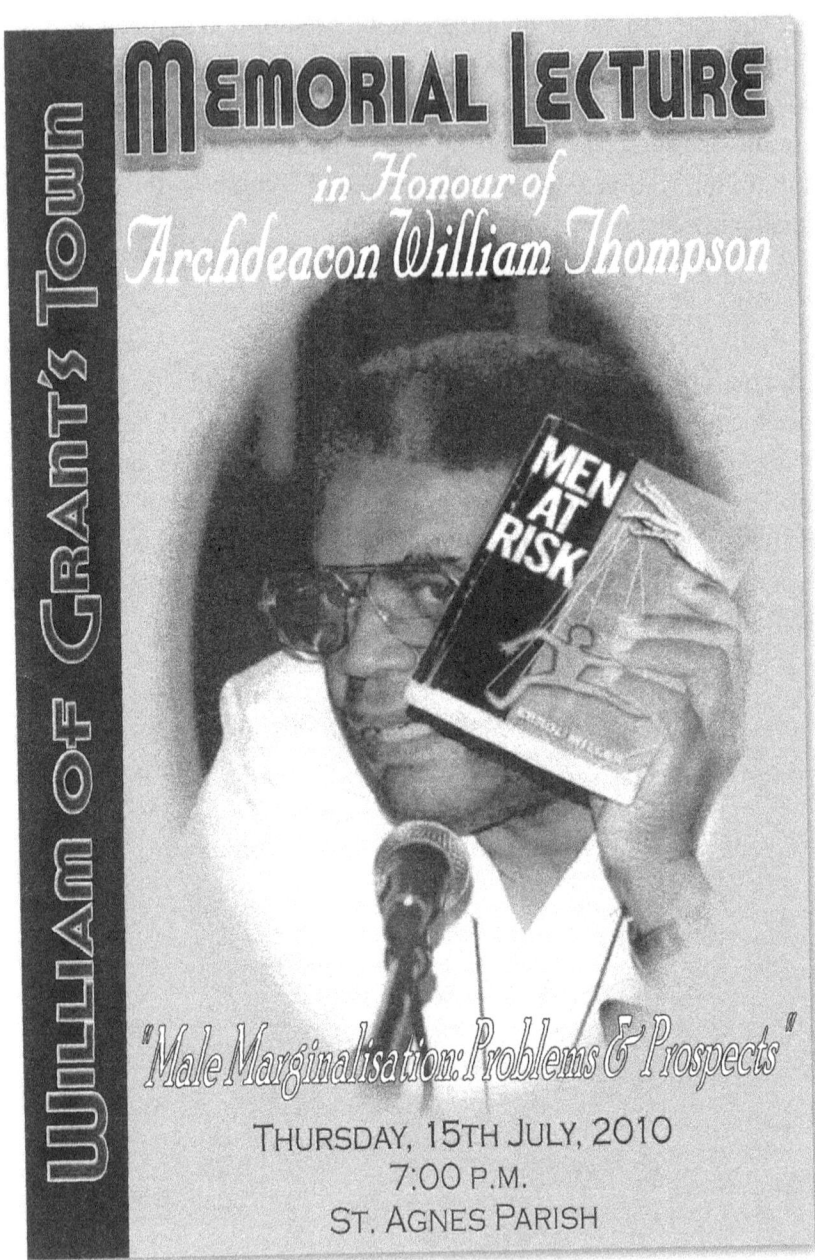

MEMORIAL LECTURE

in Honour of

Archdeacon William Thompson

WILLIAM OF GRANT'S TOWN

"Male Marginalisation: Problems & Prospects"

THURSDAY, 15TH JULY, 2010
7:00 P.M.
ST. AGNES PARISH

Memorial Lecture Programme to honour
Archdeacon William Edward Thompson.

Chapter 17

Male Marginalisation: Retrospect and Prospect

~

WILLIAM OF GRANTS TOWN
10TH ANNIVERSARY MEMORIAL LECTURE
July, 2010

~

Introduction

Venerable Archdeacon William Thompson was first and foremost a Christian who was called to be a priest of the Anglican Church. He embraced the priesthood with fervour and had a special understanding of its robes, rituals, rites, bells, smells and genuflections. Venerable Archdeacon William Thompson was a Bahamian to his core and had unique insights into "Bahamianness" and the Bahamian psyche. At the same time he was a Caribbean man. He loved cricket. He often came to Sabina Park in Jamaica to watch Test matches. More importantly, he was a Caribbean scholar, historian and theologian with a depth, and breadth of knowledge of Caribbean society and the role and work of the church that was a resource to all who tapped into that reservoir of wisdom.

Venerable William Thompson was one of those persons who fell into the category that Malcolm Gladwell in his book, *The Tipping Point*, labeled as connectors. Archdeacon Thompson knew a vast number of people from all walks of life. He had a passion to make connections between people. Having read two of my books, *Men at Risk* and *Marginalisation of the Black Male*, he initiated the connection with me through a mutual friend, Dr. Keva Bethel. I then became a beneficiary of the great hospitality of Mrs. Rose Thompson, his wife, and himself and also of his great fount of knowledge and wisdom. As we conversed, it became clear that he had great passion for young people and deep concern about what was happening to young men here in Nassau and also for Bahamian society. More importantly, is that he had a heart of gold. As he shared with me some of the things he was doing, I can remember saying to him: 'Father Willie, this is great work. It is God's work but be careful it is dangerous work.' I had had my own taste of that danger having been held up with my family in our home in Jamaica by four young men with guns. One of those young men was intent on hurting us, but two of his colleagues talked him out of it. It is not the kind of experience that you are likely to forget or not warn others about.

You have conferred on me the great honour to deliver this Anniversary Lecture and through it to revisit a subject in which Venerable Archdeacon Thompson displayed deep interest. In his life it is an issue that he sought to address. Indeed, it is a matter that factored in his untimely death. It is an issue that is not going away and with which we must contend. Hopefully, by highlighting this subject in memory of Archdeacon William Thompson we will both increase understanding and promote meaningful and effective action. The assumption here is that if we better understand the driving forces in contemporary society then we are better able to both cope with the circumstances and take more appropriate actions in attempting to change the present and shape the future. In this regard it is very important not to limit our understanding to Bahamian, Jamaican or Caribbean society but to understand Bahamian, Jamaican and Caribbean societies within the context of human social history and contemporary global society.

Male Marginalisation Defined in Contemporary Society

Probably the most economical way to define the phenomenon of male marginalisation, in contemporary society, is to do so by highlighting some of its most visible social manifestations:

- More male babies being abandoned than female babies
- More boys suffering from stunted growth than girls
- More boys starting school later, attending more irregularly, dropping out of school earlier, repeating more grades, having lower rates of

completion of schooling and lower levels of achievement than girls on most measures of educational achievement.

- Fewer males than females being enrolled in and graduating from tertiary institutions

- More boys and men being patients in psychiatric wards or psychiatric hospitals than girls and women

- More men being homeless than women

- More boys and men committing violent crimes than girls and women

- Much larger numbers of boys and men being incarcerated in correctional institutions and maximum-security prisons

These negative social features do not apply to all men, only some. They are shared by some women but not many. There can be no question that some men still hold the pinnacle of power, wealth and status in most societies. Further, some women remain among the most marginalised in practically all societies. In other words, neither males nor females can be treated as unitary or monolithic categories. What these manifestations highlight is an increasing or even disproportionate number of males in a growing underclass in many societies.

Male Marginalisation in Retrospect

If particular negative social symptoms are the most economic way to define male marginalisation in contemporary society, a brief and broad socio-historical scan is appropriate to explain its general causal roots.

The Patriarchal Beginnings of Human Society

The anthropological evidence overwhelmingly points to a patriarchal beginning to human social history. Patriarchy can be defined as the rule of one of the oldest fathers of the kinship collective. In other words, one of the oldest fathers of the extended family, lineage, clan or tribe has the final authority in deciding the welfare and survival of these blood-bonded groups and the responsibility to protect and provide for these groups. This is best explained by the fact that in antiquity, when the human population lived in small isolated groups, adaptive advantage resided in group living and not individual existence. The individuals that stayed together, and comprised the group, were related by blood, that is, shared common ancestors. Further, because of the high risks of childbirth in these aboriginal situations, men lived longer than women. In this primitive era, therefore, age constituted an important group resource in terms of knowledge and experience. Older men became a strategic resource in the survival of the extended family, lineage or clan. Many wisdom sayings attest to the fact.

Not to be overlooked is the fact that men and women, of the kinship collective, worked cooperatively for survival of the group. These small isolated groups were forced to deal with all matters, including the critical matters of life and death. The life-preserving roles fell to the women of the group. Women gave birth to members of the group. It was also natural that women should be tasked with and become skilled in life preservation. By default, life-taking decisions fell to the men, to one of the oldest fathers, the patriarch. Life-taking proved more decisive in group dynamics in that while gratitude is almost always felt for those who give and preserve life, the power to take life generates fear and deference that supersedes gratitude. For all of these reasons, patriarchy emerged in antiquity.

From this brief description of early human social formation, it is critical to keep in mind four very important factors because they are critical to our understanding of the present:

1. Early human groups were structured on the basis of genealogy, generation and gender. Genealogy bound the group together by virtue of blood relationship and separated that group from other groups similarly organised. In other words, genealogy defined the external boundaries of the group in terms of 'us' and 'them'. Generation and gender differentiated the groups internally and created rank order within the group.

2. All members of the kinship collective worked cooperatively for the survival of the group. Individual well-being depended on group solidarity and group survival. As a result, reciprocal duties and obligations were developed. If one of the eldest fathers had the duty to make final decisions for the group, his obligation was always to make decisions in the best interest of the group and not merely for his own benefit. The power to make final decisions was balanced by the obligation to protect and provide for the group.

3. Gender roles were first defined in terms of life-giving and life-taking

powers within the group. It is understandable therefore, that the traits normally associated with being feminine such as caring, nurturing, kind and non-confrontational are essential to life preservation. Those that are normally associated with being masculine such as confrontational, decisive, hard-hearted and brutal are essential to life-taking.

4. Patriarchy represents deep culture in human society; it was a foundation stone at the beginning of human social formations.

Male Marginalisation in Ancient History

While men were centralised in extended families, as the human population grew and groups became larger, some extended families, lineages and clans became more dominant than others. When the matter of domination/subordination was resolved, within the covenant of kinship then the dominant extended families, lineages or clans were justified in terms of being the elder brothers and the subordinated extended families, lineages and clans accepted the designation of being the descendants of the younger brothers.

Resolution of conflicts between groups within the covenant of kinship increased the patriarchal hierarchy, such that one of the eldest fathers exercised authority way beyond his immediate family and therefore over other fathers as well. While this introduced a measure of male marginalisation, such marginalisation was muted, moderated and mitigated by the fact that the marginalised fathers were still central in their extended family, lineage or clan, and given the patriarchal hierarchy that was established, room was left for the possibility that fathers of the more marginalised lineages could move up the hierarchy, even to the top position over time as a result of some circumstance. On the other hand, women's marginalisation was deepened as the patriarchal hierarchy was expanded. But that is another Lecture.

The point that has most frequently been missed is that male marginalisation is an integral feature of patriarchy. It is most marked when families, lineages, clans and tribes contend, conflict and confront each other outside the covenant of kinship, that is, where no blood bonds or common ancestry are acknowledged. When lineages and clans confronted each other outside the covenant of kinship in circumstances where one or both groups sought dominance, the subordination of one group by the other always had more brutal and severe consequences for the men of the group that was subordinated. In *Men at Risk*, I documented the consequences for the men of the group that was subordinated. These included:

- The killing of all the men of the group while capturing the women and children and integrating them in the lineage of the conquerors
- The castration of the captured men, allowing them to keep their lives but denying them the possibility of perpetuating their lineage
- The almost permanent enslavement of the captured men.

In retrospect, male marginalisation is not a new phenomenon in human society's organisation. It is as old as human society itself. Indeed, it is an integral feature of patriarchy, the aboriginal type of human social organisation.

Contemporary Human Social Formations

Leaping from antiquity to the present, it is clear that the vast majority of human beings no longer live in small isolated patriarchal groups. However, it must be noted that in South America, Africa, Australia, and on Pacific islands, there are small groups that are not far removed from the circumstances that are characteristic of antiquity. Such groups have been excluded from, or decided not to participate in, the transformation that has taken place in human social formations.

Currently there are 203 nation-states in the world, 193 of which are sovereign states. The Montevideo Convention of 1933 stipulates that the qualifications to be a state are:

- A permanent population
- A defined territory
- A government
- The capacity to have relations with other states.

The vast majority of these 203 nation-states have urban and rural areas; varying numbers of ethnic groups; and adherents of different religions. All 203 have men and women of different ages. All 203 states have written, or in a few cases unwritten, constitutions, laws, bureaucracies, police powers, and provide public services such as health and education. The 'us' and 'them' in the national society is between citizens and foreigners—aliens. Among citizens there is, or ought to be, equality of rights guaranteed by constitution and common law.

Directions in Societal Transformation from Antiquity to the Present

The poles of the transformation from 'traditional lineage society' of antiquity to the 'modern national society' of the nation-state can be set out succinctly as follows:

1. From societies organised on the basis of blood bonds and kinship as manifested in extended family, lineage, clan, tribe, and caste and to societies organised on the basis of voluntary institutions such as the school, church, political party, trade union, company and civil service which assures access to all persons irrespective of blood bonds or kinship relationship, whether factual or fictive.

2. From societies in which the basic unit of social organisation was the kinship collective, to societies structured on the individual as the basic unit of social organisation.

3. From rights in people held by the kinship collectives to which they belong, to rights of individuals enshrined in constitutional law.

4. From the purpose of life being the perpetuation of the lineage, to individual material progress being the benchmark of success and fulfilment.

5. From government predicated on descent, from a royal lineage, to government by consent of the citizens who hold sovereign power.

6. From kingdoms premised on patriarchal structures to nation-states predicated on utopian values of equality, freedom and justice.

In a nutshell, patriarchy centralised men because societies of antiquity were organised on the basis of genealogy, generation and gender. Genealogy defined the group and differentiated it from other groups, while generation and gender established rank order within the group with older males occupying the pinnacle of the rank order. Age is mutable.

In time, young men succeed older men. Gender is fixed. Women were almost permanently marginalised within the group. The only exceptions occurred if there were breaks in male succession which would endanger loss of power, possessions or positions by the group. In such circumstances, specific women of the group by virtue of being mother, wife, sister or daughter, succeeded to central positions in order to retain power, possessions or position by the group.

Modern national society based upon individual citizenship, the rights of all citizens, and institutions accessible to all, either based on merit or voluntary association, has on paper and in principle, rendered genealogy and gender both obsolete and illegal. The high ethical vision of national society does not automatically accord men position based solely on maleness, nor does in automatically marginalise females solely for being female. Neither, should any family, lineage, tribe, clan or caste own any occupation of structure of the state based upon biological descent.

While men were centralised in the lineage society of antiquity, on paper and in principle they are equalised in contemporary national society. All the powers that were assigned to the patriarchs of numerous small lineages and clans are now concentrated into institutions of the state and national society. Physical defence is assigned to the police and military; ritual defence to the church, synagogue, mosque or temple; education to the school; administrative matters to the civil service; and capital punishment and adjudication in major matters to the courts. In this transformation, many men have been dispossessed of powers that by patriarchal traditions over several millennia were regarded as conventional male roles and powers. The general implication of this transformation has been negative for many men. The opposite has been the case for many women, but that is the subject of another Lecture.

Now that human population has expanded to the point where most people live in urban areas, individual existence has become possible. Further, as patriarchy is being dismantled in the nation-state, the life-taking roles that formerly resided with fathers, and enshrined in law up to the time of Roman law, have become major issues in contemporary society. Hence, capital punishment once the prerogative of fathers was first transferred to kings, chiefs and emperors, and then later to the State. But States are now being challenged with respect to the right to take life. One of the major issues embedded in the abortion issue centres on women entering the life-taking arena. Ironically, while the right to life is being strongly advocated by many disaffected and marginalised, young males are increasingly engaged in life-taking, whether through murder or terrorism as means of reclaiming power and position in society.

The transformation in human society is global. However, it is not to the same degree in all societies. Further, the transformation from the patriarchal society of antiquity to contemporary national society has neither been smooth nor logical nor is that transformation complete in any society. The critical question is in which societies is this transformation most and least marked?

There are three criteria that appear to differentiate societies in the transformation between lineage patriarchy and contemporary national societies. These can be listed as follows:

- Societies that have maintained continuous connection with their antiquity apropos societies that have been substantially disconnected from their antiquity.

- Societies marked by homogeneous populations that share common identifies, cultures, and world views as against heterogeneous societies comprised of numerous ethnic groups from different cultural backgrounds and holding different world views.

- Societies in which conflicts are more or less settled within the covenant of kinship, with one group accepting the hegemony of the other in exchange for autonomy within their group, apropos societies in which conflicts are between 'us' and 'them' and settled on the basis of domination, and subordination maintained by force and ideologies of superiority and inferiority.

The general and global pattern is that patriarchy tends to be conserved to a greater extent in national societies marked by continuous connection with their antiquity and in which the vast majority of people share a common identity, culture and world view and in which conflicts resolved within the framework of the covenant of kinship. On the other hand, patriarchy is transformed to a greater degree in societies with heterogeneous populations where the vast majority of people are disconnected from their roots in antiquity, and some groups dominate others by means of force and ideologies of superiority and inferiority. As such, the phenomenon of male marginalisation will be most marked in the latter and least marked in the former. Examples of the former are China and the Nordic countries of Europe, and examples of the latter are Southern Africa and New World societies, including the Commonwealth Caribbean. Given the particular focus of this Lecture, let us focus on the phenomenon of male marginalisation within the Commonwealth Caribbean.

Male Marginalisation in the Commonwealth Caribbean

Based on the general and global pattern outlined, the Commonwealth Caribbean is one of the regions of the world in which male marginalisation should be, and is, clearly manifest. Almost all the groups that compose modern Caribbean societies came, or were brought to the region, over the last 500 years. As such, there is considerable discontinuity between these groups and their ancestral societies as well as with Caribbean antiquity. The heterogeneous composition of modern Commonwealth Caribbean societies is underscored by the fact that different ethnic groups came and were brought from several different regions of the world. Further, modern Commonwealth Caribbean societies in the seventeenth century were established with great disparities of power, resources and status between the groups that came or were brought. Historical discontinuity, ethnic and cultural diversity and conflict between these diverse groups have been the ingredients of the melting pot of modern Commonwealth Caribbean.

Male Marginalisation in the Slave Society

At the inception of Commonwealth Caribbean societies in the seventeenth century, there was a relatively small English segment that commanded the legal, economic, military and social systems by virtue of imperial power. There was another British segment that carried out the administrative functions of both government and plantation. British indentured servants and African slaves were marginalised in this social formation, with the Africans, by virtue of being slaves, occupying the most marginal positions. With the growth of the slave trade, Africans gained one power—that of numbers. In a spirit of resistance, they quickly established the power of numbers as a real threat through the use of violence mainly by riot and rebellion. These expressions of the power of numbers were deemed illegal, and sanctioned by very stiff penalties, but acted as a countervailing force in the exercise of the so-called legal economic, military and social powers.

By the time of Emancipation, the basic structure of Caribbean society had emerged. There was a British ruling class comprised mainly of planters, planting attorneys and bureaucrats running the colonies; a middle group comprised of whites of modest means, Jews, freed coloureds and a few freed persons of African ancestry, living mainly in towns and involved in commerce; and the marginalised groups consisting of a few poor whites, some coloureds and the large slave population of African ancestry. Injustice, conflict between groups, the use of force to maintain the structures in favour of the ruling British minority, and episodes of violent resistance by the marginal African majority were hallmarks of the slave society in Commonwealth Caribbean countries.

Within this milieu, five paradigmic stereotypes of men emerged by the end of the slave society:

1. **The pirate:** the man who plundered the treasures of foreign powers in the name of the British monarchy while helping himself generously in the process. He used violence as his tool of trade, travelled from port to port in the region and lived recklessly in each port. Violent expropriation, recklessness, restlessness and licentious living were the trademarks of the pirate.

2. **The grandee:** the man who made investments in the slave colony, drank a lot, rode fast, gambled hard, had a lot of 'Brown skin' progeny, made it rich and then left the Caribbean to live in grandeur, sobriety and civility in the Mother Country. Business investments, licentious living and material success in the colony followed by departure from the colony to retire to a life of affluence and genteel aristocratic pursuits in Britain were the schizophrenic characteristics of grandee.

3. **The missionary:** the man who by background, belonged to the privileged segments of society but who by conviction, decided to devote his life's work to the cause of defending, and advancing the interests of the dispossessed in society, even against severe opposition from his own group. The missionary was marked by the ascriptions of privilege, and moral rejection of the status quo which required personal sacrifice in his life's undertaking and real risks in pursuing the causes he espoused.

4. **Anancy:** the man of the marginalised who outfoxed the oppressors by his wits. Irrepressible, resourceful and not hesitant to cross ethical boundaries in order to succeed. Anancy is marked with little or no

formal education, enormous 'street smarts', an abundance of common sense and an amoral approach to gaining advantage even among close friends and family. Anancy is the trickster to be wary of yet admired for his cunning and unorthodox stratagems.

5. **The rebel:** the man of the marginalised who was the author of resistance, and rebellion against the injustices imposed upon the people; not withstanding that such action would surely bring reprisals, including the loss of his life. Boldness, courage, an indomitable spirit and the use of violence characterised the rebel.

The pirate and the grandee were stereotypes of centralised white men. Anancy and the rebel were the heroes of resistance by marginalised black men. The missionaries were the heroic broker apologist that straddled the terrain between both sets of men. These stereotypic heroic men were all textured within the general society with numerous nuances and adjustments. There were pirates who did not sail to foreign ports to plunder but rather stayed on land in their own colonies and plundered the resources of their colony largely through coercion based on position, possessions, connections, and sharp business practices. There were grandees who lived in grandeur in the Caribbean with all the trappings of civility and sobriety on public show. However, they privately and covertly had several illicit relationships, fathering outside children in these relationships.

There were many of class that spawned the missionaries who did not work for the upliftment of the marginalised but on the contrary strived hard to keep the marginalised in their place by erecting myriad barriers to obstruct possible upward mobility of the marginalised. They fashioned numerous badges to mark their own superiority and to confer inferiority on the masses. Anancy did not only outsmart the pirate and the grandee but on many occasions the missionaries and rebels as well. The rebels did not always fight noble causes on behalf of the marginalised but sometimes acted just for their own advantage. A good example of this being the Maroons of Jamaica who fought the Maroon Wars of the 1730s to the point of gaining Treaties, giving them autonomy in prescribed areas. However, the Maroons subsequently sided with the British in putting down several slave rebellions. In a nutshell, the stereotypes only highlight tendencies that were embedded in a complex web of social relationships.

With these caveats in mind, it is fair to say that largely because of the combination of moral critique of slavery by the missionaries and their sponsors in Britain, the violent resistance of the slaves culminating in the Sam Sharpe Rebellion in Jamaica, in 1831. The Rebellion triggered the fear of another Haiti, and the increasing questioning of the economics of slavery as an efficient means of production. Slavery ended in August 1838. The missionaries and the rebels triumphed while the grandees acquiesced to end slavery.

Male Marginalisation in the Free Colonial Society

Emancipation guaranteed personal freedom for all members of the colony. It promised upward social mobility for those who were previously enslaved. The chief allies of the ex-slaves in immediate post-emancipation period were the Protestant denominations and the imperial government. The churches worked with the ex-slaves in ways that could be said to restore patriarchy among the people of African origins. The churches promoted marriage, helped ex-slaves to purchase property, led the movement to establish free villages, mobilised men to purchase property that made them eligible to vote, and gave some males access to the limited upward mobility opportunities that were available through the elementary education leading to teachers' college and then to theological college. This route of upward social mobility became one of the main pillars of the small Black middle class that emerged in this period, later to be joined by policemen, nurses and public health inspectors.

While the planters and their representatives in the Assembly had acquiesced to Emancipation, they adopted several measures to ensure that ex slaves would continue to be a cheap source of paid labour on the plantations. These included:

- The importation of indentured workers from India to ensure an over-supply of labour thereby keeping wages low.
- Facilitating the immigration of Chinese, Portuguese, Lebanese and Syrians to fill niches that opened up in shop-keeping, dry-goods and retail trades thus clogging the avenues of upward social mobility to these areas.
- Creating a preparatory and high school system between the 1870s and 1890s for whites of modest means, Jews and Coloureds.

- Enacting rules that imposed huge financial penalties that prevented elementary school teachers from using their teacher education to obtain jobs in the civil service and other occupations that required post-elementary education.

- Shifting the bias in teachers' colleges from male to female teachers, thus changing the main avenue of upward social mobility for Blacks from male to female. This was clearly evident by 1900.

- Restricting access to university education only to those who could afford to pay for such education in overseas institutions.

By 1900, it was clear that while the guarantee of personal freedom had been honoured, the promise of upward social mobility had not been kept. Further, the possibility of another Haiti had been averted and the products of missionary grace were now talking back to their erstwhile sponsors, hence both the Imperial Government and the missionary societies either changed sides to support the planting interest or moved to satisfy the demands of the small middle class that had emerged. This disappointment stirred the largely marginalised Black population to be sympathetic to the Garvey Movement and UNIA. They gradually turned to trade unions and political parties to represent their interests and to find common cause with the Middle Class in working towards political independence.

By the end of the colonial era, what had developed in the Caribbean was a colour/class pigmentocracy constituted of an almost white/brown upper class, an ethnically mixed middle class and an almost black/Indian lower class. While the society remained largely male dominated, the men occupying the dominant and marginalised positions were basically of different racial/ethnic backgrounds. In addition, as Miller (1984 and 1990) showed, there was a clear female bias that had developed in the structure of opportunity such that it was the females of the lower strata that had great access to the educational avenues of upward social mobility. This was not only so with respect to those going through the route of elementary schools and teachers' colleges but in some countries like Jamaica, the female bias was also visible in the prep school, high school system. Further, Black resistance to exclusion, first manifested in the Garvey movement, had morphed into spiritual resistance in the form of the Rastafarian movement, with strong tendencies toward reasserting patriarchal norms and forms.

Male Marginalisation in the Post-Independence Era

Political independence and national sovereignty were premised on the proposition that the countries would shape their own destiny, directed by the prerogatives of their citizens and not for the vested interests of any imperial power. The promise of national sovereignty was that of equal rights for all; the correction of past injustice especially to people of African and Indian ancestry; and material progress for all. It is the will of the majority that would prevail and not that of the privilege few. These objectives were to be achieved through the transfer of power, from the British ruling class to government elected by the people through adult suffrage.

National sovereignty exists; however, it is constrained by the fact that Commonwealth Caribbean states are small states within the global political economy without the military, economic or geopolitical means of ensuring equal treatment from the major powers of the world. Equal rights are enshrined in constitutions and in laws. The transfer of power has taken place. The British colonial administrators, and local planting elite, have been replaced by representatives elected through electoral systems based on adult suffrage. Consequently, most Commonwealth Caribbean countries have strong two-party democracies.

Initially, the leadership of the political parties strongly conformed to the missionary stereotype, from a sociological perspective. Where some political representatives had their roots in the marginal African or Indian majority groups, they earned missionary status through formal education credentials and the professions, especially law, medicine and teaching. Having joined the ranks of the socially advantaged, they developed a track record of working on behalf of the marginalised.

The changed structure of Commonwealth Caribbean society, in the post-independence era, can be summarised briefly as follows:

1. The pinnacle of political power increasingly resides in the hands of descendants of African slaves and Indian indentured workers, the vast majority of whom are university educated and have professional qualifications. This group is male predominant.

2. The pinnacle of economic wealth still is within the white/brown segment of the society although not exclusively so in that there are

noticeable numbers of blacks and Indians now included in this segment of society.

3. The middle cadres of professional, administrative, technical and artistically talented people who operate independently or populate the private and public bureaucracies within the countries. This segment is majority female. It is also multi-racial, multi-ethnic and multi-coloured.

4. The lower socio-economic groups that are overwhelmingly Black or Indian or both depending on the country. However, this segment of society is majority male.

There are a number of critical observations about the structure of Commonwealth Caribbean society in the post independence era that must be noted:

- Adult suffrage, which led to representative government, has produced a political class drawn from the majority groups of the society. Bluntly put elected office, whether at the national or local government level, has become a new avenue of upward social mobility. This avenue was not available to the majority segments of the society under the restricted franchise that existed in colonial times.

- The white/brown segment which dominated almost all areas of colonial life is now only dominant in the economy.

- National government has brought about a substantial expansion of the middle classes and also of the education system at all levels. However, the female bias in access to upward social mobility that was created in the Free Colonial society has continued unchanged in the Independence era. Because of the expanded education system, the female bias is even more marked in Independence. The result is that upward social mobility accessed through education is predominantly female.

- One segment of the marginalised majority has carved out its own avenue of upward social mobility, through a combination of spiritual resistance and the application of its creative talents, in the areas of music, entertainment and sports. This segment is predominately male.

- Another segment of the marginalised majority has sought to bring about material progress through crime and violence. This segment is predominately male.

Prospects:
Understanding Marginality and Centrality

Having reviewed male marginalisation, in retrospect, from its patriarchal origins in antiquity to its manifestation in contemporary Commonwealth Caribbean societies, let us shift focus to its prospects. Prospects begin in the mind. So let me approach it from two perspectives. First, to employ theory, this is the scientific way of explaining facts and predicting possibilities. Second, to seek revelation, this is the religious way of going beyond the facts and reality to identify potentials and possibilities.

Understanding Marginality and Centrality
Employing the Theory of Place

Marginality is not a disease. It is not a social pathology. Marginality is not a terminal or fatal condition. It is not a disabling factor. Certainly marginality presents obstacles and hurdles. However, it represents obstacles and hurdles that can be overcome. In essence marginality is a social fact of human society.

The human life cycle has marginality built into it. First we are dependent babies, infants and children. Then we are more independent adolescents, young adults, adults and middle-aged persons. Then many become dependent old persons. In other words, the beginning of the human life cycle is marked by marginality while, if we live long enough, the end is oft-times also marked by marginality in terms of being able to take care of one's self, independently. Then again we are not all equally endowed with the same talents and abilities, hence in some areas we are all less than others. Further, largely by accident of birth, many are born into groups that, as a result of historic circumstances, are marginalised. In these respects, marginality is a universal human social phenomenon.

The history of the human social organisation can be written from the perspective of the rise of the marginalised. As a student, in elementary school on Empire Day we were made to sing "Rule Britannia, Britannia rules the waves, Britons never never shall be slaves". But the sun has set upon the

British Empire. Britain no long rules the waves or the world. Truth be told, Britons were slaves. Britain was an outpost of the Roman Empire, that the Romans quickly abandoned by the fifth century when Rome began to be challenged by the barbarian Germanic tribes. From this marginal position Britain rose to super power status during the eighteenth and nineteenth centuries.

Two hundred years ago, the United States was a part of the Third World of those times. It was a highly indebted newly independent country whose future was not assured. From this marginal beginning, the United States rose to be a superpower in the twentieth century. Many are now saying that she had begun her decline. Indeed, before our very eyes, we are seeing the rise of China, India and Brazil in the constellation of nation-states. Further, I would be bold to say that everything that we now categorise as being part of human civilisation are the inventions, innovations and creations of particular marginal groups overcoming marginality that has now become part of the common stock of human kind. But that is another Lecture.

In the nation-states of the Caribbean, and several other parts of the world, many women are rising on the tide of marginal momentum. Having been marginalised for thousands of years by lineage, and clan patriarchy, many women are now seeing, seeking and succeeding in the opportunities presented by the constitutional and legal provisions of the nation-states that are breaking down gender barriers. Conflicts between groups have resulted in relaxing patriarchal closure in dominant groups and increase access to opportunity to women of marginalised groups.

Migrant groups are the classic practitioners of marginal energy. Having moved from their own societies to seek opportunities in other societies, their efforts are captured in the Avis motto "We strive harder". There is no better example of marginal energy displayed by migrant groups than first generation Caribbean peoples in North American and Britain. The point being made is simple. Marginality need not be a permanent condition. Neither is centrality permanent. Indeed, archeology could be described as the discipline dealing with the decline and disappearance of the central societies of the past. The list is long. But to name a few: the Sumerian, Ancient Egyptian, Indus Valley, Babylonian, Assyrian, Persian, Greek, Roman, Inca, Aztec and Mayan empires.

From the *Theory of Place*, that I have formulated, the explanation is simple. The prime motivation in society is for individuals and groups to gain and retain central places. In pursuit of gaining and retaining central places, individuals and groups will employ legitimate or illegitimate means. This is at the expense of individuals holding marginal places.

Over time, therefore, in any society, the centre becomes marked by:

1. **Comfort**, as those centralised appropriate to themselves the highest and better standards of living.

2. **Corruption**, as holders of central places seek to ensure central places for their children, relatives, clients and allies through nepotism, patronage and clientelism.

3. **Incompetence**, as persons without merit are retained in or promoted to central positions.

4. **Conservatism**, holding on to ideas, practices, technologies and methodologies well beyond their relevance and effectiveness.

In other words, over time the centre has the tendency to become marked by decadence: enjoying luxury, embracing incompetence, engaging in immoral practices such as nepotism and patronage, and conservative by holding on to obsolete and outdated ideas, methodologies and technologies.

On the other hand, the margin over time becomes marked by:

1. A lower standard of living than the centre.
2. Competence, as some members strive to overcome marginality based on merit and talent.
3. Moral force, because it is discriminated against.
4. Inventiveness and risk taking tendencies because it has nothing to lose and everything to gain.

In time the margin develops strong motivation to succeed, competence in most avenues of human endeavour, moral force in the face of discrimination and prejudice, creativity in confronting adversity and the will to and momentum to change the circumstances. In other words, the marginal develops the energy to overcome marginality, marginal energy.

Understanding Marginality and Centrality Employing the New Testament

Allow me to use the Life of Jesus, as recorded in the New Testament, to address the issue of marginality and centrality and therefore of the prospects of marginal men.

In the beginning was the Word, and the Word was with God and the Word was God. He occupied the central position in bringing the world into being, became flesh and dwelt among human kind. However, when God took on human form He did so as a marginal man.

Jesus was conceived out of wedlock. His mother and his stepfather were persons of relatively low social rank. Both were persons of very modest economic means. He was born in an unimportant rural village in the most inauspicious circumstances. He went to school but did not go above the elementary level. After leaving school, he did vocational training and became a carpenter. He was an itinerant preacher and teacher, not sanctioned by the High Priest. He was charged with a crime but declared innocent by the judge. Yet, he was condemned and executed like a common criminal. There was no public protest of this gross injustice. Indeed, the crowd shouted for the release of a guilty man instead of Him. He was executed on a cross, the most ignominious form of capital punishment employed by the Romans. He was buried in a borrowed tomb. Everything about his conception, birth, rural origin, upbringing, occupation, death and burial is marked by marginality. Marginality marks the entire life-cycle of Jesus, and with it all the abuses, brutality, humiliation, betrayal and brutality that men of power heap on marginalised men.

The pronouncement and declaration of God on marginality is abundantly clear. Marginality is a creation of man, not of God. Marginality does not limit our humanity. It does not determine who a person is. Marginality presents obstacles but it is not the final arbiter of what anyone can become. Marginality is not an excuse or justification for evil. On the contrary, the life of Jesus demonstrated that marginality is the circumstance in which God's enabling, and redemptive power is most readily visible and His Goodness and Grace is most easily seen.

Jesus was not a warrior. He did not take up arms against those who opposed him. His power did not come from killing others. He did not belong to or embrace the culture of death. He did not see the elimination of those who got in his way as the solution to any problem nor did he employ destruction of others as a tool by which to advance. On the contrary, He was the standard bearer and champion of life, abundant life, everlasting life, life devoted to the goodwill and upliftment of others. His mission was to demonstrate how life ought to be lived to its fullest. Spirit and the life principle applied against the obstacles and hurdles stacked against the marginalised are the means of defeating the odds, exceeding the expectations of the naysayer, overcoming prejudice, demystifying myths of inferiority and showing what can be accomplished by those that are despised by society.

Life and spirit are the antidotes for the happenstance of marginality.

Jesus exemplified that a man's worth cannot be estimated or measured in terms of material possessions. His was the lot of the majority of human kind. He owned no property. His possessions were just about enough to take care of his daily existence. By life and lip, Jesus declared that it was what you did with what you had: the one talent, the five talents or the ten talents that really counted. How you used your talents was the key, not the amount of talents that you had. The life of Jesus revealed that character was supreme. Character is measured by the extent to which one's life is obedient to, in compliance with and congruent to the Word of God, the Way of God and the Will of God. His life of holiness, purity, selfless service and sacrifice still speaks to every generation through the years of the best in human personality, of nobility in action, of goodness in relationship and of righteousness in all circumstances. The evil that was done to him stopped with him. What came from him was good and through that goodness mankind is redeemed.

He observed no convention or respected no social barrier where these would hinder him from serving the needs of those who needed his assistance. Nationality, race, residence, class, gender and social ostracisms did not frustrate his ministry or service. His approach was inclusive. Whosoever will could come and be healed, or fed or be redeemed. He conversed and communed with lepers, women of ill repute, tax-collectors the so-called traitors and fifth columnists of Jewish society, Samaritans, Scribes, Pharisees and Publicans. He respected the common humanity of all human kind and included them in his ministry.

Why would God's way of the transformation of society be the lamb that was slain?

I offer one possibility. It is because marginality is not divinely ordained but constructed by human beings who have power.

Change, involving the overthrow of the powerful by the marginalised, usually involves replacing the people holding power without any alteration in how power is used.

Power is seductive.

Power is prone to reprisal.

Power invariably looks after it own and falls to the temptation to overreach itself. There is something special when one finds out that one is able to get one's way even against opposition.

Power has a euphoric and exhilarating feeling. This is even more so when the tables are turned. Vengeance often follows empowerment because power has such a great propensity to repay wrongs of the past, and to quickly become self-centred, self-serving, selfish and arrogant.

God's way of transformation is not simply to replace the actors but also to change the play. The resurrection of the lamb that was slain gives power to those that have felt the full abuse and cruelty of power, while remaining faithful to God's instruction that "vengeance is mine, I will repay saith the Lord." God's method of transformation is to put power in the hands of those who can be depended upon not only to replace those who previously held power, but who will exercise the power gained in a manner that will change the play. These are the Mandela's of this world, whose lives are beacons, shining in the darkness of vengeance.

Concluding Comment

Ladies and gentlemen, brothers and sisters I have shared with you this evening, some of the content of conversations between Archdeacon William Thompson and myself. Those conversations enriched my own thinking on this difficult subject. He understood that in looking at the long run of history, male marginalisation was not new in society, only that its manifestation in these times was different. He understood that male marginalisation was real. Not all men are dominant. He knew that the difficulties that this phenomenon posed for those experiencing it, were both enormous and unjust. However, he had a profound grasp of the fact that male marginalisation was not a hopeless condition although many marginalised males had lost hope. Inspired by his belief in Jesus the Christ, Archdeacon sought to bring hope especially to young men who had lost hope and to challenge those who had successfully ascended the political and economic structures to correct the historic injustices by using their strength to do what is right, just and noble.

Male marginalisation and female marginalisation are not simply gender issues. Rather, they are profoundly related to the structure of society and other axes of social injustice with deep rooted histories. The prospects of all forms of marginalisation reside in the extent to which we confront the present. We then decide to construct the future based on just social structures, the equal value of all human beings, and the necessity for the individuals of each generation to develop their endowments and potential without regard for the happenstance of their birth.

The lesson we should take from male marginalisation, in retrospect, is that human social organisations that only seek the welfare of their own, invariably marginalises those who are not 'us', but 'them'. Applying this lesson within our own times, we can say that political parties that only use political power for the benefit of their stalwarts and financial supporters; corporations run for the benefit of their managers; schools run for the convenience of principals and teachers; churches operated for the welfare of their pastors and unions that serve mainly the interest of union representatives and delegates will marginalise others. However, by so doing, they sow seeds of their own decline and demise. Look no further than Lehman Brothers and Bear Stearns for recent examples. Theoretical analysis shows that looking after one's own, at the expense of others, breeds corruption, tolerates incompetence, introduces complacency, leads to conservatism and ends in decadence and decline.

The lesson we should take from the Scriptures, and particularly from the life of Jesus, is that marginalisation is not a justification for evil. Neither is marginalisation a determinant of who people are, or what they can become. Marginalisation is there to be overcome. The pitfalls to be avoided are the adoption of a victim mindset and becoming overwhelmed by a sense of hopelessness. The path to follow is marked by an indomitable spirit, assertive confrontation of the circumstances, creativity in construction of possibilities and reliance on God who is the champion of the marginalised.

The lesson we should draw from the life and work of Venerable Archdeacon William Thompson, Father Willie, William of Grants Town, is that those who follow Christ cannot stay neutral in the mission to construct human society of just, noble and righteous foundations. Despite the risks involved on all sides, and the dangers that lurk around many corners, the mission is not just to change players but to change the play itself. The life that is truly worth living is the life sincerely engaged with giving hope to the hopeless, bringing relief to those who are suffering, providing opportunities to the young especially those that are marginalised, giving voice to the voiceless, defending the weak against the powerful, challenging the centralised to do justly, and engaging in acts of practical holiness that are not for publicity or personal gain but for the enrichment of the lives of those we seek to serve.

Tragically, William of Grants Town, Venerable Archdeacon William Thompson died by the hand of a misguided marginalised young man who did not know that a 'purse' given at a retirement event did not mean cash in the rectory. Father Willie lives forever with his Saviour and Lord, who gives life eternal to those who believe and who live so that others can live life abundantly.

~

Chapter 18

Sixty Years of Teacher Education: Lessons for the 21st Century

~

THE INAUGURAL CONFERENCE OF TEACHERS' COLLEGES OF JAMAICA
October, 2013

~

Master of Ceremonies, Mr. Leaon Nash, Mrs. Yvonne Clarke, Dean of the Teachers Colleges of Jamaica, Dr. Mark Nicely, President of the Jamaica Teachers' Association, Dr. Marcia Stewart, Manager of the Joint Board of Teacher Education, Mr. Garth Anderson, Principal Church Teachers' College, Mr. Edward Shakes, Principal G. C. Foster College of Physical Education and Sports, Dr. Christopher Clarke, Chairman of the Organising Committee of the Conference, specially invited guests, fellow awardees, and colleagues all, I thank you most profoundly for the immense privilege to be given an award as well as for the honour to be the Guest Speaker at this special Awards event. I have worked with each of the other awardees, know their worth, eminence and the unique contribution that each has made to the teacher education enterprise.

A backward reach made with the intention to inform a forward leap has wisdom at its core. The theme for this inaugural Conference is most apt. However, allow me to take the liberty of resetting the timeframe of review from fifty to sixty years. This extension of the timeframe permits a clear distinction to be made between teacher education as it existed from its creation in the 1830s and continued up to 1953, and the period since the establishment of the Ministry of Education in 1953, when Ministerial Government came into being in Jamaica. This clear distinction between

TEACHERS COLLEGES OF JAMAICA

THE MICO UNIVERSITY COLLEGE, KINGSTON
ESTABLISHED 1836

BETHLEHEM TEACHERS' COLLEGE, ST. ELIZABETH
ESTABLISHED 1861

SHORTWOOD TEACHERS' COLLEGE, KINGSTON
ESTABLISHED 1885

ST. JOSEPHS TEACHERS' COLLEGE, KINGSTON
ESTABLISHED 1897

MONEAGUE TEACHERS COLLEGE, ST. ANN
ESTABLISHED 1956

CHURCH TEACHERS' COLLEGE, MANDEVILLE
ESTABLISHED 1965

SAM SHARPE TEACHERS' COLLEGE, MONTEGO BAY
ESTABLISHED 1975

CATHOLIC COLLEGE OF MANDEVILLE (CCM)
ESTABLISHED 1992

teacher education at the end of the colonial era, and as it has been transformed in the era of political independence is critical and fundamental to any lesson that must be taken into the twenty-first century.

A Brief Sketch of Teacher Education in Jamaica in 1953

In 1953, the totality of the established teacher education capacity in Jamaica was four small single-sex teachers' colleges that trained elementary school teachers: Bethlehem, St. Joseph's and Shortwood and Mico that trained male teachers. Three were located in Kingston and the fourth, Bethlehem, was rural. Because Mico was the largest college, the overall ratio of female to male teachers in training was about 60:40. However, the total enrolment of the four colleges was about 300 students. The heads of the colleges were expatriates and the staffs a mixture of expatriates and Jamaicans. Admission required the Third Jamaica Local Examination set by the Department of Education. The teacher education programme was three years intra-mural. Successful students were awarded a diploma which was generally equated to be equivalent to the Senior Cambridge Examination taken at the end of Fifth Form in high schools. In essence, teacher education was articulated with the elementary school system and equated to secondary education.

The four teachers' colleges constituted the second rung of the education ladder for Black people, or small settlers, or little people or the ordinary people, whatever euphemism that you wish to use. Teachers' colleges constituted one segment of the socially segregated education system, the other segment being the preparatory/high school system that catered to the small middle class. Within the framework of Jamaican and Caribbean pigmentocracy, the elementary school/teacher college segment was of darker hue and the prep school/high school system was of lighter shade. Just over 40 percent of teachers in the elementary school system had graduated from college.

By 1953, the education system, although still socially segregated, was more nuanced in terms of colour/class than it was in the 1880s. The principal difference was the growing number of children of darker hue in high schools. Invariably, these students were children of Ministers of Religion or of elementary school teachers. Indeed, many Ministers of Religion, particularly of the non-conformist denominations, were first trained as elementary school teachers. Ministers of Religion and elementary schools teachers were able to assist their children to pass the high school entrance examinations, which sometimes included Latin, and, at great sacrifice, to pay the school fees that were charged. In a nutshell, teachers' colleges were the fountain head of the small Black middle class that existed following emancipation and up to independence.

1953 marked the year in which the capacity to train secondary school teachers was inaugurated. Prior to 1953, Jamaica had no indigenous capacity to train secondary school teachers. Almost all of the principals and most of the qualified teachers were recruited from Britain. While there were some qualified Jamaican and Caribbean high school teachers, most Jamaicans teaching in high schools were past students of the schools who had been successful in either the Cambridge Higher Schools or Senior Cambridge examinations. Overall, most of the Jamaicans teaching in high schools were unqualified. Further, the turnover of high school teachers was very high as some expatriates returned home and unqualified Jamaicans moved to other jobs or went on to further studies.

However, in 1952, the Department of Education of the University College of the West Indies, UCWI, was established to offer a one year Diploma in Education to persons with Bachelor's degrees in the subjects that they proposed to teach in high schools. As such, UCWI was initially articulated with the high school system. The Department admitted its first students in October 1953.

To complete this sketch, it must be pointed out that elementary school teaching and high school teaching were socially two separate occupations. Elementary school teachers came from one social segment of the society and high school teachers from the other. Further, elementary school teachers and high school teachers were also paid differently, the former salaries being lower than the latter. However, male and female elementary school teachers were paid the same salaries while male high school teachers were paid slightly higher salaries than females. Moreover, university graduates were debarred from teaching in elementary schools. Also, only a few teachers college graduates taught in high schools.

It is this small, segregated and deficient system of teacher education, inherited from the colonial era that has been transformed, over the past sixty years, into the current enterprise.

A Brief Sketch of Teacher Education
as it Exists in 2013

The broad contours of teacher education in 2013 can be mapped briefly as follows:

1. There are ten public colleges, one public university, two private universities, at least two private colleges, the regional University of the West Indies and off-shore universities that are engaged in teacher education.

2. All institutions engaged in teacher education are co-educational, with about 80 percent of students enrolled being female.

3. Colleges and universities that train teachers are distributed across the country from east to west and north to south.

4. The indigenous capacity that has been developed produces teachers for schools at all levels of the education system: early childhood, primary, secondary and special education.

5. Entry to teacher education is defined in terms of successful completion of high schooling as measured by the Caribbean Examinations Council.

6. Teacher education is firmly and solidly part of the tertiary education level of education.

7. The teacher education capacity which was developed, now produces more teachers than the school system needs.

8. Jamaica has become a net exporter of teachers particularly to the United States, Canada and Britain.

9. Teachers, male and females, at the early childhood, primary and secondary levels are paid within the same salary scales depending on academic qualifications, professional training and years of teaching experience.

10. At the primary level, 93 percent of teachers are trained, with just over 50 percent holding at least a bachelor degree.

11. At the secondary level, 82 percent of the teachers are trained, with 60 percent having university degrees.

12. Currently, hundreds of qualified teachers with Diplomas and Bachelor degrees are unemployed.

Accomplishments of the Last 60 Years

There can be no gainsaying the fact, that when teacher education in 1953 is compared with teacher education in 2013, a great transformation has taken place in size, scale, scope, and standard.

What has this transformation achieved?

- The teaching profession, in Jamaica, has been Jamaicanised and made self-sustaining. Many teachers, in all types of schools, are Jamaicans, including the teacher educators.

- Teacher education not only supplies teachers for the school system but also qualified personnel for a wide range of occupations that serve people in the public and private sectors. Over the 60-year period, about 90,000 have been trained by colleges and universities for a school system that operates with 25,000 teachers. Taking the working life of a teacher, prior to retirement to be 35 years, the output of the colleges has been in excess of the demand for teachers by the school system over this 60-year period.

- The products of Jamaican teacher education have proven to be internationally competitive. Without preferential arrangements between governments, Jamaican teachers, on their own initiative have established the validity of their education, training, and credentials by competence and performance in the international market place, in a manner not dissimilar to our musicians, entertainers, athletes, sportsmen and informal commercial importers.

- The Jamaican teacher education system leads the Commonwealth Caribbean in its scope, governance, and methods of validation. Several of its innovations and elements have been copied by a number of countries of the sub-region. Jamaica was the first country to begin training secondary school teachers through its teachers' colleges. Its special education capacity has allowed Jamaica to prepare teachers in this area especially for the Eastern Caribbean countries. The model developed for training personnel, at the early childhood level, has been copied by several countries. Jamaican early childhood educators played a leading role in writing International Labour Organisation (ILO) standards for early childhood education.

- The teachers produced by the expanded system have been high calibre citizens in Jamaica and in every country to which they have migrated. Most have been deeply involved in the communities in which they work and live. The Jamaica Teachers' Association is the largest and among the most effective union in the country. Its credit union has the highest capital base and the lowest default level among credit unions in the country. Among the Jamaican diaspora, past students of teacher-training colleges have been among the best organised in the different countries.

The short answer to the question of what has been achieved over the last 60 years is that we have firmly established a teacher education industry with proven export capacity. Further, the products of Jamaican teacher education have been well educated, competent professionals of character, committed to community and to service wherever they live and work. Indeed, teacher education has been one of the great successes of the Independence era.

The Enabling Factors of the Transformation

Given the remarkable nature of the transformation that has occurred in teacher education over the last 60 years, the question becomes, what have been the major enabling factors? These in my opinion are the following:

1. Insulation of the teacher certification apparatus from direct political influence. This was deliberately and explicitly adopted as policy in 1953 at the inception of the Ministry of Education. The Board of Teacher Training was established with the chairman and the majority of members being drawn from the profession and from outside of the Ministry. Immediately following Independence, to provide even greater insulation, and with help from the Ford Foundation, the teacher-certification function was devolved to the Institute of Education of the UWI. This was done with ceremony and fanfare in 1965 with the establishment of the Institute of Teacher Education, later renamed the Joint Board of Teacher Education.

2. An ongoing legally constructed institutional partnership with the partners being the Ministry of Education, the Colleges training teacher-, the Jamaica Teachers' Association and the University of the West Indies, which presided over the partnership. This institutional partnership brought together in constant interaction, policy-formulation, implementation, professional interests and research and development resources. Further, the partnership involved multilayered working relationships through Boards of Studies, which over time, created an organic community of teacher educators.

3. Responsiveness of the partnership to the imperatives of the Jamaican education system as the system expanded, required improvements in quality, demanded innovations, reacted to resource constraints and needed human resource development. This partnership has been structured, interactive, and participatory and has involved: The chief technical officers of the Ministry, particularly in curriculum development and school supervision, college principals and lecturers, professional development officers of the Jamaica Teachers' Association, and University researchers from difficult faculties.

4. Functional cooperation in teacher education, beginning with the Bahamas and Belize, and later extending to Cayman Islands, Turks and Caicos Islands and other countries of the Commonwealth Caribbean. This not only helped to share costs but also involved contrasts of circumstances resulting in cross-fertilization of ideas in problem solving.

The Inhibiting or Resisting Factors

Seldom is there great gain, without severe pain, caused when enabling factors clash with inhibiting factors, resulting in tensions and contentions. From my experience, and without seeking to be exhaustive, allow me to identify five inhibiting factors within the teacher education partnership

i. The tendency of partners, in seeking to reach agreement, to give up a preferred position in order to gain from similar action by other partners, but then seek to renege on their commitment during implementation. Failure to keep the partnership honest and honourable has dire consequences for trust. Maintaining the integrity of agreements is a major responsibility of those who presided over the partnership.

ii. The tendency of teacher training institutions to embrace collaboration and cooperation for reasons of benefit, but not on the basis of principle, resulting in the breaking of pacts for the advantage of their particular institutions.

iii. The tendency of institutions to be so focused on their own interest, and advantage, only to lose sight of the greater and common good of teacher education.

iv. Myopia, which cannot see beyond the short-term and the existing problems. Therefore, there is a lack of any long-term vision of the opportunities to be seized and the prospects to be explored.

v. Resource constraints, which are in no need of further elaboration.

Persistent Patterns

Neither success nor transformation is ever complete. What patterns of teacher education of 1953 still persist or may even have deteriorated?

Briefly the most glaring are:

1. The gender bias in favour of females. In the 1880s there was considerable difficulty in finding suitably qualified young women to be trained as teachers. By 1900, structural reforms were enacted and implemented to rectify this problem. By the 1950's, a distinct bias had emerged in favour of females. Since 1953, this bias has become even more pronounced. No structural reforms or provisions have been implemented to ensure better gender balance among teachers at any level of the education system. The policy intention of the late 1890s continues in the twenty-first century.

2. The cross-purpose between providers and participants. Teacher education is provided to supply teachers to schools. Many students gain admission to train as teachers because it is the most affordable option that they have in pursuit of their desire for upward social mobility.

3. Entrants to teachers' colleges now take an educational route through high schooling, attaining higher admission requirements and are

largely from the same sociological origins as their peers of 1953. In other words, teacher education remains a principal means of upward social mobility for the same social segments it has served from its inception, the difference being that they now take a different education route and teach at all levels of the education system, not only the primary level.

Lessons for the Twenty-First Century

Lessons from the last 60 years of teacher education ought to be taken into the twenty-first century. They can and should be drawn from the advances made, the factors that enabled these advances and the inhibiting factors that had to be overcome. These lessons are legion. Given the time limitations of this Address, to avoid being abstract, allow me to apply some lessons to two persistent problems and two current hot-button issues.

The Gender Gap among Teachers

In 1953, there were four single-sex colleges that trained teachers: three female and one male and the gender-ratio among elementary school teachers was 60:40. Over the last 60 years, all colleges and universities training teachers have become co-educational and the ratio is now 80:20.

One lesson is the matter of single-sex and co-educational institutions being immaterial to the gender gap. Another lesson is that the expansion of the teacher education enterprise, within a co-education framework, has widened the gender gap. A third lesson is that despite much talk, no measure taken so far has yet been effective.

In this regard, it may be instructive to revisit the deliberate and intentional policy measures taken in the late 1890s to shift the gender bias from being male to female. These included structural changes, incentives and sustaining these until the desired shift was achieved. These are well documented in Miller (1994), Marginalisation of the Black Male. The fact is that the intentions of the late 1890s have prevailed for the entire twentieth century and continue into the twenty-first century. The reason appears to be the absence of the will to train more men as teachers. Proof of will may well be the provision of more boarding accommodation for male students.

The Unemployment of Significant Numbers of Qualified Teachers

The roots of this current situation are four-pronged:

1. The annual output supplied by the teacher education capacity is greater than the annual needs of education system for teachers

2. The economic downturn in Jamaica, the Commonwealth Caribbean and North America has constrained attrition from the Jamaican school system as well as resulted in the return of teachers who had left teaching during better economic times.

3. The steady decline in student enrolment at the primary and secondary levels due to the steady decline of live births, resulting in the steady decline of the number of students of primary and secondary school age in the population.

4. The legal right of unqualified teachers to remain in teaching for six years. A similar situation occurred, to a lesser degree, in the early 1980s. This experience also provides some lessons that should be taken into the twenty-first century. These can be listed as follows:

    a. Extreme caution should be exercised in considering proposals to cut back or reduce the teacher education capacity that has been built. This should only become an option if there is no economic recovery in the Jamaican, Caribbean, and North American economies over the next five to ten years and if other measures taken prove unsuccessful. Should such economic recovery occur within the next five years to ten years, another exodus of teachers can be expected. Cutting back capacity would then result in deficit to supply the demands of the school system, such as occurred in the late 1980s.

    b. Even in circumstances of unemployment of qualified teachers, teachers' colleges will remain attractive as an avenue of upward social mobility for able and ambitious young people of modest means, especially from rural areas. Teacher education provides developed talent at the tertiary level for occupations other than teaching. Further, it is tertiary education that gives competitive advantage in the global economy. Cutting capacity in any segment of tertiary education in Jamaica would be a huge mistake. As I have said and written, Jamaican and Caribbean education has an unusual deformity—a very broad body of early childhood, primary and secondary education upon which a pinhead of tertiary education sits. Our level of provision and participation in early childhood, primary and secondary education match the high income countries, but our level of provision of tertiary and higher education lags behind other so-called developing world.

c. Dismiss the idea of privatizing teacher education, as recently raised in the Senate. It is a socially retrogressive thought given the history and sociology of teacher education. In addition, the conditions and constituencies are there to mobilise resistance to this idea such that the political cost at the polls could be huge for any government or opposition that embraces it. Any political party that dares to do this should be made to pay.

d. The teacher education industry that has been created has produced teachers who, on their individual initiative, have competed successfully within the Caribbean, North America and Britain. They have the potential to be further developed, enhanced and fine-tuned to supply teachers to these countries as well as to English-speaking countries, in Africa and elsewhere, which have growing demand for teachers. In this regard, the Diaspora of past students across the world, and the initiatives already taken by some colleges and universities constitute a great resource. The opportunity should be taken to significantly expand the export of teachers to both traditional and non-traditional markets. In addition, Jamaican teacher education has the competence and capacity to attract students from areas of the Anglophone world that needs to produce more teachers. Jamaican teacher education should deliberately enter the global competition for such students.

Given the teacher education capacity that exists, it is possible to complete the transition to a fully qualified teacher force in the foreseeable future. Careful attention will be needed in how this is done and begins with providing the means to achieve full accreditation.

The Licensing of Teachers

The recommendation of the Transformation Task Force in Education to establish a Teaching Council to license teachers is positive and sound. Licensing teachers in a manner similar to other professional groups will advance teaching as a profession. The clear beneficiaries of a Teaching Council, setting and maintaining professional standards for teachers, will be children and young people who are taught and the teachers who teach them.

Recently, the JTA sent me the Draft Bill of the Jamaica Teaching Council, and accompanying documents, as part of their request for my opinion. I found the Consultation Paper most instructive. From my limited layman's knowledge, the Bill seems well drafted. However, my advice to the JTA was to reject the Draft Bill in its current form. It is my considered opinion that if enacted, as is, the proposed Teaching Council would create far more problems than it solves and would be an absolute disservice to the teaching profession. In a nutshell, the Draft Bill is not ready for broadcast much less prime time. The reasons for the advice given are as follows:

1. The composition of the Board of the Council is a throwback to colonial times. The largest single block is seven ex-officio members including the Financial Secretary and Solicitor General. This is not a matter of voting rights but strength of voice in arguing issues. This throwback indicates no knowledge of the lesson of institutional partnership.

2. There is no requirement for the great majority of Board members of the Council to be nominated, or elected by the professional association, and for them to be licensed members of the teaching profession.

3. The Consultation Paper states that the Council is an agency of the Ministry of Education, which is somewhat unusual for conceptualisation for such a body. However, the Draft Bill goes even beyond this and makes the Council the creature of the Minister. Please note, I am not making any reference to the current holder of the post of Minister of Education. I am taking issue with the powers proposed to be given to Ministers of Education hereto forth. The draft Bill proposed that the Minister:

- Appoints six members on his own judgment
- Can appoint a person to act temporarily in the place of any appointed member in case of absence or incapacity of that member
- Appoints the Chairman from among the members
- Grants leave to members
- Set the remuneration of members
- Approve the appointment of standing committees and specify their terms of reference
- Approve the appointment of special committees
- Can revoke the appointment of any member subject to any one of six specified conditions, and
- Ensure that the Council is evenly balance between men and women.

4. The Draft Bill not only ignores the lesson of insulating professional matters related to teachers from political influence, it creates a highway for such influence.

5. The proposed Teaching Council is in no way comparable to any of twelve Councils legally established to regulate the other professional groups in Jamaica.

6. Taken at face value, the Council would require a massive bureaucracy to carry out its functions. With over 25,000 teachers, teachers constitute by far the largest professional group in the country. Just to carry out its core function of licensing will require a much larger bureaucracy. Nevertheless, this Draft Bill takes a greenfield approach. No recognition is given to teacher education comparable to say legal education, or medical education or pharmacy education in their respective roles to those professions. Accordingly, the Draft Bill gives the Council powers to set up testing and examination systems at very basic levels, for example, to test literacy and numeracy. This would significantly increase the bureaucracy required. Then again, instead of providing for a Disciplinary Committee as is standard, the Council is given the power to take over directly, and centrally, the disciplining of teachers from public and private school boards and employers.

This again would require substantial bureaucracy. A massive increase in the public bureaucracy could neither be justified nor financed in circumstances of IMF requirements that the public sector must be cut, significantly. Powers granted with no prospect of the resources needed, will cause the proposed Council to be impotent at birth.

Note that I have shared with you the opinion and advice that I have given the JTA upon their request. Professionally, I have learned not to give advice to persons or entities that do not request such.

Abandoning the Development Paradigm: Constructing Caribbean Civilisation

Allow me to conclude with an issue that runs deep within my soul and constantly exercises my mind. I crave your indulgence for a hearing and your patience if you conclude that I am talking foolishness. My only defence is that I truly believe this foolishness.

Some of our forebearers, over several generations, had a clear vision of personal freedom and their mission to resist and strive to abolish slavery. Later and likewise, they have had a clear vision of national sovereignty and their mission to strive for political independence. Today, we enjoy both personal freedom as individuals and collective freedom as a nation. However, in the twenty-first century we appear to be lost in freedom. We do not appear to have any central focus, consensus or clear vision on how to use our personal freedoms for the common good of our country or region.

I believe that our forebearers would weep at the senseless slaughter now common among our young men. They would be driven to despair at the physical violence, practiced by the dons, and the structural violence that continue to be inflicted by those who have inherited powers once exercised by the colonial masters. They would unanimously agree that these are not what their sacrifices were intended to achieve.

We share with the rest of the Caribbean a blessed location on planet earth. Warm climate year round; great beaches; sands of various colours but mainly white; countless sunny, cloudless days each year; cooling land breezes; refreshing sea breezes; and an alluring bio-diversity. The Caribbean as a place is often and rightly described as 'paradise'. Yet, our modern history is that of generations of people catching hell on a daily basis. It is time to bring the human condition in sync with the beauty of the flora and fauna of the sub-region.

What have we learned about our first efforts in political freedom over the last 60 years?

The short answer is that the development paradigm is a dead-end.

The essence of the development paradigm is that the former colonial powers are well developed and their former colonies are underdeveloped. A shift in this paradigm can only occur when the former colonies imitate the colonial powers' policies and systems, taking guidance, and using grants and loans from their institutions.

The fundamental flaw in this development paradigm is the assumption that there is a terminus to human society, and that these powerful countries had reached that terminus by the genius of their people and the systems that they had created. Others can reach this terminus by imitation and without the powers used to achieve their position of dominance.

Understand, there are no genes within the human genome that define and determine the form and terminus of human societies. The form, share and destiny of societies result from the learned behaviours and the outcome of the choices made by their members.

Another lesson we should have learned is that as a small marginal country in the geopolitics of this world, imitating the powerful, relying on their people, resources and institutions simply perpetuates dependencies and grow debt. What development paradigm thinking does is:

- Obscure the power relationships in the world
- Foster dependency on aid and loans that benefit the donors more than the recipients
- Stifle local enterprise
- Encourage debt and then blame the victims for their lack of progress.

Essentially, it keeps us locked into relationships, almost exclusively, with the former colonial powers and their successors.

Yet, the ultimate lesson is, that our people have made the greatest advances in areas in which they have not depended upon preferential treatment by the powerful nations, nor benefitted from getting massive waivers from our governments.

These advances have been made by those of our people who have accepted and met the demands of the international competition, honed their talents, used enterprise and initiative, mastered new technologies and been confident in their abilities.

Teachers are included in the band of persons who have learned this ultimate lesson.

Now, it is time to chart a new course and to adopt a different world view. China, India and some countries of Africa, are on the move in the twenty-first century. These are continents and countries from which some of our ancestors came. How should we relate to them? Hopefully it is not as mendicants. In this hemisphere, countries like Brazil, Mexico and Chile are in the process of becoming regional powers. Within Latin America, we are an addendum as reflected in 'Latin America and the Caribbean'. How do we relate to these Latin American powers, outside of attracting tourists?

The circumstances of the world in the twenty-first century demand new thinking, new relationships and new understandings, including of ourselves. We are being confronted by civilisations in a manner as never before. We will need to deal with these civilisations as a civilisation and not principally as nation-states. These are not matters to be relegated to the exclusive province of political leaders. They affect all of us. Allow me to suggest the broad terms and general directions that should guide our thinking in the twenty-first century:

1. Recognition and confidence that there is, and we are a part of, a Caribbean civilisation that has already made us distinct from those of our ancestral origins and hemispheric neighbours. At the same time, common threads connect us with the fabric of those civilisations, thus, enabling conversations that are not those of strangers.

2. Obligation and commitment to construct Caribbean civilisation by advancing Caribbean institutions, creating linkages between national institutions such that insularity is surmounted, and there is continuing and constant engagement in confronting and transforming the sources of structural violence that have caused so much pain to generations of our people.

3. Duty to inspire, motivate and encourage our people, especially the young, to devote their personal talents and endowments to the common good of just and civilized relations and to ensure the advancement of the region in the world community.

4. Determination and will to sever the remaining colonial vestiges, like the Privy Council, which retain self-doubt in our capacity to creatively and constructively address the existential challenges of our times.

A Vision of Teacher Education in the Twenty-First Century

Education is about vision, values and virtue.

Education is about mobilising a people to construct their future in noble ways.

Education is about civilisation, at its most elemental level, producing civilized people.

Schools, colleges and universities connect people across generations with common identities, bonds of solidarity, core values and a shared sense of destiny, thus, allowing the mobilization and the civilizing mission to be sustained over decades or even centuries. Teacher education occupies a unique position in this process because it is the source of cultivating the agents of this mobilising and civilizing mission.

Over the last sixty years, a Jamaican teacher education enterprise of sufficient size, comprehensive scope, and improving standards has been established. It has produced competent professionals of character and commitment to community and to service. The mission and the role of teacher education in the twenty-first century are to take this established enterprise, complete its unfinished business, direct and focus its energies and resources to the challenges facing the country and its people in this new century. This is not only with respect to knowledge, skills and competences but also with respect to the identity, solidarity, outlook, character, mindset and sensibilities that teachers and citizens must possess, and model, in order to survive and prosper in this century.

The urgency of this task is underscored by the obligation of colleges and universities to effectively educate and prepare their students for the world

CHECKLIST FOR TEACHER EDUCATION

1. Providing high quality education designed to foster creative and critical thinking skills, ensure solid knowledge of content in required subjects, ensure sound pedagogic content knowledge and the required mastery of teaching skills

2. Ensuring competence, proficiency and mastery in the use of information and communication technologies in learning, teaching and everyday life. This requires that each staff member, and all teacher trainees, are in possession of several electronic devices that are networked, connected to its intranet, and the internet, and are used routinely in all aspects of learning, work and life.

3. Having centres of excellence marked by the critical mass of staff, facilities, equipment and students needed to prepare world class teachers at particular levels of the education and in specializations within these levels, and with doors open to students from across the region. In other words, resisting the urge for each college to be all things to the education system of its country.

4. Being part of the agreed collective of institutions covering the entire spectrum of teacher education needed by the education systems of Jamaica and the Caribbean

5. Being integrated into the Caribbean community of practice in teacher education with multi-layered connections involving students, professional staff, administrators, past-students, policy advisors, professional associations and education researchers.

6. Being integrated into a Caribbean placement service which provides college graduates with assistance in accessing job opportunities in countries of the Caribbean and across the world.

7. Being integrated into the knowledge networks of the world through the Caribbean Knowledge and Learning Network (CKLN).

that faces them on graduation. This is not an academic exercise. It is duty and responsibility. Therefore, within the context of the mission of continuing to construct the Caribbean civilisation, allow me to conclude with a simple check-list against which teacher education institutions should assess themselves in the education of their students.

God bless you all in this effort.

Chapter 19

The English-Speaking Caribbean in its Journey of Discovery of our Common Humanity

A REPLY TO
THE EDUCATION INTERNATIONAL
ALBERT SHANKER EDUCATION AWARD 2004
JULY, 2004

President, Mary Futrell; General Secretary, Fred van Leeuwen; and distinguished colleagues all, it is with sincere gratitude and deep humility that I receive the Education International Albert Shanker Education Award for 2004. Lifetime awards for service cannot be attributed only to the individuals who receive them, for no one is an island nor self-made. So tonight, let me immediately acknowledge my family, represented here by my wife, Sharon, and daughter, Catherine, who nothing could keep from being present. Their love and support have been integral to any achievement of mine. Equally, let me also acknowledge the support, friendship, and dedication of all the teachers in the Caribbean, that it has been my privilege to serve with, and whose contributions and achievements are intricately intertwined with my efforts. Teaching is a social profession, and no achievement attributed to me could be accomplished without the collaboration and cooperation of my colleague teachers.

So let me ask all teachers from the English-speaking Caribbean present in this banquet hall tonight, to stand with me in receiving this prestigious award.

EI Albert Shanker Education Award

Education International
Internationale de l'Education
Internacional de la Educación
Bildungsinternationale

Mary Hatwood   Fred van Leeuwen
FutrellPresident   General Secretary   PROFESSOR ERROL MILLER

Dear Dr MILLER,

It is with great pleasure that I inform you that the Executive Board of Education International (EI) has designated you as the recipient of the 2004 EI Albert Shanker Education Award.

The Albert Shanker Education Award is attributed to a teacher or other education employee in recognition of an outstanding personal contribution to education. His or her professional action will have demonstrated that quality education requires quality teachers and education employees. That professional action will have reflected a commitment to educational excellence and the promotion of democracy, social justice and equality through education. The recipient's educational action will reflect the ideals and aspirations which are articulated in Article 2 of the Constitution of Education International and will be an inspiration to colleagues. In principle the recipient will be a class room teacher or an education employee working directly with pupils or students.

The Albert Shanker Education Award will be presented to you during the EI Awards Dinner, which will take place in the evening of Sunday 25 July in the framework of EI's Fourth World Congress in Porto Alegre, Brazil (22-26 July).

Education International has been generous in recounting several activities in which I have been engaged. Let me put them in the context of the English-speaking Caribbean, the principal arena in which I have served. The English-speaking Caribbean consists of 18 small or tiny countries stretching from Bermuda and the Bahamas in the north, to Trinidad and Tobago and Guyana in the south, and from Barbados in the east, to Belize in the west. Belize is in Central America, and Guyana is in South America but they are linked to the chain of islands in the Caribbean Sea by history, culture, and language. The total population of this sub-region is about 5,000,000 people. Anguilla is the smallest country, with just about 10,000 people, while Jamaica is the largest, with 2,600,000.

With respect to social composition, we are Africans without tribes, Indians without castes, Chinese without dynasties, and Europeans without classism. By this, I mean, that we, as a people in the Caribbean, have been disconnected from the internal divisions of the continents and cultures from which our ancestors came. Loosened from these traditional social ties, we as a people have been forced to embark on the journey to discover the common humanity of all humankind and to build bonds of solidarity across these social divisions.

On this social journey of the discovery of our common humanity, our countries are constrained by small size, separated by wide expanses of sea, marginalised in terms of global political economy, have no military might whatsoever, and are burdened with the legacy of the injustices bequeathed by slavery, colonialism, and the plantation economy. However, neither the enormity of the challenge of the social journey, nor the severe limitations imposed by the constraints, have dimmed or inhibited our resolve to succeed. We are a people who understand that our destiny lies in defeating the odds. Further, we have never allowed the limitations and constraints of our circumstances to determine what we think of ourselves, or how we define the goals and aspirations we embrace and strive to achieve. Let me illustrate the point being made by a few examples:

- Since the UNDP Development Index began to be published in the early 1990s, little Barbados with a population of 250,000, has ranked between 24th and 30th of the 190-odd countries listed worldwide with respect to basic human needs indicators in health, education, and other social services that constitute the Index. Hence, Barbados has lower rates of infant mortality, higher rates of life expectancy, and higher-levels of adult literacy than some Western industrialized countries

- Tiny St. Lucia, with a population of just over 150,000, has in the last 30 years produced two Nobel Laureates: one in Economics and the other in Literature

- Trinidad and Tobago, with a population of about 1,300,000, has given the world the only new musical instrument invented in the twentieth century: the steel drum. With it comes calypso and soca—a withering social commentary that causes politicians to quake in their boots when caught in the cross-hairs of their lyrics

- Jamaica has given the world a new religion, Rastafarianism, and a genre of popular music, reggae, that has expanded the choice of young people worldwide beyond the music coming out of North America and Western Europe. Indeed, Bob Marley's song, *One Love* was selected 'Song of the Twentieth Century' by the BBC, and his album Legend was selected 'Album of the Century' by Billboard in the United States

Jamaica is still the smallest country in population, and the only one without a professional league, that has qualified for the FIFA World Cup for football. Also Jamaica's tally of medals in the sprints of the Olympics and World Athletics Championship is surpassed only by the USA.

When the Rhodes Trust celebrated 100 years, and Oxford University awarded four honorary doctorates to outstanding Rhodes Scholars, it was Professor Rex Nettleford, Caribbean icon, and Vice-Chancellor of the University of the West Indies, who replied on behalf of the four awardees that included U.S. President Bill Clinton.

But beyond these achievements that belie the small size and lack of political and economic importance of our sub-region, it's the Caribbean audacity which obliges us to stand up and be counted. Even in circumstances that may seem ridiculous, or hopeless to others, we make our mark. For example, Jamaica was the first country to impose economic sanctions against the apartheid regime of South Africa. While in terms of substance this may have appeared laughable in the 1950s when it was done, it sets a precedence that the majority of nations in the world community followed in ensuing decades.

My reason for citing these examples of Caribbean achievements is to underscore the fact that Caribbean expectations and accomplishments have never been constrained by our marginality in the political economy of the world or our relative unimportance in terms of size. Further, in our journey of discovery of our common humanity, we have embraced education as a principal means of progress. The Caribbean is a shining example of the theme of this Congress. However, we have gone further than embracing education as a means of progress, we have learned that education is a vital instrument in harnessing the power of the weak.

You see, colleagues, we in the Caribbean have a long history of resisting the powerful. This orientation is immortalized in the lyrics of many of our songwriters and in the verses of several of our poets. It is not surprising therefore, that when Winston Churchill sought appropriate words with which to rally the British people during World War II he turned to the poem, *If We Must Die*, written by the Jamaican poet, Claude McKay:

If we must die, let it not be like hogs

Hunted and penned in an inglorious spot,

While round us bark the mad and hungry dogs,

Making their mock at our accursèd lot.

If we must die, O let us nobly die,

So that our precious blood may not be shed

In vain; then even the monsters we defy

Shall be constrained to honour us though dead!

O kinsmen! we must meet the common foe!

Though far outnumbered let us show us brave,

And for their thousand blows deal one death-blow!

What though before us lies the open grave?

Like men we'll face the murderous, cowardly pack,

Pressed to the wall, dying, but fighting back!

However, constrained by small size and marginality, our major instruments of resistance have never been war and wealth. Our principal instruments of resistance have always included the mind and the spirit. It is the indomitable spirit of our forebears that broke the shackles of slavery. It is the mastery of the mind that finally liberated us from the assertions and assumptions of colonialism. Our forebears prized literacy and sought to be literate even when reading was a punishable offence among slaves. The Caribbean achieved levels of education that rivalled the imperial world while we were still colonies.

The development of the mind and the cultivation of the spirit, constitute the very substance of the education enterprise. The power of the weak resides in:

- Forging a strong sense of identity, and enduring bonds of solidarity among those of diverse backgrounds and circumstances but who share a common destiny

- Developing the intellect
- Fostering the creative imagination
- Inspiring commitment to integrity
- Cultivating an indomitable spirit that refuses to be broken or crushed by adversity or immobilised by daunting odds.

Teachers in the Caribbean have been in the forefront of harnessing the power of the weak among people in our societies. It is through their sacrifice that many children from very humble circumstances have become adults who have escaped the cycle of persistent poverty. It is through their vision that many Caribbean leaders have been inspired to break barriers of social injustice, to reach intellectual heights that many thought could not be attained, and to establish that excellence as a resident domiciled in our region. It is within this framework that I have had the opportunity, and the privilege, to serve and to lead. Hopefully, it is for these reasons that Education International has honoured Caribbean teachers and myself through this Albert Shanker Education Award for 2004.

Finally, President Futrell, allow me to show some small gratitude by presenting you and General Secretary, van Leeuwen, with copies of my latest book, launched earlier this year: *The Prophet and the Virgin*.

The book is a historical sociology of the teaching occupation that adopts a gender perspective. It begins with the Sumerian civilisation, and traces the masculine roots of teaching to the lineage traditions of this ancient civilisation and through the prophetic traditions of Judaism, Christianity, and Islam. It traces the feminine roots of teaching to the ascetic traditions of Islam and Christianity. It concludes by tracing the transformation of teaching in the nation states of the United States and the Caribbean. In a real sense, this book records my own exploration into what it means to be a teacher and what is involved in the training of teachers. It is my considered view, that, in the final analysis; teaching is about how vision, values, and virtue are construed and constructed in every era of human history.

~

Chapter 20

The Spirit of the Mico is the Source of its Longevity: The First Chancellor's Address

~

The Mico University College Graduation 2008
December, 2008

~

It is with real joy, for you who are graduating in this ceremony, and with a sense of personal and institutional history, that I welcome all present this afternoon to the second graduation of The Mico University College, in the 172nd year of the Mico Institution. For you who are graduating, your families and friends, today marks a major milestone in the commencement of your journey as teachers and as professionals. We commend you for your achievement and celebrate your advancement in the academic and professional community. To our two honorary graduands, Dr. Karl James and Dr. Dudley Thompson, we salute you, your lives of service and accomplishments which have enriched so many other lives.

For the first time in its 172-year history, the Mico has a chancellor. This marks the first occasion where a graduation of the Mico is being presided over by a chancellor. For the first time, the Mico will be awarding honorary doctorates. This evening is institutional history in the making. These signal the advancement of the Mico in the constellation of colleges and universities in Jamaica, the Caribbean and the world.

In the knowledge society that is now emerging across the world, it is tertiary education that confers comparative and competitive advantage. Faced with the challenge of expanding tertiary education opportunities, countries across the globe have been transforming and upgrading colleges.

(ABOVE) Mico College, along Marescaux Road, in Kingston, Jamaica, was founded in 1836, with Trust Funds from the bequest of Lady Jane Mico. The buildings were reconstructed by Mais and Sant after the earthquake of 1907.

It stands today as one of the strongest buildings of Victorian architecture in the island and the oldest Normal School/ Teacher Training College in the Western Hemisphere.

(LEFT) Professor Errol Miller at the ceremony of installation as the first chancellor at the Mico University College.

©*The Gleaner Company Ltd.*

The Mico, with its history and performance, qualifies and deserves such upgrading. The Government of Jamaica, by Act of Parliament, and Scheme of Arrangement concurs and has upgraded the Mico from college to University College. President Dr. Claude Packer, the staff and the Board, deserve the highest commendation for this advancement of the Mico.

Then again, there is personal history. When my email and voice mail showed messages to the effect that Mr. Henry Buxton, direct descendant of Thomas Fowell Buxton, the great emancipator, and Chairman of the Trustees of the Lady Mico Trust, wanted to talk to me, I took it that it was just another of those conversations between the Chairman and myself as a Trustee. Words cannot express my utter and complete surprise when he informed me that he and the other Trustees had decided that I should be the first Chancellor of the Mico University College. The thought of being a chancellor had never once crossed my mind. I argued but to no avail. I pleaded for time to discuss the matter with Dr. Packer and the Chairman of the Board but I was told that the deal was sealed. I had no option.

My only recourse was to think about it. Then I realised that the significance of being named the first chancellor went far beyond me. For the first time in Jamaican history, a university college or university, will have as its chancellor, a Jamaican who received his education in Jamaica, has always resided in Jamaica and has no residence of citizenship elsewhere. This made me recall when, as young Caribbean nationals of the staff at the University of the West Indies, we faced the 'publish or perish' practice of the University in spite of the fact that the 'British Journal of This' and the 'American Journal of That' had the elevated status of international journals, but Caribbean Journals were regarded as local publications.

We resolved that our obligation was to show that excellence resided in the region by conducting high quality research and publishing the results in Caribbean journals. Looking back, not only have the Caribbean journals we supported, gained international recognition and acclaim but almost every one of us who had come to the resolve, also gained international recognition for our academic research and publications.

At a time when our nations seem to have lost its confidence as it continues to hold on to obsolete colonial vestiges, such as the Privy Council in England as our final court, the English Trustees of the Lady Mico Trust have vested confidence in the Trustee that resides in Jamaica. They have elevated him to the highest office in the upgraded Mico. At a time when we as a people seem to be returning to the old view that what comes from abroad is better, that solutions reside outside of ourselves, and that those of us who choose to reside in Jamaica are of less calibre, the leadership of the Mico is united in affirming confidence in home grown accomplishment.

The point is, in this moment of institutional history, the Mico Community is simply acting true to its character. As it has always done, the Mico community is swimming upstream against the tide and not downstream with the tide. It is acting in the same manner as it did at the founding of the Mico institutions in 1836 to educate former slaves. The Mico adopted the approach of training the ex-slaves' most able children as teachers. Acting in the same manner as it did a century later, in the 1930s, the college offered the classics in its programme, allowing some students to obtain university matriculation and read for bachelor degrees as external students of London University. In achieving University College status, the Mico is simply looking to the future and its possibilities as it has always done.

This graduation, taking place in December 2008, comes at a time of great global economic stress. The world's leading economies are in recession. While recessions are cyclical, this one is special. It could lead to the first depression of the twenty-first century. Stock markets are convulsing. Major banks in the richest countries are on life support. Markets that are supposed to be self-regulating are out of control. Governments are now called upon to intervene as losses are socialized after profits were privately enjoyed. The answer of the Central Banks in these rich countries is to print huge sums of money in order to bail out the banks and stabilize the markets. All of these contradict the stated tenets of free market capitalism and sound economic practice. What is certain, however, is that all of us across the global are going to pay for the folly of those in the rich countries who have created this economic and catastrophic situation.

It is extremely important for us to note that this global economic crisis, with implications for all of us, is not the creation of illiterate and uneducated people of the so-called third world, although they too will have to pay. Rather, it is the brainchild and the work of very smart and highly education people with MBAs and other highly prized post-graduate degrees from some of the most prestigious universities in the so-called first world. These architects of the economic and financial crises were supported by a combination of politicians: those who pandered to the people and those who adamantly pursued their doctrinaire ideological inclinations.

If we take a step back we could summarise the essence of their folly by saying that they tried to create:

- Wealth not based on work
- Prosperity while outsourcing production, and passing produc-tivity gains to the wealthy and not to the workers
- Debt and credit, not savings, as the source of economic growth
- Home ownership based on future value.

While this gave the illusion of prosperity, and mesmerised many, what has actually been produced is commercial paper without value. The sad conse-quence of this folly are workers who have lost their jobs, homeowners who have lost their homes, pensioners who have lost their pensions, investors who have lost their investments and the many who have lost hope for a better life.

The lesson we must all learn from this, is that university degrees and high offices in the public and private sectors, do not by themselves constitute wisdom and sound judgment. This brings us to some central questions:

What is the meaning of this re-invention of the Mico as a university college?

What is the meaning of graduating into this community of scholars and professionals?

What remains of the Mico that we have known? As we gather at this Graduation of the Mico University College in 2008, the words associated with the Passover, leaps from the pages of the *Book of Exodus* and lands squarely in our midst. "What mean ye by this service?"

Allow me to attempt to answer these questions:

In the 1830s, four Mico Normal Schools for training teachers were established in the Caribbean. Only this college in Kingston has survived. When colleges training male teachers were closed in 1899 in Jamaica, only Mico College survived. The question then becomes what has allowed this Mico institution to survive and be transformed from being a normal school, to being a college, to being a university college? The point is that normal school, college, and university college are but institutional levels of academic and professional operation. They do not provide the reason why an institution is transformed from one level to the next or explain why it has survived over generations. Such transformations are but evidence of its viability and sustainability.

The real answer to Mico's survival and transformation resides in its 'spirit'. As a non-Miconian, who happened to have had the great honour to have led this institution for eight years and six months, let me tell you what I learned about 'the spirit of the Mico'.

1. The 'spirit of the Mico' is courage and confidence to look beyond human frailty, flaws and faults and to see the potential and possibilities that reside in the human personality and society. It is the courage and the confidence to see beyond the misery that surrounds us, the enormity of the challenges that confront us, the odds that face us, and catch a glimpse of the nobility, strength and beauty that resides among us—and be so inspired by that vision. This brings out the best in us and demands the best from us. It is the courage and the confidence to confound those who would hold us in low esteem and think little of our chances to achieve the ambitious tasks we undertake.

2. The 'spirit of the Mico' is commitment to build capacity among the vulnerable in society, especially the children of the disadvantaged and marginalised, by seeking to change their life chances, by challenging the conventional stereotypes and images they commonly have of themselves, by working to lift the horizons they set for themselves, and by cultivating the mind to explore the full measure of the intellect and the creative imagination. It is the commitment to build capacity among the vulnerable in society. In so doing, accidents of birth and legacy of social history are not perpetuated across generations but rather allow each new generation the opportunity to discover and achieve their full potential.

3. The 'spirit of the Mico' is conviction that service to community is the source of individual and personal fulfilment. Individual intellect, imagination, invention and innovation are the sources of all advancement in human society. However, rampant individualism, unrestrained pursuit of self-interest and worship at the shrine of individual rights, result in anarchy. The 'spirit of the Mico' is the conviction that when individual enterprise, energy, enthusiasm and entrepreneurship are directed to serve the common good of community not only the community benefits, but individuals find meaning and fulfilment in their endeavours.

4. The 'spirit of the Mico' is capability to chart new courses where these are needed and demanded. The 'spirit of the Mico' is a pioneering spirit. It is a trailblazing spirit. It is the capability to perceive what is needed and provide what is necessary. It is the willingness to risk failure in order to achieve the success that is demanded by the circumstances.

The college song exhorts all Miconians to "Breathe not the spirit of the Mico in vain." Graduating Class of 2008, let this refrain sink deep within the lungs of your souls. May it come to consciousness where ever you are, and in whatever you do. What this refrain is asserting is that all who have come within the sphere of Mico's influence, its programme of instruction and its mode of operation, ought to become imbued, possessed, and inspired with its 'spirit'. Further, having breathed 'the Mico spirit', you are obligated to bring forth fruit worthy of this 'spirit'.

The obligations of breathing 'the spirit of the Mico' are made even more binding and compelling by past Miconians. Miconians have given excellent service in so many fields, in so many countries of the world and have changed so many lives across the world that time would fail us to recount their deeds. Allow me to mention just a dozen of them who have passed on:

- Mr. John Savage first Superintendent of Schools appointed in Jamaica. He was a member of the first batch of students of the College in 1836.

- Mr. F. W. Bailey leading light in the formation of the Jamaica Union of Teachers in 1894, the first union of any kind formed in the Commonwealth Caribbean and at a time when unions were illegal.

- Reverend Lackland Augustus Lennon, Archbishop of Lagos, Nigeria in the early twentieth century and one of first black bishops of the Anglican Church.

- Reverend W. A. Thompson, one of the translators of the Bible in several African languages in the early twentieth century.

- Reverend Henry Ward, renowned teacher, pioneer, social worker and founder of Meadowbrook High School.

- Mr. Cyril Potter, Guyanese Miconian, renowned education and after whom the Cyril Potter College of Education in Guyana is named.

- Sir Harold Allan, first Minister of Finance in Jamaica

- Professor Reginald Murray, first Jamaican Chief Education Office, Director of UNESCO's Regional Office in West Africa and Director of the Institute of Education, University of the West Indies.

- The Honourable Tacius Golding, famous teacher and later Speaker of the House of Representatives.

- Sir Clifford Campbell, Member of Parliament and first Governor General of Jamaica and Sir Howard Cooke, also Member of Parliament, Minister of Education and Governor General of Jamaica.

- Professor Laurie Reid, pioneer of educational measurement in the Jamaica and the person responsible for setting the Common Entrance Examination from its inception in 1957 until his death in the 1990s.

- Professor Aubrey Phillips pioneer researcher in social psychology in Jamaica, teacher educator par excellence and President of the Jamaica Teachers' Association.

- Honourable Glen Owen, member of the Privy Council and first Miconian to be Principal of the Mico.

The 'spirit of the Mico' has lived within thousands of Miconians who have passed on, and not just the dozen named. It continues to live in the vast majority who are still alive. It is expected to live in you who this evening formally join the Mico Community.

The lives of our two honorary graduands, Dr. Karl James and Dr. Dudley Thompson, exemplify the 'spirit of the Mico'. One breathed and was infected by it as a student. The other was overtaken by it as member and Chairman of the Board for over 20 years. My wife and family join with me in congratulating you both.

As the Mico moves and changes from one level to the next, as an institution, may 'the Mico spirit' remain constant to ensure its character as it imbues and inspires all who join its rank.

Chapter 21

A Vision of UWI
and Living in Life's Intersections

~

UNIVERSITY OF THE WEST INDIES, MONA
2012 GRADUATION ADDRESS
November, 2012

~

Introduction

Chancellor, Principal of the Mona Campus and other Campuses, Members of the Academic Community of the University of the West Indies, Dr. Joy Spence, invited guests, family, friends, well-wishers of the Graduating Class of 2012, and most important, members of the Graduating Class of 2012 of the University of the West Indies. I am triply honoured this morning. First, to have been awarded Doctor of Laws, Honoris Causa, from my alma mater. Second, to say thanks to the University of the West Indies on behalf of Dr. Joy Spence who is not only the first female master-blender in the world, but in 2012 has been awarded honorary doctorates from both universities from which she graduated. Third, to be given the opportunity to address this Graduating Class of 2012.

No one is self-made. No one achieves anything without the support and sustenance of others. That includes Dr. Spence and me. We therefore acknowledge our parents, teachers, spouses, children, siblings, colleagues, mentors and friends who have contributed to the persons we have become and what we have achieved. In whatever spirit you take it Dr. Spence and I are blended, thanks to you and to the Almighty.

University of the West Indies with campuses throughout the Caribbean. Established 1948.

Vision of UWI

For the last 30 years, following my return to the University, having been Principal of the Mico and Permanent Secretary of the Ministry of Education, I have had a vision for the University of the West Indies. This vision is comprised of Campuses, University Centres, National Colleges and University Colleges, combined in a University System with a collective enrolment of over 100,000 students, ranking among the top 100 research universities in the world. While the national colleges and university colleges would be administratively autonomous they would be articulated, affiliated and integrated within the UWI academic brand of degrees and its quality assurance mechanisms.

In my own field of education, the Schools of Education of Mona, Cave Hill and St. Augustine, would be the integrated Graduate School of Education, producing the higher-level professional personnel needed in the education sector, generating, through research, the knowledge needed to advance learning and teaching, and providing the developmental services in education, required by our countries and people.

Public national higher education institutions and UWI are all heavily supported by the taxpayers of our countries. From my perspective, the articulation and affiliation of these public institutions into a single UWI system constitutes the most effective and efficient way to deploy the resources from the respective national budgets. The point that must not be missed is that for Commonwealth Caribbean countries to configure their higher education system, their public national higher education institutions or small to medium size entities operating in relative isolation, and trying to cover as many disciplines as possible, is a most ineffective and inefficient deployment of resources.

Further, there are real limits to the physical expansion of the UWI campuses, hence the areas in which expansion takes place is of great strategic importance in the international competitiveness of the region. Neither the public national institutions, nor UWI, can overlook the fact that they must compete internationally. An unarticulated fractured public system of higher education in the Commonwealth Caribbean is to the detriment of all.

Clearly, to this point I have largely lost the argument for this vision of UWI. I have come to recognise the structural and idiosyncratic factors that impede its realization. However, I am convinced that the imperatives of universal secondary education, improved quality of secondary school leavers, the increasing fees for international students in the US and UK, international competitiveness in the knowledge economy, issues of accreditation, and validation of credentials and the fact that the Caribbean Knowledge and Learning Net is now a reality, will force a reconsideration of this conception of the future of UWI and public national higher education institutions.

Chancellor, I crave your forgiveness for this trespass. Yet, I could not forgive myself if I did not steal this last opportunity to express a view with which UWI, governments and national higher education institutions of the region must contend.

Living in the Intersection of Life's Contradictions

Members of the Graduating Class of 2012, I am acutely aware that you are graduating in difficult times locally, regionally and internationally. Characteristic of the times is the joke my daughter told me of a thief who broke into a woman's house recently and was searching for money. The woman woke up, challenged the thief concerning what he was doing and after he told her, she joined him in the search. However, life and education are not just about the short-term. Let me therefore share with you briefly what I have learned about life over the long term.

Life is lived in the intersection of three pairs of irreconcilable contradictions: equality and excellence, individuality and community; and reason and revelation. Once we are alive we cannot escape the conundrum they represent and present.

Equality and Excellence

Equality resides in that which we share in common with all other human beings. It is the sense in which we are all ordinary people, in ways in which we are the same as everybody else. The notion of equality embraces the idea of the common humanity of all human kind. Equality is inclusive. It is egalitarian. It is comforted by norms. However, equality is threatened by difference. To live and never experience that sense of being like everybody else requires the lifestyle of the hermit.

Excellence is rooted in ways in which we exceed others, in the extraordinary performance that surpasses all others, in prized differences in endowments compared to others. Excellence is exclusive. It is elitist. Excellence is intolerant of the ordinary and dismissive of norms. It thrives on difference. Part of the motivation to excel is the inner urge to discover and develop the best in ourselves. Yet, to live one's life always trying to exceed others in everything, to outstrip colleagues, friends and family, and to emphasize and celebrate prized differences is to become an insufferable bore, obsessed with being special and increasingly alienated from society.

It is impossible for everybody to be equally excellent at anything. Neither is it possible for anyone to be equally excellent at everything. It is in the intersection of equality and excellence that we find space to be truly human. That is, to be able to share fellowship with others based on our common humanity, deserving and requiring mutual respect; while at the same time exploring, discovering, and developing to their zenith, the best that we can be in at least some things.

Like Whitney Houston sings, we all yearn for at least "one moment in time when we are more that we thought we could be, when we are racing with destiny and the answers were all up to me". At the same time the challenge is living with all those other moments in time when we are no different from anybody else, when our own destiny is in doubt and the answers are outside of our control.

Individuality and Community

Individuality is defined by uniqueness. It is the source of personality. Individuality is the fountain head of initiative, innovation, invention and imagination in society. It is the source of collective energy, enthusiasm, enterprise and effort. Yet, left unfettered and unrestrained, individuality tends to run to selfishness, greed, anarchy, barbarity, and amorality where the strong devours and destroys the weak and only the strong survives.

Community is one of the necessary pre-conditions for civilised living. It is community that establishes the common good of its members. It is community that ensures the continuity and conservation of a people across generations though identity and bonds of solidarity. It is community that fetters, and restrains individuality, through codes and conventions, idealising conformity to some norms and values. Yet the conformity and uniformity demanded by community can stifle individuality, and promote robotic and humanoid behaviours without soul.

Individuality divides. Community unifies. Reverend Dr. Burchell Taylor in a sermon pointed out that these two contradictory realities are vital attributes that cannot be resolved. They must be held in constructive tension. It is the intersection of individuality and community that provides opportunities to discover how individual initiative, innovation, invention, energy, enterprise and effort, can serve the highest ideals and conventions of community. It is in the intersection of individuality and community that diversity is revealed as an agent of the common good, and conformity is understood as the border and boundary of freedom.

Reason and Revelation

Reason is nailed to current reality. It relies on empirical data derived from the five senses, confirmed by measurement and the application of either deductive or inductive logic. Reason revels in facts. To use current jargon, it is evidence based. But reason is bound to what is. It is highly sympathetic to the status quo. Then again, many things in life are not reasonable, or logical or subject to measurement.

Revelation is stubbornly resistant to facts. Its penchant is to ignore current reality. Its starting point is to assert what ought to be. It seeks to provide meaning and purpose and is openly optimistic. Its *modus operandi* is faith: Reaching for what is not, and hoping and striving until it is. Revelation seeks always to transcend reality, often calls upon the divine and is challenged by proof.

In the final analysis, reason and revelation cannot be reconciled, although some may entertain the idea of reasonable faith or revelation that is subject to logic. Also, there can be little dispute that reason and logic have led to major achievements and advancement in the human condition, especially in the domain of science and technology. But even in this domain many achievements and advancements have come through transcendence as intuition, insight and refusal to accept received wisdom or conventional explanations; led to new scientific theories which thereafter have garnered empirical support.

It is also indisputable that both reason and revelation have led to some of the most abominable atrocities in human history by some who claim irrefutable evidence or impeccable logic or direct instruction from God. Whether by reason or revelation, they have acted with finality and great brutality in many situations. At the same time, it is in the intersection of reason and revelation that there is scope to address some of the most pressing issues facing us, personally and collectively.

The Intersection Forces Choices and Coping with Inconsistencies

The intersection between individuality and community becomes compounded when it is also crossed by the intersection of equality and excellence. Excellence in any area takes on the aura of a general superiority of such persons in the community. The geography of birth becomes a prized difference and become the basis for either inclusion or exclusion, as citizens or aliens. Equality becomes the writ by which to prosecute injustice, and to identify unethical and immoral practices.

When reason and revelation are added to the intersections of equality and excellence as well as individuality and community, the situation is confounded. The latter provides no definitive and absolute base on which to resolve six-fold interacting contradictions.

One consequence of living in the intersection of life's major contradictions is that choices have to be made. Choice is the fundamental requirement in addressing these contradictions. Another consequence, over time, is inconsistency in us and others. It is impossible in making choices with respect to these three pairs of irreconcilable contradictions to be entirely consistent over time. On some issues, the choice will be based on the claims of equality, on others on the imperatives of excellence, on others on the needs for individuality, on others on the demands of community, and still on others, by applying reason and on others by exercising faith. Making choices and coping with inconsistences is the existential conditions of all of us. This brings us face-to-face with the limitations of the nature of our humanity and our mortality.

Love as the Source of Wholeness

What then allows us to become and remain whole persons, living constructive lives in community, having inner personal peace and experiencing moments of true joy? My best answer is love. By that I mean:

- Maintaining goodwill and good intentions to all. In the negative, this means not working for anybody's down fall, although a few may wish or work for yours.

- Using the exceptional talents we possess to undertake sacrificial deeds on behalf of others particularly the voiceless, the 'voteless', the vulnerable and the victimized in society.

- Acting justly and showing mercy in relationships,

- Holding firmly to our convictions, whether based upon reason or revelation, while respecting others of opposing convictions

- Walking humbly among family, friends, colleagues and strangers understanding that we are no different from them.

Concluding Comment

Members of the Graduating Class of 2012, the concept of living in the intersections of these three pairs of irreconcilable but fundamental human constructs is neither abstract nor academic. Recognise it or not, these intersections constitute the context and subtext of our daily existence. The choices we make in confronting these contradictions, determine how we cope with inconsistences in ourselves, others and society; shape our being; our becoming; our relationships; our work; our achievements; our peace; our joy; and our happiness. Look within and be kind to yourself. Look around and care for and about others. Look up and find the strength and inspiration to persevere whatever the circumstances.

God bless you.

Acknowledgements

Thanks to the 21 organisations that gave me the opportunity to contribute to their important and significant milestone events. The honour bestowed on me was tremendous. That honour demanded that I should prepare assiduously for each occasion. In the process I was educated, instructed and enriched in many ways that were both uplifting as well as useful in my own formation and work. My hope is that the presentations recorded in this volume will contribute in some small way to the continued success of the institutions as well as continued recognition of the work and worth of the leaders that were celebrated.

Thanks to Professor Sir Kenneth Hall, former Governor General of Jamaica and past Principal of the University of the West Indies, Mona for so graciously agreeing to write the Foreword and for producing in it such a timely manner. I am more than flattered by what he wrote. Generosity has been an integral part of Sir Kenneth's *persona* and his many, varied and seminal contributions to Jamaican and Caribbean society.

Thanks to Mr. Winston Wright for the work done in editing the manuscript and also for efforts he will make in marketing. I am grateful that he introduced me to Miss Lena Rose of Minna Press.

Thanks to Lena Rose, and the Minna Press team, for the work that has been done in editing, publishing and globally distributing this book, in both print and electronic formats. I have been impressed with the very professional manner in which the various tasks have been undertaken and the commitment shown in meeting timelines. Hopefully, the first undertaking together will result in many others.

Many persons contributed to these 21 speeches but none more so than my wife Sharon. She was the initial sounding board, first critic and editor. She was the first test I had to pass before delivering many of the speeches. I trusted her judgments implicitly. It she passed the speech I knew that it was okay. On several occasions, because we were living in different places, she was unable to attend the events. On every such occasion, I would have to give a report of the event and the speech. Thanks Sharon for your unfailing love, constant support and unswerving loyalty.

Professor Emeritus, the Honourable Errol Miller B.Sc, MA, Ph.D has had a distinguished career as an educator and public servant. He is also author of *The Prophet and the Virgin,* and 17 other books and monographs, 30 chapters of books and over 70 papers and reports in peer-review publications.

A renowned, charismatic speaker, his keen interests in history, education and nation-building, co-mingled with unwavering Christian sensibilities, have manifested into his becoming one of the *de facto* keynote speakers for commemorative, milestone events in Jamaica, the Caribbean and the diaspora. In this book, *Marking Milestones: 21 Keynote Speeches about Successful Institutions and Outstanding Leaders,* Professor Miller honours these organisations and leaders. The book is created to inform and inspire a wider audience than those who heard the speeches.

Achievements in Education

Professor Miller has conducted ground-breaking research on issues of race, class, gender and other social issues that impact education systems. He developed the "Theory of Place" out of which the research on male marginalisation and other issues have been examined. His outstanding service in education includes:

- Chancellor, Mico University College: 2007 to 2015

- Professor Emeritus, School of Education, University of the West Indies, Mona, since 2006

- Professor of Teacher Education, Institute of Education:1981 to 2005

- Principal, Mico University College: 1972 to1980

- Past President of the Jamaica Teachers Association

Achievements in Public Service

In whatever capacity he has served, Professor Miller is known for his non-partisan approach to government and politics. As Permanent Secretary in the Ministry of Education, Jamaica, he has provided leadership for the implementation of major reforms such as free secondary and tertiary education; the integration of schools serving children with various disabilities into the public system; and the conversion of three-year junior secondary schools into five year secondary schools across the country. As a member of the Electoral Advisory Committee (EAC), and first Chairman of the Electoral Commission of Jamaica, Professor Miller has provided leadership in Jamaica's electoral reform process over twelve years, and has contributed to the high regard now currently enjoyed by the Electoral Commission and Jamaica's electoral system.

Major Awards

Professor Miller earned the Super Lion Award (1974), for being a Distinguished Graduate of Chancellor Hall, University of the West Indies, Mona. Since then, he has been the recipient of numerous awards, locally and internationally, for his contribution to education and public service. These include: Two Fulbright Fellowships for Senior Academics; Commander of the Order of Distinction and Order of Jamaica; the Vice Chancellor's Award for Excellence at the University of the West Indies; UWI Doctor of Laws Honoris Causa; the UWI Alumni Association Pelican Award 2006; Jamaica Teachers Association Honour Roll and the Albert Shanker Education Award for 2004 by Education International.

Despite all his accomplishments, Professor Miller is widely known as simply "Prof", especially to his peers, and the students he has taught and mentored throughout his career. Now in semi-retirement, he is focused on writing, fully exploring the subjects that are dear to his heart.

Prof is a Calabar High School 'Old Boy' who retains a great interest in his alma mater. He is a member of the Bethel Baptist Church, Half Way Tree, Jamaica since July 1956 and is a lay preacher. He is married to Sharon, and has two sons Garth and Ye Kengale and one daughter, Catherine. He is also a proud grandparent of Phillip, Jheanelle, Gabriel and Chantel.